Intimacy in Crisis

Intimacy in Crisis

Men and women in crisis through the life cycle and how to help

JANE RIDLEY
BA(HONS), PQSW

W
WHURR PUBLISHERS
LONDON

First published 1999 by
Whurr Publishers Ltd
19b Compton Terrace, London N1 2UN, England

British Library Cataloguing in Publication Data
A catalogue record for this book is available from the British Library.

ISBN: 1 86156 113 X

Printed and bound in the UK by Athenaeum Press Ltd, Gateshead, Tyne & Wear

Contents

Dedication

This book is dedicated to
Elly Jansen OBE, a problem solving woman
and
Dr Malcolm Pines, a very nurturing man

Preface

This book is divided into two parts. Part I is a practical guide for therapists, counsellors and professionals. Relationship and sexual difficulties are explored in detail through case material and gender differences are highlighted. Alternative interventions are offered. Part II provides a theoretical and research oriented backdrop to gender and individual development of women and men through the life cycle.

Parts I and II are designed to overlap and supplement each other and have been cross-referenced so that the reader can move easily between practice, theory and research. The practically oriented therapist may wish to dip into Part II following particular areas of interest rather than reading it in sequence.

Gender development, life cycle and life events are specialisms within which other specialisms occur; central aspects of each area have been summarised. Key references are cited for readers with particular interests. Some life stages have attracted greater interest than others; for example, pregnancy and its impact upon the woman has been studied in detail, as has male aggression, giving a partial and unbalanced picture of female/male relationships at some points on the life cycle. Clinical experience has been used to fill this gap. It is hoped that future research will pay greater attention to the impact of life stages and events upon both partners.

Chapter 1 introduces the book and argues that any definition of intimacy should take into account the different intimacy needs of women and men.

Chapter 2 considers five key elements of intimacy and how each gender seeks to transmit and receive what they need from each other. The concept of an invisible screen between the woman and man containing these five elements of intimacy is used. Case examples illustrate the five elements, followed by alternative ways of helping when things go wrong.

Chapter 3 describes 'critical periods' in the life cycle of the individual or couple when her/his essential femaleness or maleness may be vulnerable.

Examples are given in Chapter 4 demonstrating ways in which life events such as illness, abuse or violence can have a major impact upon the intimacy needs of each gender.

Part II, Chapter 5 reviews alternative ways of thinking about gender. Chapter 6 describes the physical and biological development of the female and male. The accompanying personal and emotional experiences are outlined to emphasise that intensely personal responses cannot be divorced from the physical development of the female or male.

The material presented acknowledges the need for greater equality of opportunity for both women and men, but suggests that many of the basic biological and physical aspects of femaleness and maleness are being ignored in this process.

Acknowledgements

Special thanks to Jack Nathan, Keith Nicol and to family members John, Sarah, Jonathon, Karen, Michael, Meigan and Tony for their encouragement and support.

Part I

1 CHAPTER

A Working Hypothesis

1.1. Introduction

Whilst the statistics for divorce suggest that the concept of marriage 'till death do us part' is under question, many individuals continue to strive towards a special permanent relationship with a member of the opposite sex. This intense search is the subject matter of this book.

It is not easy to understand what is happening when a woman or man seeks out a partner with whom to share her or his life, or what drives women and men to seek again for such a relationship when a first or long-term relationship has ended in disappointment or rejection. Some inner compulsion seems to keep the search alive that somewhere, somehow, this 'desired' relationship can be found. However, as more women and men experience the failure of a long-term relationship the search for intimacy may itself be in crisis.

This book argues that a failure to understand the opposite sex's intimacy needs can contribute to relationship distress. Not only are women and men different in their physical and biological makeup, but gender differences in resources, needs and perspectives mean that each gender seeks different satisfactions and responses from their intimate long-term relationship with a member of the opposite sex. Intimacy within a long-term relationship has different meanings for women and men.

The intimacy needs of one partner in a heterosexual relationship often go unrecognised by the other partner. Gender differences are then considered as irritations or deliberate attempts to avoid, punish, dominate or control the relationship. Where each gender's different intimacy needs are recognised and respected they add depth and resilience to a long-term relationship.

This book suggests ways of recognising gender differences, and ways of helping when things go wrong.

A simple format, the invisible intimacy screen, is described. This format is designed so that it can be used by counsellors, therapists and professional helpers with specific individuals or couples seeking help.

This invisible intimacy screen describes five elements of intimacy that women and men seek, but each of which may be viewed from divergent perspectives.

1.1.1. Dilemmas

Four problems should be addressed before describing the book in more detail. The first is the necessity to understand physical sexual relationships in some detail. Physical sexuality describes the desire, arousal and orgasmic phases of the female/male physical sexual relationship. Physical sexuality is separated out to highlight gender differences which affect the male and female in these phases (Kaplan, 1981; Gillan, 1987; Heiman and Lo Piccolo, 1988; Bancroft, 1990; Quilliam and Grove-Stephenson, 1992; Stanway, 1993).

There are disadvantages in separating physical sexuality from the totality of the relationship as in reality there is a powerful interdependence between the different elements of the relationship and sexuality. The reader is asked to be mindful that this separation is made in order to explore female/male differences; paradoxically, however, physical sexuality and the totality of the relationship are deeply intertwined.

A further disadvantage in separating out physical sexuality and exploring female/male sexual differences is that the language used is clinical and, for those unfamiliar with these details, may seem intrusive or insensitive. As a society we are discouraged from being open about physical and sexual needs, which can lead to embarrassment. Powerful negative messages from church, family and society make adequate discussion difficult. In spite of these disadvantages the differences between the female and male desire, arousal and orgasmic phases of sexual relationship are described. Physical sexuality is often ignored by researchers and psychotherapists; divisions exist even amongst sexual and relationship therapists, making its integration into a discussion of intimacy difficult. Female/male long-term relationships are often assessed in great detail without reference to the sexual life of the couple (Gottman, 1994).

The third difficulty is that the language of interpersonal relationships can seem remote and confusing jargon. For example, to describe this book as about 'intersubjective experience' may distance the reader from the material. The aim has been, where possible, to use everyday language and avoid the use of jargon.

Finally, much of what is written is based upon clinical experience. Where clinical material is used all identifying characteristics have been altered in order to protect the confidentiality of the client.

1.2. Intimacy

1.2.1. What does intimacy mean to women and men?

What does intimacy or the search for intimacy mean? Is it possible to know whether women and men seek intimacy? Do they seek the same elements within the concept of intimacy?

There are many contrary or overlapping definitions of intimacy. Hudson and Jacot (1995) explore 'similarity in difference and difference in similarity' and define intimacy as their exploration.

> Buried in this semantic cluster is the sense of a reciprocal traffic in thoughts and needs that springs up between those who know one another well and remain erotically alive to one another.

Virginia Satir's philosophy correlates intimacy – the connecting of one self with the other – with the ability to value and nurture the self (Brothers, 1991). Mijuskovic (1991), on the other hand, suggests that:

> intimacy, as a feeling, of course, it cannot be described any more than the sensation of yellow can be conceptually conveyed to one congenitally blind.

He goes on to describe intimacy as:

> conceptually, it is a sense of belonging, of being 'one' with another and yet at the same time each must preserve his or her own separate and distinct identity.

or,

> the conviction that we've shared passions, thoughts, and actions before and I want to share them with you again, together, forever.

Kersten and Himle (1991) think that while intimacy is to some degree subjective, most theorists studying intimacy:

> would agree that there are common elements in most intimate relationships such as mutual self-disclosure, frequent interaction, compatibility of values and needs, intense liking or loving, value or resource exchanged, 'we-ness', and knowledge of the innermost being of another, interdependence, trust, commitment, and caring.

The above definitions do not take into account gender differences. They are global and as such do not assist practitioners and professionals working with individuals or couples in distress.

This book addresses the question of intimacy through the differing needs of women and men which are sometimes complementary and sometimes in conflict. In doing so, a definition of intimacy must take account of these differences. Intimacy and its development then depends upon each partner feeling sufficiently satisfied by the partner's responses to their needs. Five key elements of intimacy are identified.

Intimacy can then be understood as a developmental process within a relationship in which the needs of the woman and man are recognised, respected and responded to within these areas. Over time, a sense of mutual trust, respect and understanding grows in which each partner is able to respond in a way that is 'good enough' to the physical, emotional, social and interpersonal needs of the other. 'Good enough' because each individual may have differing needs for aspects of relatedness such as separateness and closeness and for 'upperness and lowerness' (Birtchnell, 1990, 1993; Crowe, 1997).

> Attention is being drawn here to those couples who are in difficulties, and who may benefit from recognising, respecting and responding to their partner's gender needs.

1.2.2. Falling in and out of love

How does this fit together with current ideas that falling in love is a sufficient basis for a long-term relationship? The Egyptians 3,500 years ago wrote poems of love (Bergman, 1987), and falling in love is a recurring theme throughout history. In the late nineteenth and twentieth centuries 'falling in love' has become a reason for marrying. For many in the West personal well-being and happiness is sought through 'falling in love'. According to Hatfield (1996) this idea is spreading throughout the world.

> Regardless of the pros and cons of the various possibilities, young women and men throughout the world seem to have made their choice. Young women and men are insisting on marrying for love.

Reibstein (1997) describes five elements that make love last and argues for the persistence of a romantic belief in an egalitarian, supportive and intimate partnership which marriage and long-term cohabitation represents today. Some therapists also support this idea that long-term relationships should be based upon mutual affection and equality (Rampage, 1994; Rubin, 1996).

Mansfield and Collard (1988), investigating a group of couples marrying for the first time in church in two London suburbs, did not find that all marriages are based on 'falling in love'. They suggest that this selected group of couples marrying in the 1980s, 'are pragmatic, choosing to marry because they are ready for marriage'.

How far the concept of marriage for love has spread around the world is not clear.

> In much of India, Africa, many parts of Latin America and Asia marriages are still decided for primarily economic, social or status reasons. Consideration for the other and the possibility of a love relationship may develop later. Love is not a *sine qua non* of such marriages. (Crowe and Ridley, 1990)

The upward trend in divorce statistics suggests that 'falling in love' does not necessarily provide the basis upon which satisfactory long-term relationships develop; and cross-cultural studies suggest that arranged marriages also have their difficulty (Xiaohe and Whyte, 1990).

Falling in and out of love are felt to be out of the control of the individual and she/he is therefore not responsible for her/his feelings. The concept of intimacy as presented here is one in which both partners are responsible for learning about the other and finding out how to be responsive to each other's needs.

It is argued that falling in love may provide the beginning point for a long-term relationship but not the solution. At some point in the relationship (usually within the first three years), each partner begins to realise that she/he does not know the other and that expectations of how the other will respond are not met. At this moment an acknowledgement of, respect for and a preparedness to respond to gender differences are essential to the development of satisfactory mutual intimacy. Love and affection rapidly disappear when faced with inexplicable behaviour that does not attend to basic intimacy needs.

1.2.3. A contextual model of intimacy

Gender differences do not affect all couples detrimentally. The concept of 'sentiment override' (Heider, 1958; Weiss, 1980) may explain this. Weiss suggests that couples within satisfactory relationships are able to process their partner's behaviour in a way that does not lead to a negative interaction.

Bradbury and Fincham (1990) suggest that partners judge their marital quality negatively when there are perceived conflicts in goals.

Using the invisible intimacy screen (see 2.2.1) as a checklist for examining couple interaction, a conflict in goals often occurs when women and men approach the same situation from very different perspectives.

Where gender differences are not recognised and respected, much unhappiness can grow out of a longing for the partner to be 'like me'. It is with distressed couples, where gender differences are an obstacle to intimacy, that it may be most useful to start from the premiss that 'I do not know the gender which I am not'. (See Chapter 5 for further discussion.)

1.3. A working hypothesis

(See also Chapter 6.)

In his ground-breaking study, Daniel Stern (1985) describes his approach as a:

> working hypothesis which remains to be proved, and even its status as a hypothesis remains to be explored.

His hypothesis underpins some of the key ideas discussed here. Firstly, that there are 'sensitive periods' during which the experiences of the child are of utmost importance. These are times when the 'emerging self' makes sense of the experiences.

Secondly, Stern suggests the life task of the individual is to move from a position of separateness towards a sense of connectedness. Rather than seeing the baby as needing to work towards separation, Stern (1985) sees the baby as inherently having the psychic equipment (through perception, touch, and ability to learn and differentiate) to develop the ability to connect with others as a result of inherent separateness.

Using Stern's hypothesis, the task of the male or female becomes that of learning about the other from an inherent position of separateness and difference (Keller, 1985; Benjamin, 1988; Sheinberg and Penn, 1991).

Taking seriously both Stern's (1985) contention that the emergent child has the potential to experience itself as a separate entity and Rutter's (1980) view that a child's gender identity is well developed before he or she has a proper appreciation of sex differences generally, one can think of each gender as containing a separate and distinct understanding of either their own femaleness or their own maleness.

Benjamin (1988) makes an important contribution to the study of human behaviour in her discussion of 'intersubjectivity'. She writes elegantly of the need to develop a new theory of human development in which:

> the individual subject no longer reigns absolute must confront the difficulty that each subject has in recognizing the other as an equivalent centre of experience.

She continues:

> Intersubjective theory postulates that the other must be recognised as another subject in order for the self to fully experience his or her subjectivity in the other's presence.

If one introduces the concept of gender differences it becomes necessary to recognise that the 'other' (partner) has a separate centre of self which is gender based. By emphasising the intersubjective nature of human development, Benjamin (1988) makes a link with Chodorow (1978), who writes:

> We cannot understand gender differences apart from this relational construct.

It is argued here that the female knows how she perceives, feels and makes sense of the world, and the male knows how he as a male perceives, feels and makes sense of the world. To understand the opposite gender each must find out through connecting with the other and perceiving, feeling and making sense of the other gender through this ongoing life long connection (see Chapter 6).

This is a shift in thinking about female/male interrelationships. It begins with the premiss that each gender has shared knowledge about its own gender but not of the opposite gender.

Each gender can say,

1. I have the ability (whether male or female) to know myself as a separate human being, and to know my gender.
2. I do not know the gender which I am not, except through contact with and experience of that gender, during my life cycle.
3. My task within a heterosexual relationship is to learn about the other gender and not to assume a knowledge which I may not have.

I do not 'know' the gender which I am not.

> The importance of this new work on infant psychology is that it overturns the old developmental shibboleth of 'separation' as the ultimate goal and it defines the process of maturity as an alternating state of both connections and differentiations within the context of ongoing relationships (Sheinberg and Penn, 1991).

The view is advanced here that each gender may, at times, perceive, feel and make sense of the world in gender-specific ways, and a life task for women and men may be to learn about the other gender. Gender-specific differences may arise out of basic biological needs (Money, 1986) or 'through socialisation alone' (Lips, 1997) or as a 'dynamic interplay among processes that operate across time frames, levels of analysis, and contexts' (Cairns et al., 1995).

Many couples are able to take for granted gender differences and to make appropriate adjustments. For these couples, 'emotional override' (Weiss, 1980) may be in operation.

Gay and lesbian relationships are not the focus of this book but may indicate that 'intimacy' with the same gender can be easier than engaging in the struggle to know the unknown (Faderman, 1981; Hite, 1981, Wellings et al., 1994, Van Arsdall, 1996).

To facilitate thinking about differing intimacy needs, the concept of an invisible intimacy/gender screen is introduced in Chapter 2. The invisible intimacy screen is a filter through which each gender perceives the other and whose reactions require translation before the other is understood.

> Couples have struggled with the question 'why does she/he not behave like me?' Perhaps because in some very simple ways she/he is not like me.

In describing this screen there is an implicit acceptance of the interconnections between the sexual and social. A greater understanding of this may help couples in their search for intimacy.

1.4. Implications for therapists, counsellors and professionals

Several concerns emerge for professionals who work with couples, the first of which is the gender of the therapists. Within couple therapy in Britain a majority of therapists are women who, unless attuned to both female and male intimacy needs, may value the female's intimacy needs most and consequently encourage the couple to accept a female approach to intimacy. Sharing of feelings, touch and tenderness and reciprocal speedy communication may then become central to therapy. Autonomy and independence within the relationship, problem solving, good regular sex, respecting the male's use of language and slower approach to communication, and male aggression, may be seen as negative aspects of a couple relationship. Should this occur the man may feel disadvantaged and disinclined to seek help.

Women tend to be the help seekers (Briscoe, 1982, 1986, 1987) and clinical experience suggests that it can be difficult to persuade men to seek help for relationship difficulties.

One can only speculate what impact a balanced approach to female/male intimacy needs may have. Would men be more inclined to become relationship and sexual therapists themselves and be more prepared to seek help for relationship difficulties?

Professionals working with relationships and sexual difficulties can ensure that, within therapy, a balance is sought between male and female intimacy needs; and that they are prepared to acknowledge gender differences and to work with the couple towards this end. Being aware of gender prejudices enables professionals to work towards an accepting and respectful attitude to the needs of both partners.

A further concern is that some aspects of behaviour are learned and may be unlearned, and other aspects of behaviour are defined by the maleness or femaleness of the person and are less amenable to change. Theoreticians disagree amongst themselves regarding these issues and few clear guidelines are available.

Professional workers, without being overwhelmed by this lack of clarity, can help both partners respect and take seriously the gender needs of the other. This means keeping a balance between each partner and assisting both without trying to 'make-over' the other in 'my own image'. At the same time, small changes are possible, and may more easily occur within an accepting relationship where differences are acknowledged. Although one cannot change the colour of one's eyes.

This is a challenging paradox in thinking about and working with couples in distress – understanding the interaction between the biological and physical inheritance, the uniqueness of the individual, and the social and culturally learned aspects of behaviour. A key issue for the therapist is to assist each gender with this paradox while being aware of her/his own gender prejudice.

1.5. Individuality and gender

The individuality of each female or male may seem at variance with the intimacy screen since the variety of human resources and potential cannot be classified simply or conclusively. Exceptions stretch the imagination and question any, and all, generalisation.

The woman who is a professor of mathematics, a high powered female executive or mountain climber may feel, quite rightly, that gender as described does not fit her. However, she will still have to consider how she wants to cope with issues such as pregnancy and childbirth. The man who is a homemaker, and finds the competitive world of work a hostile and forbidding place, will still have to cope with his own sexuality and his need to find a sexual partner with whom he can feel safe enough to enjoy a confident sexual life. In these ways the issue of the physical and biological inheritance will colour their life choices.

For men or women who feel that they are gay, lesbian or bisexual the issues are confusing, particularly since society tends to isolate and stigmatise them. However, for many lesbian women the desire to become pregnant does not disappear as a result of being physically attracted to other women rather than to men. Similarly, men who are gay may wish to assert their rights to father children.

The need for a physical sexual outlet for men has been emphasised by the homosexual community, in their demands for legalising sexual relationships between consenting adults in private, whereas many lesbians emphasise their relationship as primarily emotional (Faderman, 1981).

While recognising the uniqueness of each individual, these differences in the physical makeup of women and men cannot be avoided.

1.6. Summary

Chapter 1 suggests that a definition of intimacy which is helpful to heterosexual relationships may need to encompass gender differences.

2 CHAPTER

The Invisible Intimacy Screen

2.1. Introduction

Chapter 2 introduces the invisible intimacy screen. Intimacy is described as involving five key elements, each of which a man or woman may view from divergent perspectives. These five elements form the invisible screen through which women and men relate.

Additionally, there may be overarching gender differences in which the woman may act to connect with others within a network of relationships and be concerned about who gets hurt by any decision (Bar-Tal and Frieze, 1977; Gilligan, 1982, 1987; Nolen-Hoeksema, 1987; Prager, 1989; Markus and Oyserman, 1989).

The man, on the other hand, may interact from a position of separateness and make choices which maintain his independence and autonomy. He may focus on the impact of any decisions upon his own position within a hierarchy of authority (Ruble and Frieze, 1978; Gilligan, 1982, 1987; Ruble et al., 1988; Tannen, 1990; Jack, 1991; Kuebli and Fivush, 1992;).

Female/male intimacy needs and responses are influenced by the elements of the intimacy screen, which operate to add excitement and uniqueness to a relationship, or frustration and a feeling of being misunderstood.

In presenting the elements of the invisible intimacy screen there is no intention to suggest that these are the only influences upon the couple. Many other factors (described in Chapters 3 and 4) such as personal abilities, culture, religion, education, personal and family experiences of poverty, overcrowding, poor housing, social and economic factors may all play their part in overriding or modifying these elements.

What is being suggested is that where couples are in distress or are seeking help with relationship difficulties, the invisible intimacy screen can be used as a checklist or aid to consider whether gender differences are causing stress and getting in the way of a deepening intimacy.

Each element is described here as a discrete entity for greater clarity, although in reality they interconnect and are interwoven.

2.2. The invisible intimacy screen

2.2.1. The elements of the invisible intimacy screen

A definition of intimacy that takes account of gender differences may help couples come to terms with their different ways of relating.

Intimacy was previously explored in four areas – sexual closeness, physical and non-verbal closeness, emotional empathy, and operational closeness (Ridley, 1993). Within these four areas men were described as placing greater emphasis upon sexual closeness and women upon physical and non-verbal closeness. A woman may seek emotional empathy and a man will usually try to solve a problem rather than listen to her feelings. Where this occurs, both partners feel that empathy is lacking.

> It may be more useful to think about heterosexual intimacy as encompassing five elements. These are emotionally arousing situations, social and interpersonal pressures, within a physical sexual relationship, communication, and aggression. Defining intimacy then becomes a more complicated reality-based exercise.

It is as if there is an invisible screen between the woman and man through which each observes the other, and expects the other to behave 'like me' or respond by mirroring their own responses. When this does not occur and each gender responds from a gender base, confusion and dismay can occur. Because the screen is invisible, there is ample scope for distortion, misunderstandings and crises of intimacy.

For some couples gender differences enhance the relationship. Others prefer to think of the opposite gender as being deliberately disagreeable, obstinate, or downright stupid. Many relationship crises arise out of an inability to understand or reinterpret their relationship in gender terms.

> For intimacy to develop there is a need to reinterpret couple interaction in gender terms.

	Female tendencies	Male tendencies	
1F	**In emotionally arousing situations** tends to want to speak about emotions and wants to be listened to	**In emotionally arousing situations** tends to look for the problem and wants to find solutions	1M
2F	**Where there are social and interpersonal pressures** tends to seek connectedness within a network of relationships and pays attention to who gets hurt	**Where there are social and interpersonal pressures** tends to seek autonomy and separateness and considers his own position within a hierarchy	2M
3F	**Within a physical sexual relationship** tends to want emotional sharing, touch and tenderness and whole body involvement, and seeks exclusivity	**Within a physical sexual relationship** tends to need to feel confident and to seek penetration, is penis focussed, and does not necessarily seek exclusivity for himself	3M
4F	**Within communication** tends to find words quickly and seeks mutual responsiveness	**Within communication** tends to be slow to find words, seeks a non-verbal understanding	4M
5F	**Within aggression** tends to be verbally aggressive	**Within aggression** tends to be physically aggressive	5M

Figure 1: The invisible intimacy screen

The key elements contained in the screen that may interfere with intimacy can be summarised as shown in Figure 1.

The elements of the invisible intimacy screen can come into play during every female/male interaction throughout the life cycle. Using a different metaphor, within these five areas, women and men may speak different dialects while assuming they speak the same.

2.2.2. Using the invisible intimacy screen to think about couple interaction and gender differences

Sections 2.3 to 2.7 describe the separate elements of the invisible intimacy screen. To avoid repetition number/letter combinations (1 F, 1 M, etc.) are used to highlight female (1 F) and male (1 M) responses and needs within an emotionally arousing situation; 2 F, 2 M to indicate female and male responses and needs when there are social and interpersonal pressures on the couple; 3 F, 3 M for female and male responses and needs within a physical sexual relationship; 4 F, 4 M for female and male responses and needs within communication styles; and 5 F, 5 M to indicate female and male needs and responses in relation to aggression.

2.2.3. Taking account of the invisible intimacy screen

Using the invisible intimacy screen as a simple, if crude, guide to each gender's priorities, a definition that balances the needs of each gender becomes possible.

A definition of intimacy would encompass an ability of each partner to understand, respect, actively care for what the other needs in several key interactions. These are in response to emotionally arousing situations, to social pressures and interpersonal situations, within a physical sexual relationship as well as interactions that require good communication or where feelings of aggression are heightened. A sense of mutuality can then emerge from the acceptance and celebration of difference and of vulnerabilities.

Stated in this way, a shared sense of intimacy may seem difficult to achieve. Falling in love is easier. It is out of the control of the individual and 'just happens'. 'Falling out of love' also 'just happens'. In contrast, intimacy as understood here is the product of learning about and coming to a deeper understanding, appreciation of and commitment to the gender needs of the other. Hard work and painful experiences can be the seedbed for this greater understanding and a deepening of intimacy.

Couples who have faced and survived tragedy together often say that their relationship is stronger as a result.

> Much damage can be done by taking sides, assuming one gender to have all the good qualities, while putting pressure upon the 'bad' gender to change (see 2.3.1).

In presenting this material one is not attempting to say that all couples will have these difficulties. Many couples engage creatively to find out about the other, and much of the pleasure within the relationship derives from their differentness. Each learns to depend on the other for their strengths and to be aware of their vulnerabilities. For these couples, much of what is said here may be either known to them or irrelevant. They will have found an acceptable way to accommodate to each other.

Although each element of the invisible intimacy screen is described as if it is a discrete and separate entity, there is an obvious overlap and interaction between these elements and other factors. The personal experience of each partner, the impact of life events and the current life cycle stage of the participants will affect all of their interactions.

The five elements of gender differences play their part in defining the quality of a couple relationship in the same way that age, health, personal or family history or culture affect a couple. Where intimacy is being threatened a review of the elements of the intimacy screen can indicate ways in which intimacy can be enhanced. Alternative ways of helping are offered.

2.2.4. Couple interactions

The couple interactions described are selected specifically to demonstrate gender differences. For many couples the differences are not so clear. Therapists are encouraged not to fall into the trap of assuming that differences always cause problems, but allow her/himself the flexibility to be aware of gender differences and to focus on them when they occur and cause relationship difficulties. The examples given are specifically chosen to highlight how gender differences can interfere with intimacy.

The following is a simplified example showing how gender differences can affect an ordinary couple interaction. The number/letter combinations 1 F, 1 M refer to the invisible intimacy screen (see 2.2.1 and Examples 2d, Tim and Tina; 2h, Janice and Roy).

2.2.4.1. Example 2a, Alan and Amy

This is a common female/male interaction in which Alan shows his sympathy by wanting to have sexual intercourse, which is perceived by Amy as insensitive.

Alan (26) and Amy (25) represent a common female/male interaction. They have lived together for three years and think of themselves as 'an item' and do not intend to marry. Amy has a five-year-old boy, Kevin, from a previous relationship. Kevin is visiting his father for the weekend for the first time in several months.

During the evening meal they argued about how often Kevin should be with his father. Alan feels that he is the real parent and prefers Kevin not to see his natural father. Amy both agrees and disagrees. She is upset and tearful.

Alan notices her distress and suddenly feels warm and protective towards her instead of being angry. He tries to show his concern and affection for her by making sexual advances (3 M).

Amy is shocked and offended that he can be so insensitive to her distress. She wants to feel understood emotionally, and in harmony with herself and Andy before relaxing and enjoying Andy's sexual advances (1 F, 3 F).

Additionally, she feels that Andy should understand the intensity of pressure she is under when thinking of her son's relationship with his father (1 F, 2 F).

The above scenario sets the scene for misunderstandings unless each can accept that the other is responding from a gender perspective and be respectful of the other's needs.

2.2.4.2. How to help: general guidelines

i. Introduction: respect gender differences

While working with couples it may not be necessary to speak about gender differences. What is relevant is that the therapist is able to recognise and work with gender differences, keeping a balance between the positive abilities each partner brings into the relationship and drawing upon both partners' resources. Since many relationship therapists are women it is important, for both female and male therapists, that any personal biases or any tendency to take sides is discussed and monitored within supervision.

ii. Seek agreement from both partners

It is necessary to seek the agreement of both partners that they wish to engage in working together, and to find a safe and confidential environment in which to work together without interruptions. It is also important to ensure as far as possible that the couple are helped to refrain from going over old ground, or allowing one partner to dominate the interaction. Interventions can be gentle but persistent, aimed at keeping conversations mutual, reciprocal, future focused, time limited, practical, and positive. It is helpful to keep the focus and pace interventions appropriately. At the same time, sensitive issues which are being avoided can be addressed by the therapist when appropriate. Using a light touch and a sense of humour, bringing playfulness and an ability to experiment into a couple relationship, even in heated or conflictual situations, can lessen the tension.

See Crowe and Ridley (1990) for greater detail on how to work with couples.

iii. Decentre and observe the couple interaction

In the session, encourage the couple to face each other and to talk together about the difficulties they face. This enables the therapist to observe the couple's communication, and notice non-verbal interaction as well as the power dynamics between the couple, and elements such as who speaks first, and how seriously they take each other.

iv. Learn about the couple by asking them to talk together about their current difficulties

By observing couple interaction in this way it does not take long to notice whether they tend to use gender-specific skills in communication.

v. Reviewing their sexual relationship

Not all couples present with sexual difficulties. However, where couples are experiencing difficulties, the sexual relationship is often also at risk. It is therefore helpful to get an early understanding as to whether this is occurring. The therapist needs to feel comfortable and confident in her/his attitude to sexuality and be able to raise this issue without embarrassment. Too many therapists are untrained in this area and often neglect sexuality as an aspect of couple intimacy.

vi. Talking about gender differences

In my experience it comes as a relief to couples that difficulties experienced are understandable when gender differences are taken into account. Instead of feeling deliberately misunderstood, couples can then help each other to respond more effectively to the gender needs of the other (see Examples 2d, Tim and Tina; 2g, Bob, Cynthia and Bruce; 3g, Belinda and Ben; 3h, Zoey and Zack; 3i, Harry and Helen).

2.2.4.3. Using the invisible intimacy screen to think about Alan and Amy

To overcome misunderstandings, Amy can be helped to communicate her needs to Alan (4 F) without being too verbally aggressive (5 F), or too anxious about other issues (1 F, 2 F). Alan can learn to respond by listening empathically (1 M, 4 M) without being aggressive physically (5 M).

It also means that Alan can be encouraged to 'put on hold' his sexual desires and find a way to listen to Amy's distress verbally (1 M) rather than showing his concern sexually (3 M); Amy can be invited to understand that a man often feels sexual if his emotions are aroused.

2.2.4.4. Introduce the concept of gender differences

A simple statement can be made, such as, 'what may be happening is that you are each behaving like many other women and men, each showing very different needs and responses. Amy wanting to be listened to and have her feelings attended to and Alan wanting to show how much he cares through his sexual responses'.

> The interaction of the man who tries to show his empathy through physical sexuality but is perceived by the woman as insensitive, is common.

It is rarely necessary to have complicated discussions about gender and gender differences. However, where couples want to explore the question of gender differences further they can be referred to books and articles.

Many couples understand these differences. For others, this simple scenario slowly escalates until the woman goes off sex and the man becomes aggressive, or also goes off sex (see Example 2h, Janice and Roy).

2.2.5. Simplifying in order to draw attention to interaction

In drawing attention to potential gender differences complex issues are simplified. The need to simplify to identify patterns of interaction is taken from systems thinking. Sluzki (1978) writes that a systems model requires an ability to simplify by:

> focusing on certain behaviours and interpersonal processes at the expense of

> others – selectively observing events, filtering in those observables that are relevant to the model.
>
> This simplification makes systems work attractive, but also raises doubts about the arbitrary exclusion of data which do not fit the hypotheses being considered (Crowe and Ridley, 1990).

Much other information is temporarily excluded and can be reintroduced when making an assessment of a couple's interaction. However, gender differences are too often ignored or set aside as irrelevant.

2.3. Emotionally arousing situations

2.3.1. Women and emotionally arousing situations (1 F)

Intimacy is sometimes defined around the mutual sharing of emotions. Reis and Shaver (1988) suggest that a fundamental characteristic of intimacy is the discloser's feelings of being understood, validated and cared for, and Sternberg (1988) considers intimacy to be the emotional component of love, which refers to feelings of warmth, support, and commitment to the relationship. Levinger (1988) defines intimacy as a combination of affective and behavioural interdependence of two partners.

> In the United States and Canada today, the emphasis is on psychological intimacy and emotional sharing, in addition to task performance (Ingoldsby and Smith, 1995).

Brown and Harris (1978) were among the first to define and research women's need for an intimate relationship. They concluded that a 'confiding relationship' with a husband or a close relative was protective against depression even in the presence of other precipitating factors such as the early death of a mother, or having three children under 7. In defining a confiding relationship, they drew upon Weiss's (1969) definition of secure attachment which is provided by ties from which participants gain a sense of security and place and where individuals:

> can express their feelings freely and without self-consciousness.... For a relationship to provide intimacy there must be trust, effective understanding and ready access.

Brown and Harris's research indicates that for women there is a need to share feelings, within a trusting relationship, perhaps what Bradbury et al. (1996) calls emotion focused coping. Interestingly, Brown and Harris (1978) expressly state 'this does not mean that a sexual relationship is necessary'.

> The concept is considered throughout, that for a woman there may be a need to share feelings within a trusting relationship as an essential aspect of intimacy which is not necessarily required by men (Charnofsky, 1992).

Kersten and Himle (1991) think that mutuality is an aspect of intimacy which is agreed upon by most theorists, yet experience of couples seeking therapy often suggests that this is not necessarily a priority for men. The tendency for women and men to respond differently within emotionally arousing situations can make 'mutual sharing of emotions' a stressful experience for both partners. It may be that women place more value on mutual sharing than men currently do. Men do not exhibit the same need, nor do they necessarily approach emotions in the same way (Jacobson, 1983; Gottman and Levenson, 1988; Manstead, 1992; Brody and Hall, 1993; Noller, 1993; Gottman, 1994).

A more functional response from a male perspective may be to solve the underlying problem that is thought to be the cause of the feeling (Gilligan, 1982). Men may also place greater emphasis upon other aspects of a relationship, for example a safely available and encouraging sexual partner (3 F, 3 M).

For the woman to seek emotional sharing may be so natural to her that she does not understand a man who rarely speaks about his feelings. For the man who communicates through physical sexuality it is equally difficult to understand why his female partner prefers to talk first about her feelings. Too often, each gender sees the other as inadequate or deficient, rather than having complementary abilities.

Markman and Kraft (1989) have suggested that women often experience intimacy by verbal self-disclosure of affect, whereas men experience intimacy by sharing activities together.

> It is suggested here that, rather than thinking of men as inadequate because they speak less about feelings than women, it would be more realistic to accept that men approach emotionally arousing situations from a different perspective and with different resources.

With different early education, men may learn to be more attentive to their own and their partner's feelings. However, it may be unrealistic for women to expect men to achieve the same level of awareness and interest in feelings as they themselves have.

> Realistically women may need to turn to other women for greater emotional support, in the way they did in the past, in order to satisfy their need for emotional sharing.

Charnofsky (1992) encapsulates this discrepancy between the way women and men treat emotional situations. He records the experience of men whose wives have left them, giving repeated examples of men who did not respond to the discontent of their partner.

2.3.1.1. Example 2b, Mort

> Mort was asked 'And with all those indications that something was wrong between you, what did you do about it?'
>
> His answer was 'Oh, I didn't really do anything, I thought she was going through some mid-life crisis or something. I mean, we agreed on politics and religion and child-rearing and stuff like that, so I figured we'd stick it out for sure and maybe she'd get over her weird moods. Look where that strategy's got me'.

If one uses a male perspective one can hypothesise that he respects what he believes she needs, which would be to preserve independence and autonomy. He also confuses her responses to their relationship with the onset of the menopause and assumes her 'weird moods' are because of 'some mid-life crisis'.

This simple example draws attention to two ways in which women and men respond differently. The woman wants to talk through the aspects of their relationship which upset her. If this does not happen she feels ignored, undervalued and rejected. Because she is attuned to others' feelings and attending to who gets hurt, she finds it difficult to accept that her partner can still love her if he ignores her in these ways.

The man seems to make a calculation, firstly that she is responding to a 'female' event, the menopause, and secondly that she will get over it on her own.

2.3.2. Men and emotionally arousing situations (1 M)

Tannen (1990) taped and analysed thousands of female/male interviews and concluded that women and men face emotional issues from very distinct perspectives. When a situation arises that is charged with emotion for a woman, men often respond not to the emotion, but to the problem and women want to speak about their feelings and have them understood.

Tannen thinks that men recognise the feelings, but want to listen to what happened (not to the feelings themselves), in order to understand the cause of the upset, and to identify the 'problem'. Once the 'problem' has been understood, Tannen suggests, most men will then try to solve it. Neither partner is satisfied and both feel misunderstood.

It is as if women and men experience emotionally arousing situations differently. Women experience feelings as tangible and concrete events which must be dealt with. Men experience the problem as the tangible and concrete event to be tackled. Each gender defines a different problem.

2.3.2.1. Example 2c, Tony Moore

A somewhat extreme example of the male approach to emotionally arousing situations is that of Tony Moore (1991).

> Dr Tony Moore, a surgeon and rehabilitation specialist, was hit by a 30-tonne truck while driving to work and was severely injured.
>
> He describes vividly his first reactions to the injury, which were to examine himself in detail to discover how serious were his injuries.
>
> 'Even before anyone arrived at the wreckage my mind was racing to make sure that I survived. I moved my left arm to feel my neck and back, searching for an injury which would help to explain why I couldn't move or feel my legs. My fingers were shaking with the fear of what they might find, but while I managed to wriggle my toes inside my shoes, which told me that I had been spared a dreaded paraplegia, my fingers found fresh damage.'
>
> By the time the ambulance arrived, he had assessed the situation.
> 'Get me up, get me out', he urged with two desperate gasps.
> 'Stay calm,' said the young ambulance man.

'Stay nothing,' he hissed with grim intensity. 'Please mate, I'm a doctor, I have subcutaneous emphysema, a pneumothorax, a flail chest, and I can't bloody breathe.'
'Oh shit,' the ambulance man replied.

The above excerpt is about a remarkable man, who made a remarkable recovery. As such it may tell about only him. It may be useful to note his ability to focus on the seriousness of the situation, how it affected him, and what the solutions to the problem would be. He was of course trained as a surgeon, and his training stood him in good stead.

He did not speak about feelings, nor about how the accident might affect his family or close relationships. He focused on assessing the extent of the problem. This suggests that Tony Moore may be exhibiting a male characteristic (particularly well trained and developed in him) of focusing upon assessing what is the problem, and what needs to be done in order to fix it.

It would be helpful to know how a woman surgeon might react to a similar life event. She may respond from a very problem-focused perspective; her training would encourage her to do so, and all women do not respond alike. It would be useful to know if her initial thoughts might be about how the accident affects those who are dependent upon her. Neither response is better or worse than the other, the woman is not necessarily more altruistic and the man more narcissistic, but each may approach the same incident from alternative perspectives.

2.3.2.2. Example 2d, Tim and Tina

The following is an example from clinical experience of an emotionally arousing situation where the man feels hurt because his efforts to solve the problem are rejected and the woman is upset because her feelings are not listened to during a critical period in their relationship.

Tim (42) and Tina (39) have been married for 20 years. They have three children aged 19, 17 and 15. Tina, a housewife and mother, was referred to the sexual therapy clinic for lack of sexual desire. Having had a hysterectomy six months previously, the couple recommenced sexual intercourse after three months. Since then, Tina experienced pain during intercourse and a slow diminution of desire. Medically there was no cause for the pain during intercourse.

What follows is a segment of conversation between Tim and Tina on his return from work, which was replayed during therapy.

Tim, hopefully. 'Well how have you been feeling today?'

Tina. 'A bit down, I found myself crying at lunch time when I was listening to the Archers. There was so much talk about babies.'

Tim. 'Why would that make you cry? You've had your fair share of babies. Wouldn't it be better if you did not listen to that rubbish. Why don't you go and have lunch with Mabel instead?'

Tina. 'No, I'm not up to seeing Mabel yet.'

Tim. 'Surely, she'd cheer you up. She's such a lively person. I can't imagine her wanting to cry about babies.'

Tina. 'No, well I suppose you can't ... But she hasn't had a hysterectomy ... It makes me feel so old.'

Tim, by now a little startled. 'Old. What at your age? You are only 39. You are not old. You still look pretty good to me.'

He tries to hug her and she shrugs him off.

Tina. 'Just look at my sagging stomach!'

Tim. 'Well, why not join an aerobics class. This step aerobics seems to be all the rage. All the young things in the office are doing it. It seems to keep them in shape.'

Tina, in tears. 'Oh, you'll never understand.'

Tim. 'I do my best, but you won't try any of the things I suggest. What am I supposed to do?'

Resentful silence follows.

The above example can be understood in different ways. One is to make the assumption that they simply do not understand each other and wonder why they are in this relationship since they understand each other so little.

Alternatively one can think of Tim and Tina as doing their best to communicate through the invisible intimacy screen but failing. Failing because each assumes, incorrectly, that they are similar.

Tim tries to solve the problem of Tina's sadness and her sagging stomach, by suggesting things to do. Tina rejects Tim's suggestions, which hurts Tim and increases Tina's gloom.

As a woman she quickly compares herself, within the network of her relationships, with Mabel who has not had a hysterectomy, and to the 'young things' at work whose figures have not been burdened by pregnancy nor diminished by surgery. Rather than being perceived as helpful, each suggestion is felt to be unsympathetic.

Tina felt misunderstood because Tim did not seem to notice her feelings nor want to hear about them. Tim feels upset because none of his suggestions are taken up as helpful.

2.3.2.3. How to help

In general, where any issue is getting in the way of a more satisfying relationship, it is important to help the couple to take each other seriously. This is particularly important where gender differences occur.

The following interventions may be useful.

2.3.2.4. Taking each other seriously

(See also 2.7.2.2)

Ask Tim to listen to how Tina feels about having had a hysterectomy. Using the hypothesis that Tina wants her feelings to be listened to (1 F):

i. Decentre by asking the couple to turn to face each other so that they can talk directly to each other (see 2.2.4.2).
ii. Suggest that Tim ask Tina how she has been affected by the hysterectomy.
iii. Ask her to say more about her feelings.
iv. Encourage Tim to listen without making any suggestions as to 'what to do'.
v. Encourage Tina to ask Tim what he has understood about her feelings.
vi. Help Tim to restate in his own words Tina's feelings.
vii. See if Tina can ask Tim what it was like for him to listen to her feelings without making suggestions about how to solve the problem.
viii. When the couple have got this far (perhaps in a later session) it may be possible for Tina to be encouraged to hear one or two of Tim's suggestions for solving the problem. At some point Tina may be ready to try one out. This takes time.

ix. Discussing gender differences. Tim and Tina may be able to use the above interventions without any reference to gender differences. However, if a couple become very stuck, or are very interested in how they communicate, it can be helpful to point out the ways in which they are using gender skills that get in the way of their relationship. In this case Tim is using the male skill of problem solving and Tina that of speaking about her feelings. From experience, couples are relieved to have such an explanation and can usually accept there is a need to change.

2.3.2.5. 'Playing' with gender differences

Learning to play, bringing lightness and humour into couple relationships, is particularly important for couples whose disagreements have become entrenched and humourless. An element of play can be introduced by using reverse gender role play. Therapists who are unaccustomed to being more interventionist can practise role play with colleagues to build self-confidence.

Reverse gender is a form of role play in which each partner pretends to be the other gender. The emphasis is therefore upon each partner allowing themselves to enter 'playfully' into the idea that they can, for the moment, be physically the other gender and learn what that may be like. (See also 2.4.2.4 (role reversals), where less emphasis is placed upon the physical self and more on how each gender behaves).

Reverse gender can be tailored to each particular couple and each of the five elements of the invisible intimacy screen can be addressed as appropriate (see 2.2.2 and 2.4.2.4).

Couples do seem to enjoy playing at being the other gender. They may decide that they want to swap jackets or the man may pretend to be wearing a skirt and high heels.

Encourage the couple to be enthusiastic about getting into their parts fully so that the experience is rich and fun.

Where gender issues are being explored it may help to be open about the purpose of the reverse gender by saying, for example, 'Let's see whether you are more sympathetic to female and male perspectives by "playing" at being the other gender.'

Tim and Tina would have been asked to take the other's perspective, with Tina trying to solve the problem and Tim speaking about feelings. Each partner can be encouraged to 'coach' the other by engaging positively in the gender reversal, with the therapist intervening to ensure that the couple stay on track.

Where there seem to be severe problems in understanding the other it can be helpful to ask each partner to imagine that they have the physical attributes of their partner and to tell each other what that feels like.

This may be particularly helpful where there are physical and sexual difficulties. Inexperienced therapists are not encouraged to take this step without prior training and good supervision. Issues of envy, jealousy or resentment of the other gender may emerge which require care and patience.

The therapist should also ensure that any role play should occur during the first 20 minutes of a session, leaving time for processing and discussion of what was learned during the session.

Taking risks and 'playing' in session can help each partner 'get inside' and understand the other gender, and their own feelings, in new ways. Myths about the other gender can be explored and debunked. For example, where a woman has had a powerful and angry father she may assume that all men are powerful and angry. Within a 'reverse gender' experience those feelings may be expressed while in role and discussed in the debriefing or processing that follows (see 2.4.2.4, iii).

Reverse gender role play is best when experienced by the couple as pleasurable. It is essential to take time to ensure that the couple feel comfortable and agree to participate and are prepared to 'play with a different approach'. The therapist is required to be flexible and feel confident to participate in the experience with the couple.

Tina and Tim were able to learn more about the other by talking with each other, and a reverse role play was not required. A good outcome for them over time may be a combination initially of listening to feelings (1 F), restating those feelings in words and later problem solving (1 M). It may not be necessary openly to address the issue of gender differences.

Men often do understand their partner's feelings and, when asked, can state in detail what the feelings may be. In this sense they are not insensitive.

> However, such men need to understand that the partner will feel valued when her feelings are listened to actively and talked about; and undervalued if they are not.

The fact that he knows, but does not speak about what she is feeling, is not enough. To have feelings verbalised openly seems central to many women's intimacy needs.

2.3.2.6. Example 2e, Jim and Susan

In this example the man faces a problem and wishes to discuss it with his female partner. Assume (1 M) that when Jim tells Susan about 'the problem', he wants help in thinking about alternative solutions. He does not find it useful to explore the feelings of those involved.

Jim has disagreed with a colleague at work because a project they are both engaged in is behind schedule. It may involve the firm in extra costs, since bonuses are paid when contracts are completed on time, and penalties charged when contracts are late. Jim shares his concern, hoping that Susan can help him consider ways of speeding up the contract.

Susan begins to ask him how he feels, and what it was like to be so angry with his colleague, who is also his drinking partner. She is concerned that Jim will lose a very good friend. Consequently she tries to persuade him that he should not have been so angry, or at least that he should seek a reconciliation with his friend, as soon as possible.

Jim is astonished, feels criticised by Susan and angry that she takes so lightly his anxiety that the contracts may be late, the financial implications for the firm and for his reputation within the firm.

He tries to express his frustration with Susan that she has not understood his work situation. He speaks angrily and says, 'Oh never mind, I shouldn't have bothered you about this since you obviously don't understand my work.'

Susan is by now upset, she feels put down by this remark but tries again to see if she can help him with what she believes are his hurt feelings because of a disagreement with his best friend. She responds placatingly: 'Don't worry, Bill is an understanding sort of chap, I don't suppose he will carry any resentment for very long.'

At this Jim explodes with annoyance and leaves the room saying, 'I knew I should never have bothered asking you. It is always better to just sort it out myself.'

In this example Jim hopes for a solution to the problem of the possible delays to the contract and Susan sees the relationship difficulties with an old friend as the key issue. It is not surprising that the discussion ends unsatisfactorily.

After such an interchange one can understand that Susan believes that Jim has difficulty talking about his feelings and Jim may be reinforced in his sense that Susan could not help him to solve his work problems and that it is better to do so on one's own.

2.3.2.7. How to help

i. Use intervention designed to help Jim and Susan take each other seriously (see 2.3.2.4) Reverse the process, i.e. ask Susan to listen to what Jim is describing as the problem.
ii. If necessary, ask her to restate the problem without talking about feelings.
iii. Encourage Jim to ask Susan if she can think of ways to speed up the contract.
iv. Suggest that they do some problem-solving 'brainstorming' without censoring any of the ideas as absurd or useless. See if this can become a 'game' in which they both enjoy allowing themselves freedom to suggest alternatives. Make a list of these ideas.
v. Make a shorter list from the 'brainstorm list' of suggestions which seem practical. Encourage both Susan and Jim to think creatively and not put pressure on each other at this stage to choose one particular solution.

2.3.3. Resolving emotionally arousing situations

Feminists have encouraged a rethink of female/male relationships and as a result more attention is being paid to women's needs. The expression of feeling is increasingly seen as an area of strength within a woman's makeup and men are encouraged to develop an ability to speak about feelings as a way of releasing tension and responding to the woman's need for a shared emotional experience. Where a woman wants to have her feelings listened to, she may feel misunderstood and unloved within the relationship if this does not occur.

> Where a man approaches an emotionally charged situation from a problem-solving perspective, for intimacy to develop within a couple relationship he will need this aspect of him to be respected (1 F, 1 M).

If pressed to speak about feelings his sense of autonomy and personal worth may be undermined (2 M) and his problem-solving skills undervalued.

Realistically, many emotionally arousing situations require a blend of ventilating and accepting feelings and using problem-solving skills to face up to difficulties over time.

2.4. Where there are social and interpersonal pressures (2 F, 2 M)

Social and interpersonal pressures which particularly affect the couple may revolve around their social or cultural differences, female/male attitudes to work and the family, financial problems, different child rearing practices and relationships with the wider family. Social gatherings, family anniversaries, weddings or funerals can all become a focus for gender conflict. Where there is illness, disability, handicap or infertility such pressures can become overwhelming.

For the less traditional couples, relationships with past partners, children from previous relationships and the extended family can bring additional social pressures which are extremely demanding of the couple (Robinson, 1982; Anderson, 1994; Rutter and Hay, 1994; Harway, 1996). (See Chapter 3; Examples 3g, Belinda and Ben; 3h, Zoey and Zack.)

2.4.1. Women and social and interpersonal pressures (2 F)

Within the context of social and interpersonal pressures there are many interacting and competing forces. It is therefore difficult to claim with certainty that gender is a key factor in couple distress but gender differences should be taken into account when reviewing, assessing or working with couples who are in distress.

The couple interaction under social or interpersonal pressures may be affected by the woman's potential need to connect and to consider 'who gets hurt'; and for the male through his need to maintain autonomy and independence (Gilligan, 1982, 1987; Walsh, 1987; Tannen, 1990; Jack, 1991; Pool, 1994).

> The man relates to his social position within a hierarchy, and the woman relates to who gets hurt.

According to Gilligan (1982), there is a clear difference between women and men in how social and interpersonal situations are approached. Tannen (1990) thinks that women and men 'just don't understand' each other's communication style. Women use language to reinforce relationships and men use language to protect their independence and negotiate status within large group activities. Women and men are under different kinds of pressure within social situations.

Example 2e, Jim and Susan, illustrates this complex aspect of female/male interaction. Jim is concerned about the impact of delays to the contract on his prestige and position within the firm. Susan is concerned about the relationship between Jim and his drinking partner and colleague.

2.4.1.1. Female/male attitudes to work

Disputes often occur because of the alternative meanings women and men attach to their commitment to work, home and family. Many women place more emphasis upon their children and home whereas men tend to place more emphasis upon their work.

> For men, even unrewarding work is better than no work at all. Work is necessary to supply the needs of survival. With luck it will provide him with some pleasure of mastery. But for men unlike women, it fulfils a third essential purpose. It defines his manhood (Gaylin, 1992).

The world of employment is male dominated even though many women enter the workforce and succeed in managerial and senior positions. Traditional patterns dominate the work scene and women tend to go into caring and nurturing employment, such as nursing, teaching or social work. Men dominate senior positions in banking, politics and management, and also do physically demanding work of farming, mining, heavy engineering, and soldiering (Family Policy Studies, 1993).

Because of economic and social pressures, both women and men currently face many changes. Work opportunities vary, and redundancy or early retirement is more common. New technologies provide work for which women are suited and men face greater competition at work (Dormor, 1992). The question of equality of opportunity and wages is beyond the scope of this book, except to note that there are many social and political inequalities to be addressed within the employment field.

Relevant to intimacy is the way women and men approach issues of work and the family. A situation which one sees repeatedly is the man working long hours and the woman feeling neglected by him, even though she also works.

2.4.1.2. Example 2f, Dick and Dora

Dick (41) and Dora (41) have been married for 21 years, with two children David (20) and Doreen (18) who have recently left home. Dora was very close to the children and Dick was an accepting outsider to this relationship. A 'self-made man', a middle manager Dick prided himself that his wife and children had a good standard of living through his personal efforts. He loved his wife and children and felt satisfied with his life and family. Dora worked part time as a dental assistant since Doreen began school at five years. She recently became aware that she was unhappy with her work. She was particularly unhappy with her husband whom she felt was neglectful of her and put his work before her.

The following is a replay of an interaction of this (and other similar couple interactions) in which neither the man nor woman understand what the other is saying or feeling.

At 8.15 pm, Dick came home after a late evening management meeting where a potential takeover of the firm was discussed.

Dora greeted him. 'You are late, your supper is cold, and I'm really fed up.'

Dick, who is tired and somewhat worried about the impact of the takeover upon his position at work, responded. 'That's rich. You're upset, I'm the one who had to work late.'

Dora. 'Yes, well, you prefer staying late at work. Your work is more important to you than me.'

Dick. 'You know that is not true, you know that I have always put you and the family first.'

Dora. 'You always say that, but it doesn't feel like that. You are never here, when you are here you fall asleep all the time, you never talk to me, if you do it's about work.'

Dick. 'That's very unfair.'

Dora. 'What is unfair about it? It is unfair that you leave me at home waiting until you come in so that we can do something together, which never happens because you are always working, you bring work home and ignore me. That is what is unfair. While I spend my days in a job I don't like, with people I don't like, and you ignore me.'

Dick was by now feeling rather frightened and perplexed. He hoped that Dora understood he worked for her and the family, which gave him satisfaction, not the work itself. He began to try to explain this to her, but she interrupts him.

Dick. 'Dora, you know that I only enjoy work because it means we can have a nice house and good holidays.'

Dora. 'That is exactly what I mean, all you care about is the house and holidays, but what about me?'

By now both partners are upset and angry with each other and the discussion escalates further, each feeling thoroughly misunderstood by the other.

At one level this is an interaction that many couples experience and take for granted; at another level each gender feels deeply misunderstood about an important aspect of themselves.

For Dick, his need for independence and autonomy have largely been met by being a 'self-made man'. Additionally, he is able to protect his wife and family physically by providing them with a good standard of living (2 M). This satisfies a significant part of his 'intimacy needs', therefore he feels he is demonstrating his intimacy with Dora, or using her words, that he 'cares'. If one thinks of Dick being at a point on the life cycle where he begins to review his achievements, he feels reasonably satisfied (see Chapter 4; also 6.11).

Dora, on the other hand, not only feels neglected by her husband as he pays more attention to his work than to her and the children, she faces another demanding stage in her life cycle, the children leaving home no longer needing her so much, the lessening of her fertility and the impending menopause, with its accompanying review (see 6.7).

It is not unusual for the woman to turn her attention to her husband at such a time and reproach him for not caring. He, for his part, may be surprised as he has known her to be satisfied with her roles of wife, home-maker, mother and part-time worker. Suddenly she is not. A life cycle stage becomes a critical period for the couple.

Taking into account the elements of the invisible intimacy screen, if Dick follows a gender route he may try to problem-solve instead of listening to Dora's feelings (1 M). He may attempt to show he cares for her by seeking penetrative sex (3 M), or he may become aggressive (5 M).

Dora, for her part, should she respond from a gender base, may feel misunderstood by his problem solving (1 F). She is likely to need to have her feelings attended to before she can let herself enjoy sexual intercourse (3 F). She is more likely to be verbally aggressive than physically aggressive (5 F). A scenario can develop in which an ordinary interaction becomes a crisis and each gender cannot reach across the gender divide to care for the other.

2.4.1.3. How to help

i. Intimacy is likely to be enhanced if Dick can listen to how upset Dora is (1 F), and both share concerns about the children's absence, talk together about Dora's frustration at work and perhaps think together about their future now that the children have left home(4 F, 4 M). They may then begin to problem-solve alternative solutions (1 M). Instead of seeking sex (3 M), Dick could hold Dora gently to show he understands her feelings. She may become sensually aroused once her feelings have been listened to(3 F, 3 M). Any aggression (5 F, 5 M) may then be channelled into a passionate and tender sensual relationship which may or may not include sexual intercourse. In this way each is more able to attend to the other's intimacy needs and at the same time have their own needs met. A potential crisis can develop into a deepening of a shared sense of intimacy. (All of the elements of intimacy 1–5 have been engaged in the deepening of intimacy.)

ii. Communication training may be useful, perhaps beginning with Dick listening to Dora without interruption so that she feels listened to. This can then be reversed, with Dora listening to Dick for a similar length of time.

iii. A talking timetable can be considered, in which they can talk together for 10–15 minutes each day, with the focus being upon what it is like for them both now the children have left home.

iv. Planning forward may be helpful, discussing how they can use their newfound freedom. Can they go walking, to the theatre, swimming? What would bring some fun and pleasure into their relationship? Where couples have very different interests, they can alternate events, going together to an event that she prefers and then to one that he prefers.

In these ways they can begin the process of becoming a couple again after so many years as parent and breadwinner.

Similar scenarios reoccur in many socially pressurising situations and resentments can be stored as minor irritations, which simmer under the surface and erupt at times of tiredness or stress. They can then be used as ammunition which is thrown across the gender barrier, each partner feeling misunderstood and neglected.

How women and men respond to social pressures, or social situations, often overlaps with their physical sexual relationship (see 6.5, 6.9).

The woman may often take care of her partner's needs and not ask for what she wants because she does not want her partner to be hurt (see 6.3.6, 6.5.1).

The man's focus upon his sexual prowess is an aspect of maleness which is also subject to much social pressure and expectation (see 6.8.3, 6.10).

2.4.2. Men and social and interpersonal pressure (2 M)

An everyday example of a life event for parents is when a couple are trying to work out how best to help their child enter school on her/his first day.

2.4.2.1. Example 2g, Bob, Cynthia and son Bruce

Bruce, 4½ years old, was commencing school. Bob, his father, wanted to take Bruce to the school gates and say goodbye to him there, and Bruce's mother Cynthia would collect him.

Cynthia was very upset at this suggestion. She felt Bruce should be accompanied into the school and introduced to one or two other pupils while she stayed with him for a short while.

Cynthia criticised Bob for being insensitive to their son and for being unprepared to help him to overcome any anxieties he might have about making friends in a new situation. Bob felt that Bruce would be fine and that Cynthia was coddling him. They were unable to reconcile their differences and were each left feeling resentful of the other. Additionally, Bob felt put down by his wife as she insisted that she take Bruce to school and stay with him for the first hour or so. He had offered to take Bruce to school thinking it would encourage Bruce to feel safe. Cynthia, for her part, was also resentful and disappointed, as she again felt that she was the only parent who cared for Bruce and was always left having to be with him.

Thinking about Bob and Cynthia from a gender perspective, one can hypothesise that Bob is seeking to develop his son's sense of self-worth and independence (2 M) and Cynthia is seeking to ensure that he has a beginning network of friends (2 F). Since they were unable to respect each other's perspective each is left feeling resentful and isolated.

2.4.2.2. How to help

i. Bob and Cynthia may be helped to take each other seriously (see 2.3.2.4); i.e. ask Bob to listen to Cynthia and ask her how she feels about Bruce starting school. Decentre and ensure that the couple talk directly to each other.

ii. Use brainstorming (see 2.3.2.7, iv, v); focus on what would help in getting Bruce safely started at school.

iii. Ask each to talk about their own first day and what was good or not good about it; are there any helpful ideas there?

iv. Can the couple discuss how best they can support each other at this time? Perhaps they could each ask the other for something simple which would be supportive. They can use 'I' statements such as 'I would like you Bob to support me by ....', and 'I would like you Cynthia to support me by ....'

Focus on the couple pulling together and supporting each other at this time. In this way they learn about each other's gender perspective (see also 3.7., with reference to children).

2.4.2.3. Where there are entrenched positions

Sometimes entrenched positions arise out of a genuine misunderstanding. Resentments can arise because of a characteristic of the partner, which it is assumed can be changed. This is a central dilemma for therapists and those who work within the helping professions, because some behaviours can be changed and others are less amenable to change.

Where gender issues get in the way, the following options could be used. With Bob and Cynthia (2g, above) for example:

i. Draw attention to the fact that what may be occurring is a gendered response within their communication.
ii. While asking them to talk together about how they want to manage Bruce's first day at school, use phrases such as 'Bob, as a man and Bruce's father, can you ask Cynthia how she, as a woman and Bruce's mother, would want to introduce Bruce to school.'
iii. Suggest that Bob ask Cynthia what she hopes to achieve by accompanying Bruce into the classroom. Ensure that Bob listens (and repeats in his own words) what he thinks Cynthia has said.
iv. Reverse the above, using phrases such as 'Cynthia, as a woman and Bruce's mother, can you ask Bob how, as a man and as Bruce's father, he would want to introduce Bruce to school.' Follow this up by suggesting he explain what he hopes to achieve by his approach.
v. Suggest that Cynthia asks Bob to say more about why he wants to leave Bruce at the school gates.
vi. Ask Cynthia to repeat (in her own words) what Bob has said.
vii. Encourage them to share their thoughts about each other's suggestions and to come up with a compromise that they can both support.
viii. A light touch and a sense of humour helps; a comment about a 'battle of the sexes as to which sex wins' may be appropriate.
ix. Find out if they would agree that being independent and having a network of friends may both be useful attributes. Perhaps they can discuss this.
x. Can they discuss ways in which as a couple they can encourage Bruce to develop both of these attributes over time. In these ways, instead of a battle for which gender wins, they can jointly help their son develop strengths in both areas and at the same time respect each other's approach.

2.4.2.4. Role reversal

Another option for entrenched positions is to try a 'role reversal' where each is asked to behave like the other. The issue of gender difference is not discussed directly, as it is in reverse gender role play (see 2.3.2.5).

i. Each partner is asked to play the role of the other, with the focus being upon how the other behaves and what she or he says. It is best if this can be experienced as good fun or as a playful experiment.

ii. Each can be asked to observe the other's non-verbal posture, voice tone and facial expression in order to role play each other.

iii. Bob then pretends he is Cynthia; using her voice tone, physical position and use of language, he presents what he thinks is Cynthia's position. Cynthia, using Bob's voice tone, physical position and use of language, presents Bob's position. (The couple may be a little shy at first but with a little firm encouragement can usually enter into the role play with enthusiasm and can often bring useful insights into a very stuck position.)

iv. It is important now to process the experience by asking them what it felt to 'be' the other and what they learned from 'being' their partner.

It can be helpful to spend quite a long time 'processing' the experience. Encourage them to ask each other about the experience and to say what it was like to see themselves portrayed in this way. If the couple have never done this before they can be encouraged to try it again in the privacy of their own home. What it felt like to be the other can be a powerful learning experience for both partners.

After discussing their experience of the role play, the couple can be asked to continue with discussion of how to manage Bruce's first day at school. There is often a shift in the couple's understanding following the role play, and reaching a compromise agreement may be more possible.

The aim of the interventions is to help the couple move from a position of blaming the other, to an acceptance of each other's perspectives. Each may believe they have the best answers. Since women have often been put in charge of child rearing it is not surprising if the woman feels her approach is the best. However, neither partner necessarily has all the skills and it may be more effective child rearing if a compromise can be reached which both parents can support. This is good parenting but it is also good modelling of listening to and learning about the other gender. The couple relationship benefits as each gender acknowledges, respects and is able to respond to the other's approach. Intimacy is then deepened (see also 3.7).

2.5. Within a physical sexual relationship (3 F, 3 M)

(See also 6.5, 6.9)

In describing physical sexual relationships it is necessary to write about details that are personal and private. The language of sexuality is often crude or clinical and can be experienced as intrusive or impersonal. Many myths and taboos surround physical sexual relationships and religious or cultural beliefs can pressurise a couple and interfere with a relaxed and satisfying physical sexual relationship (Zilbergeld, 1980).

Sexual abuse experienced by either gender can interfere with physical sexual responses and pleasures.

Biologically and culturally, women are more likely to need to feel emotionally relaxed, to prefer touch and tenderness, and to have the whole body engaged in the sexual act before sexual intercourse becomes a fully satisfying part of a relationship. The man usually needs to feel confident and encouraged to be able to achieve and maintain an erection during penetrative intercourse (Symonds, 1979; Mansfield and Collard 1988; Bancroft; 1990, Crowe and Ridley, 1990; Mansfield et al., 1992).

Female and male needs, which are often at variance with each other, can be obscured in the first flush of experimentation by feelings of excitement; within a long-term relationship they can become areas of concern.

Once acknowledged, there are simple and effective ways couples can be helped to learn about each other's needs, rhythms and responses. It does require an ability to talk about sexuality and gender differences without each feeling criticised or blamed. Phrases such as 'she's frigid', 'she's a cold fish' or 'he's insensitive', 'he's oversexed' can be a smokescreen for lack of understanding of female/male differences.

In spite of the emphasis of society upon sexual openness, many couples feel that talking in detail about their physical sexual needs is the opposite of intimacy. Couples often have difficulty finding words that can be used without embarrassment to speak about their physical sexual needs, and to ask permission for and to give what they each need (see also 2.6.1).

2.5.1. Exclusivity and female/male preferences

The question of exclusivity within a relationship is complex and women and men seem to have opposing values. The Sexual Behaviour in Britain Survey (Wellings et al., 1994) describes this complexity.

> Only one respondent in fifty believes extramarital sex to be not at all wrong, and some four out of five people (78.7% men and 84.3% women) are of the opinion that it is always or mostly wrong. Only marginally fewer people – two-thirds of men and more than three-quarters of women – disapprove of sexual relationships outside a live-in relationship, and well over half of men and more than two-thirds of women see sexual relations outside a regular relationship as always or mostly wrong.

However,

> Care needs to be taken here in distinguishing attitudes from behaviour. Disapproval of behaviour does not mean that people refrain from it. Adultery is still one of the most widely cited grounds for divorce in Britain.

Hunt (1964) found that over half of the clients sought counselling from Marriage Guidance because of an affair, many of which occurred during the partner's first pregnancy (see 6.3.4, 6.8.4).

Hite (1981) reports that the greater number of married men were not monogamous. Seventy-two per cent of men married for two years or more had had sex outside of marriage: the overwhelming majority did not tell their wives, at least at the time. According to Hite the typical response from her survey of these men was:

> I believe in monogamy. It is the moral and religious thing to do. My outside sex has been unknown to my wife. It had no effect on my marriage.

Physical sexual exclusivity may be more important to women than to men although paradoxically men may expect their partner to be faithful to them. The reality seems to be that men (and some women; Heyn, 1992) engage in a physical sexual relationship outside of the marriage or long-term relationship.

An additional complication is the speed of change within family relationships. Couples are learning to accept that they and their partner have had previous long-term relationships and sexual partners. The emphasis upon virginity is disappearing and perhaps with it the ideal of 'exclusivity' in long-term relationships.

As a therapist, working with couples where one partner has disclosed her/his affair, the re-establishing of intimacy depends upon the rebuilding of trust and an acceptance that the 'affair' was not meant to destroy the couple relationship. Some men find casual sexual relationships consistent with a commitment to their partner. Their wives or partners, however, are often devastated by what is felt to be a total betrayal of trust (Hite, 1981).

Because sexual relationships outside of a long-term relationship or marriage are common, it is not clear that sexual exclusivity is an essential aspect of intimacy for both women and men. It may now be more realistic to accept the disclosure of an affair as a life event which most couples may face during their relationship.

> Physical sexual exclusivity, like the need for emotional sharing, may reflect the aspirations of women within an intimate long-term relationship.

These two aspects of intimacy, which women may seek, seem to be in conflict with current male behaviour, contributing to the present crisis in female/male long-term relationships (Bradbury et al., 1996).

2.5.2. Women and physical sexual relationships (3 F)

Brown and Harris (1978) touch lightly upon an area that is one of the more provocative differences between women and men – that of how each approaches physical sexuality. They suggest that for a woman an intimate relationship may not necessarily include a physical sexual relationship.

When considering how men might define their need for intimacy it is probable that most men would include within the definition the ability to have regular safe sexual intercourse (Nicholson and Thompson, 1992). It may be significant that the gay community have insisted that sexual relationships between consenting adults in private be accepted and normalised (Wolfenden Report, 1957). The lesbian community, however, do not seem to place the same emphasis upon sexual relationships. 'It is instead a relationship in which two women's strongest emotions and affections are directed towards one another' (Faderman, 1981).

> This may express an underlying difference of emphasis between women and men in their search for an intimate relationship. A man may usually hope for a trusting relationship within which his need to express himself physically and sexually can be contained. Women, on the other hand, may look for a relationship where the mutual expression of shared feeling is a priority.

2.5.2.1. When a woman is pressurised for sex

A woman may often be reluctant to engage in penetrative sex until her feelings have been attended to, most clearly identified in couples where the man pressurises for sex and the woman becomes increasingly reluctant to engage in sexual activity. This complaint is often seen at marital and sexual therapy clinics. (For clinical examples see Crowe and Ridley, 1986.)

The relationship often follows a pattern in which the man is active and more assertive within the relationship and the woman is submissive and less able to state her needs. They may previously have had a good sexual relationship, but the woman has begun to lose interest in sexual activity or finds it distasteful. She may express concerns about herself, fearing that she is 'frigid'. The more the man pressurises for sex the more the woman is 'turned off'.

A useful intervention developed at the Maudsley Hospital Marital and Sexual Clinic is based upon hypotheses that have gender implications. Firstly, the man and woman may have different levels of need for sexual activity. Their priorities may be different; she may prefer more touch and tenderness and he may seek penetration early within the sexual relationship. Additionally, she may use her 'nurturing' self to look after him and not necessarily ask for what she needs within their sexual or social relationship. Putting this another way, she may consider 'who gets hurt' (Gilligan, 1982) and think that he may be hurt if she suggests he should change his approach to her. The man may assume that she will ask for what she needs and is unaware of any smouldering resentments or unstated requests.

2.5.2.2. Example 2h, Janice and Roy

Janice (30) and Roy (29) have been married for one year, and have no children (Crowe and Ridley, 1986). They presented themselves at the marital and sexual clinic in crisis: 'can we survive together?'. Janice described herself as upset at losing her independence since her marriage, finding it hard to live with her husband and share their life together. She had periods of depression, particularly at weekends when they were together, and she missed her separate existence and her own flat. They described themselves as very different individuals coming from quite different family backgrounds. He was said to be quiet, practical, home loving, and needing her for himself. She was described as outgoing, needing friends at home and more academic. She also had a 'better job' and earned more money than he did.

During the first two months of therapy the work done was in relation to their different interests, backgrounds, and an attempt to find shared activities, especially at weekends.

By session three, sexual issues were emerging as central to their difficulties. Janice was feeling pressurised sexually, she felt sexually 'harassed' if he approached her crudely, or if she was 'not in the mood'. Since 'sexual harassment' was such a central issue for Janice a sexual timetable was offered to the couple as a strategy that might help them with their difficulties (see 2.5.2.3, iii, iv).

2.5.2.3. How to help

i. Touching exercises

Within therapy the couple were offered standard Masters and Johnson (1966, 1970). These are graded exercises in which both the woman and man are encouraged to find out more about their own and their partner's bodies through massage and touch. What kind of touch, what pace each prefers; so that each learns about giving and receiving tactile and sensual pleasures. In this way, both partners are able to overcome embarrassment about their sexual relationship. Equally important, for the purpose of this book, each learns that female and male sexuality are not necessarily identical. The Masters and Johnson non-genital and genital touching exercises attend to the woman's need for more touch and tenderness before penetration (3 F) and teaches the man that it can enhance both partners' pleasure (3 M).

ii. Explaining gender differences

Where gender differences are clear it can be helpful to explain to the couple that women often need to have their feelings attended to and prefer touch and tenderness before penetration is attempted and that men are often seeking early penetration and may feel that this is an understandable way to express feelings. It may be necessary to allow the couple time to discuss this together, to read around and to talk this through with the therapist. Experience indicates that couples are relieved when these complex differences are discussed openly and are 'normalised', i.e. they can see that their dilemma is shared by many other heterosexual couples.

iii. The negotiated sexual timetable

A sexual timetable, can be offered to such couples as a 'holding measure' to enable a couple to agree when they will and will not have sex. (The woman is freed from any pressuring on evenings when sex is banned, and the male partner does know that he will be able to have penetrative sex on a mutually agreed day.) This avoids the arguments and pressure for sexual activity.

iv. Suggesting a sexual timetable

This sexual timetable can be offered as a crazy idea for the couple to think about, or timetabled carefully within the session. It should not be imposed but offered to the woman as an alternative to being pressurised and to the man as a way of knowing that his partner will engage in sexual activity with him. It allows both partners to be more relaxed and enjoy touch and cuddles without additional pressures.

The couple, if they agree, are asked to choose a time and day when they can have sexual intercourse. For the rest of the time it is agreed jointly that the man will not pressurise the woman for sex and the woman will participate in sexual activity on the chosen day.

Where a couple are able to use the negotiated timetable, the focus can move from sexual battles into their social relationship. For Janice and

Roy there were many things that had not been discussed or negotiated. Their social life was non-existent because Roy preferred to stay at home and was not sociable. They had a major disagreement about a past boyfriend of Janice who wished to arrange her birthday treat. They did not discuss issues that caused resentment between them, such as their different earning capacity, the way the garden should be planned, and whether they would ever have children (4 F, 4 M). Additionally, Janice found Roy's sexual approaches to her while she was washing the dishes or making supper to be inappropriate, but had not asked him to change in case he was hurt by this.

These issues were buried under the regular arguments about sexual intercourse. During therapy, which encompassed the ability to communicate about their different needs, Roy and Janice resumed a good sexual life and were both enjoying each other's company much more.

v. Timetable for talking

As therapy progressed the couple were asked to set aside time to talk and continue at home with some of the discussions begun in session about their different needs for sociability and separateness. When setting a talking timetable it is useful to suggest between 10 and 30 minutes, depending upon the couple's ability to talk together, help the couple to decide when and where and ensure that there are no interruptions from the telephone, television or friends. It can also be useful to decide how the talking session should end. A glass of wine, a walk with the dog, time apart are suggestions, and each couple have their own ideas as to what will help. It is best to have short talking sessions initially and encourage the couple to help each other to remember to use the time and to end as agreed. These talking times can be reviewed in the next session (see also 2.4.1.3).

vi. Help the couple negotiate when they want to be sociable and when at home together.

Janice and Roy decided to have Sunday lunch as a time to invite family and friends and Roy was encouraged to go along with it. He seemed satisfied with this as their sexual relationship improved.

In the above example, both the man and the woman had similar sex drives; having sexual intercourse two or three times a week was satisfactory for both, once the resentments within the relationship had been resolved.

> One could say that the woman was able to say 'no' sexually but found it difficult to say 'no' within their social relationship.

2.5.3. Men and physical sexuality (3 M)

(See also 6.8, 6.9)
It is not clear whether some men have a higher sex drive than their partner, or whether the woman is preoccupied with family, work and other pressures that intervene. However, an issue that frequently presents at sexual therapy clinics is of different levels of desire in the man and the woman. Most commonly it is the man who is seeking more regular sex than the woman. For such couples the negotiated sexual timetable can be very helpful (see 2.5.2.3, iii).

When it is the woman who wants more sexual activity, the sexual timetable is not useful. This highlights an obvious physical difference between women and men which has a major impact upon female/male relationships and is rarely discussed openly or responsibly.

Whilst a woman can accept penetrative sex without necessarily desiring it, by 'laying back and thinking of England', a man cannot choose to have an erection. He may get erections when he does not want them but he cannot necessarily choose when to have an erection. The more he tries for an erection the less successful he may be.

Many men do have erectile difficulties:

> For men, erectile dysfunction is clearly the most commonly presented problem, whilst low sexual desire is relatively infrequent, and it is rare for men to complain principally of lack of sexual enjoyment. In women low sexual interest is the most common (Bancroft, 1990).

Male erectile difficulties are an interesting aspect of gender differences and seem to encapsulate some of the more complex and more vulnerable aspects of maleness (see 6.12).

2.5.3.1. Example 2i, George and Gillian

George (52) and Gillian (50) have been married for 29 years and have one son aged 28 living in Australia.

Gillian took her husband to the sexual therapy clinic concerned that he was no longer able to get an erection. George was reluctant to seek help; he felt that nothing could be done. They had had a good sex life until about five years previously when George began to lose his erection immediately after penetration. This difficulty increased until, at interview, he said he no longer achieved an erection.

George insisted that the problem was his alone and did not feel his wife should come to treatment with him. He was at pains to demonstrate there were no problems in the relationship, that he had a near perfect wife who was a great home manager, a great cook and an excellent mother.

Many men present issues of sexual dysfunction in this way, taking responsibility for their own erectile difficulties, and speaking from a position of separateness, autonomy and independence, even though in a long-term relationship. As part of the assessment the couple were asked about their relationship and any significant life events.

Harry, their son, left home for Indonesia about six years ago, and George's father died three years ago. Both events have emotional and practical implications. As a result of Harry finally leaving home, Gillian took a part-time job in a dress shop and became more active and outgoing. Previously she had been content to be a home-maker and mother. George was made redundant for six months two years previously and found work as a motor mechanic with a different firm. Gillian was concerned that George felt low following his father's death and his redundancy. Her response was to cajole him to go out with her, and to smarten himself up.

As a motor mechanic, George's hands and nails were often oily and Gillian nagged him about this. She tended to be spotless and pernickety about household cleanliness; George, a keen handyman, was chided regularly about leaving his tools and 'mess' around the house.

In session, it became clear that George was in awe of Gillian, as a good housewife, a caring mother and now a part-time dress shop assistant. Whilst she was constantly chiding him for his untidiness at home and his appearance, he could only speak of her in glowing terms.

He had been upset at his father's death and despondent that at 50 he was made redundant. No doubt this played some part in his general sense of self-respect and well-being.

Gillian tried her best to cheer him up. She used two very female skills, firstly looking after him even more than previously. She bought him new younger looking shirts and attending to his every daily need. Secondly, she used her verbal skills, sometimes scolding, criticising or cajoling him, hoping to help him feel better. She cheerfully told friends and their son that she had got herself a new child instead of a husband.

Cajoling, criticising and chiding are not necessarily experienced as caring by the partner.

The dynamics of the relationship had changed over recent years; Gillian became more dominant and critical and George found it hard to live up to her expectations.

Thinking in gender terms, one can hypothesise that Gillian, disappointed by George's sadness, was using her nurturing and verbal skills to try to make amends and George was having difficulty maintaining his adult independence and autonomy within the relationship (2 F, 2 M). Putting it crudely, George's penis understood this better than they did and was unable to stand up for itself.

2.5.3.2. How to help

i. Redress the balance within the relationship

With such a couple interaction, the aim is to redress the balance within the relationship, and to help the man to regain his self-esteem. For George and Gillian this means helping George to be more assertive and less in awe of Gillian, and to encourage Gillian to avoid cajoling and criticising. It is useful to note that many women are unaware that their cajoling, criticising and chiding is not necessarily experienced as caring by their male partner. Instead, it is often experienced as undermining or diminishing, a fact which may surprise the partner if confronted.

Using communication training, Gillian can be helped to use positive statements, make specific requests, avoid criticism and 'sting in the tail' and George can be helped to make positive requests for change and to speak about resentments.

The hypothesis is that, unless George is able to stand up for himself within his relationship, he is unlikely to regain the ability to achieve an erection. Gillian is not the cause of the loss of self-esteem, but is unwittingly contributing to its continuance. This hypothesis has been used successfully clinically but has not been adequately researched.

ii. Encourage a trivial argument

A useful intervention is to assist the couple to have a trivial argument about a trivial issue which the man chooses. It may be difficult initially for the man to propose anything as he has grown accustomed to thinking of his wife as near perfect and of himself as less competent. The therapist therefore can be encouraging and persistent. It is best if the trivial issue is chosen by the man and is seen by both partners as 'trivial'. Clinical examples are: asking the wife to put her shoes away rather than leaving them scattered over the bedroom floor; telling her he wants to leave his hammer on the kitchen bench overnight without complaints from her; asking her not to criticise the fact that he slops around in his slippers; suggesting that she stop cajoling him for the amount of toilet paper he uses. An example quoted in detail (Crowe and Ridley, 1990) is one in which a well intentioned but overwhelming wife insisted that her husband always put the toilet seat down after he had used the toilet. When he was able eventually to insist that he would leave the toilet seat up, and she would stop complaining, they recommenced sexual intercourse after a gap of 16 years.

> Encourage an argument about a trivial issue.

iii. When to use a trivial argument

Encouraging a trivial argument can also be a useful intervention for couples where one partner is mild to moderately depressed, where there are power differentials within the couple relationship, or where there are unstated resentments. In these situations it is best if the trivial issue can be chosen by the depressed spouse, the partner with less power within the relationship or the partner who does not express verbally the hidden resentments.

With George and Gillian, the issue was complicated by the life events of his father's death and the temporary loss of job, which added to George's sense of getting old and 'past it'. At the same time, Gillian had found a new enthusiasm for life through her job and wanted George to participate.

Cajoling and criticising, though well intentioned, added to his loss of self-esteem (4 F and 5 F). Like many women, Gillian used her verbal and nurturing skills and did not realise that this is not always supportive.

George, like many men in similar circumstances, insisted that his difficulty gaining and maintaining an erection was his problem and was reluctant, initially, to accept that his relationship with his wife was relevant (1 M, 2 M).

George was aware of physical treatments available to address male erectile difficulties but was glad to regain an ability to achieve an erection with marital and sexual therapy.

iv. Physical treatments for erectile difficulties

Many men with erectile difficulties request medical rather than relationship solutions. A variety of medical and technical alternatives are available to assist with erectile difficulties, such as penile injections or mechanical devices such as a pump or penile band, or alternatively hormone replacement therapy or medication including the recently available Viagra.

These medical and mechanical alternatives can be extremely useful. Where a man has diabetes he may experience powerful sexual desires but be unable to achieve an erection. Penile injections were developed in 1982 for these specific erectile problems and can be very effective.

With the increasing availability of medical and mechanical aids for erectile failure, more men are requesting medical solutions to erectile difficulties, rather than considering other factors that may be involved in their erectile difficulties, such as relationship or emotional problems, or simply the impact of stress or ageing.

It may be relevant to raise the question whether such men are using a male skill of problem solving to an extreme degree. Stated in gender terms, the man who is accustomed to using well honed problem-solving skills may decide that, if the problem is a flaccid penis, a solution would be one in which the penis can be artificially made erect. A technical or medical solution such as a pill, an injection, a pump or a prosthesis may therefore be acceptable. The fact that there may be other potential contributory factors which, if attended to, may enable the man to achieve an erection without a medical solution, may not seem relevant.

> The male ability to be very problem focused may protect or prevent him from looking at other potential alternatives.

His own sense of vulnerability and his need to maintain his independence and autonomy may also make it difficult for him to seek help in anything other than a problem focused way (1 M, 2 M, 3 M).

Factors such as early redundancy, the loss of a relationship through separation, divorce, or death, or negative interactions with family, friends, work, or finance are often set aside by such men as irrelevant to their problem. The slowing down of the sexual responses as a natural aspect of ageing may also play its part.

The male oriented scientific and medical profession seems to collude with this medicalisation of erectile difficulties, rather than taking into account contributing emotional and social factors.

For the couple, although the man can achieve an erection by technical means, the woman may decide that unless the erection comes from an emotional and spontaneous erection, there is little point in having sex. The male problem focus (1 M, 3 M) and the female need to have emotions attended to, again collide (1 F, 3 F) (Crowe and Qureshi, 1991).

There are couples who are able to enjoy penetrative sex using medical aids. An 81-year-old man who has had surgery for prostate cancer uses papaverine injections to gain an erection, and his 60-year-old partner of many years take great pleasure in their renewed sexual relationship. These couples have learned to understand and respect the gender needs of the partner. Further research into the interaction between the man who is given a medical/technical erection and his partner would help to answer these questions.

For many men with erectile difficulties, organic factors are involved, or there may be an interaction between organic and relationship issues. In such cases, there may be great value in using both relationship therapy and technical means to enable them to continue a good sexual relationship.

It is worth noting that the older woman may not always feel it is essential to have penetrative sex. She may feel satisfied if a physical relationship continues at the level of touch and tenderness or manual stimulation (Riley, 1996). The male partner may be putting undue pressure upon himself to gain an erection. Again we see a gender difference between the ageing male and female where he can be said to be penis focused and she more concerned about touch and tenderness.

Many older couples continue an active sexual life into grand old age. Both partners enjoy penetrative sex and the gentler more whole body participation which accompanies the older couple's sexuality (3 F, 3 M). For the couple who grow old together there is often a merging or similarity between the sexual needs of both partners. This may be as a result of their greater similarity following the female menopause and/or because they have learned, through trial and error, how to satisfy the sexual gender needs of the other.

2.6. In relation to communication (4 F, 4 M)

Not all couples experience communication difficulties, and many make realistic adjustments to each other's styles. Communication has been studied in detail. Communication problems may involve many factors: intellectual differences, cultural variation, inappropriate listening, speaking for the other, inadequate checking out of what has been heard or mind reading may all affect both genders (Satir, 1964; Gottman, 1976; Crowe and Ridley, 1990; Fincham and Bradbury, 1991; Cahn, 1992).

Additionally, gender differences can be observed which can complicate female/male communication (Tannen, 1990; Gottman, 1998; Fincham, 1994). Within communication women and men tend to have different levels of verbal ability. Although women and men may have a similar vocabulary, women can often access words or alternative words more speedily than men (Halpern, 1992; Pool, 1994). Women may also be more skilled at reading non-verbal cues (Money, 1986; Tannen, 1990).

Female/male communication can be distorted by gender differences in communication styles, particularly where other elements of intimacy are also under stress (Fincham, 1994). A variation in verbal and non-verbal skills between women and men may explain why women often complain, 'He never talks to me, I wish he would talk to me more', perhaps expressing her frustration that he does not have her verbal skills. Paradoxically, a wife may also say, 'If he loved me he would understand how I feel, I should not have to explain it to him', as if she expects him to read non-verbal signals easily. Such interactions are problematic when each gender feels that the other is deliberately withholding, ignoring or punishing the other when it is possible that each is responding from a gender base.

The male equivalent may be found in jibes about 'mother-in-law' or labels such as 'henpecked husband' describing an overly talkative or critical woman, who is not 'like me' less verbal.

Research has focused upon the pursuing woman and the withholding man (Gottman, 1994), which suggests that the woman continues to try to engage the partner in conversation while the man shuts off and withdraws. This research draws attention to the woman's ability with free-flowing verbal communication and the man's non-verbal response.

Tannen (1990) describes ways in which women and men use different kinds of language for different situations, with men being more competent at 'meeting talk' and women more competent at talk designed to build relationships.

2.6.1. Women, men and communication

Examples of male and female gender responses have so far been described separately. Communication is now treated as an interaction between maleness and femaleness, each gender impacting upon the other to complicate the communication tangle. Although presented interactionally this does not take away the responsibility of each gender for their part in the communication.

Women may prefer free-flowing mutual communication whilst men may respond more slowly, requiring time to think before deciding how to respond. As already suggested (see 2.3.1), women may want to communicate about feelings and men may prefer a non-verbal understanding of their feelings while seeking a solution to the problem. Women may also have the ability to find words more speedily and, although men may have a similar vocabulary, they may take longer to find a word, or its alternative (see 6.4).

The woman who is verbally agile often misinterprets her partner's slowness to respond as reluctance to talk or communicate with her. A wife was extremely irritated with her husband's slow responses to her. She knew that as a barrister he defended or prosecuted clients in courts of law and was skilled with words. She did not take into account that he took time to prepare his advocacy role at work. Others would help with the preparation and choice of words and their effectiveness.

In conversation with her his responses were slow; as a result she assumed that he did not like to talk to her. She accused him of this frequently. As time went by, he became silent, reinforcing her belief that he deliberately refused to talk with her.

In such a situation the partner has few options, he can respond like the barrister and resort to silence. He can use brief yes or no responses. He can 'blow up' verbally with a range of previously unstated, but well rehearsed resentments, which he may regret. Such a 'blow up', whether by the man or woman, can frighten both partners and can reinforce the conviction that the relationship is in danger.

Communication is central to all relationships. Satir (1964), one of the early thinkers about communication wrote 'you cannot not communicate' and described functional communication as a two-way process in which the individual is able to:

1. firmly state his/her own views
2. yet at the same time clarify and qualify what he/she says, and
3. be receptive to feedback when he/she gets it.

Or stated another way:

1.	I (the sender)	1.	I (the receiver)
2.	am saying something (the message)	2.	am receiving the following (message)
3.	to you (the receiver)	3.	from you (the sender)
4.	in this situation	4.	in this situation

What is important is that the recipient receives the message which was the intended message of the sender and then responds to that particular message.

Each couple described in this book is an example of difficulty with communication. Examples 3c, Douglas and Diane; 3d, Yvonne and Roger; and 3e, Peter and Paula each want different things from the other, and as a consequence they misunderstand each other. Example 2d, Tim and Tina, approach the impact of Tina's hysterectomy from quite different perspectives.

Example 2e, Jim and Susan, are also at odds because Susan is thinking about an argument with a friend, while Jim is worried about his work. Example 2f, Dick and Dora, are both upset when they try to talk about his work world. Example 2g, Bob and Cynthia, have difficulty communicating their different approaches to Bruce's first day at school; each places different meanings upon his preoccupation with work.

In Examples 2h, Janice and Roy, and 2i, George and Gillian, their communication is so asymmetric that their sexual life is affected. Example 2j, Edward and Emily, below, describes how different speeds at which words are accessed by women and men can be a barrier to intimacy. This is particularly so with couples when the woman denigrates the man verbally, and at the same time interprets his slowness, as either stupidity or a lack of preparedness on his part to talk with her.

Unless both partners can learn to give each other space to communicate in their own time, a pattern can emerge where the slower partner, in this case the man, deliberately does not respond as he has learned that he cannot compete verbally.

One hears a man say, 'I don't respond because I know I cannot win', meaning he will never be as verbally skilled as his partner. She may interpret his statement to mean, he will talk with her only if he 'wins' the argument or makes the final decision.

What begins as gender difference in the speed of accessing words becomes a communication tangle between the man and woman, each interpreting what the other does or says negatively. Communication then becomes a minefield of misunderstanding.

> An interaction which begins simply can escalate into a disagreement with hurt feelings on both sides.

When considering female/male relationships and male aggression the speed and ease with which a woman can find words also becomes a problem for the man (see Example 2i). The woman is often unaware of the impact of her verbal agility on her partner; what she is more aware of is that he does not respond in the way she wants. He is aware that he is losing the verbal battle and is not getting what he hopes for from the discussion.

2.6.1.1. Example 2j, Edward and Emily

Edward (35) and Emily (34) have lived together for two years. Both are divorced; Edward was divorced one year ago, and Emily's divorce was finalised one month ago.

Edward has two children, Terry aged 12 and Sharon aged 10, who live with their mother. Emily's children, Stephen aged 10 and Ralph aged 8, live with Edward and Emily.

Emily separated from her husband five years ago, and supported herself and the two children on her own for three years before she and Edward decided to live together. They agreed that they would not marry, but now that both divorces are finalised there is no obstacle to a second marriage for them both.

With regard to the disciplining of the children, a pattern has developed in which Edward is not involved with Emily's disciplining of her two boys. They have not talked about this, it just evolved.

On Edward's half day holiday at home, he decided to talk with Emily about their future together as a more permanent couple, now that Emily's divorce is final. He is also a bit upset at the way Emily's boys treat him and thinks it would be helpful to tackle the two subjects together, thinking Emily may now want his support. He hopes they can become more of a family with Edward involved in disciplining the children. He thinks they need the firmer hand of a man as they reach teenage.

Edward. 'Emily, can we talk?'

Emily. 'Yes, what about, I'm due to take Stephen and Ralph swimming and then to the dentist. Will you be able to get tea for us when we get in as we'll be a bit late?'

Edward. 'OK. I'll be glad to do that. Are you sure that Stephen deserves to go swimming, he has been very rude and disagreeable over the last few days.'

Emily, a little taken aback, as Edward has never criticised Stephen before. 'What do you mean? Stephen, is not rude, at least not as rude as your Terry, you should have heard him swearing at Ralph when he was here at the weekend.'

Edward decides he doesn't want to say anything more about Stephen, and wants to introduce the question of Emily's divorce and their future together.

Edward. 'Well, I probably should not have said anything, I wanted to ask you about your divorce, and what that means...'

He is interrupted by Emily, now a bit angry.

Emily. 'Just because I am now divorced doesn't mean that you can criticise Stephen; he is usually very well behaved, so you had better tell me what happened to make you think he should not go swimming.'

Edward. 'I didn't mean to upset you, I was just thinking that your divorce means that we can be more settled'.

Emily. 'I am upset; you know how long I had to look after Ralph and Stephen on my own, without any help from anyone, let alone you. Now you tell me he is rude. You should hear your Terry.'

Edward, realising that Emily is upset, tries to start again. 'Look, I'm glad your divorce has come through, we can talk about us as a family. I want to help you and the two boys.'

Emily. 'You can help most by offering to take the boys yourself to the swimming pool, and then to the dentist, and then I can stay at home and make tea, and maybe watch a bit of telly at the same time. My divorce doesn't make any difference to me. I have been separated for five years, there was no way I was going to depend on that man. You men are all alike, you find it easy to criticise but rather harder to help out. We've done fine the way we've been.'

Edward, looking rather glum. 'I will take them both to the swimming pool, but I thought ...'

Emily, interrupting. 'No, I'll do it as usual. Was there something else you wanted?'

Edward, ...pause... 'Well, ... I was wondering ...'

Again he is interrupted by Emily. 'Wondering what? Can't you see that I've got a lot on my mind at present, just because you have an afternoon off from work, doesn't mean that I have time to stand around waiting to know what is on your mind. But you could do something for me, ring the school – a teacher, Mrs Wallace, wanted to talk to me about something. Will you tell her that I will ring her tomorrow when I have more time.'

Edward could have chosen a better moment to introduce his topic, and he could have realised that finalising the divorce might remind Emily of past difficulties, a time when she had to learn to support herself and her two children on her own. (Emily may have felt that since she would have understood, had the situation been reversed, Edward was being particularly insensitive (1 F).) His inappropriate choice of timing, Emily's quick responses and protectiveness of her children all got in the way of open communication (4 F, 4 M). Each felt the other did not understand. What they communicated was unsupportive and defensive. Observing their verbal responsiveness, Emily was quick to find words and less prepared to wait for Edward, who struggled to find the words he needed.

Many other things occurred within the above scenario, not least of which is the impact of the life event of divorce upon each partner (see 3.3.2). Each knew the pain of a failed relationship. Each may have been worried about re-commitment in case it went wrong again. Emily may have been deliberately using her verbal skills to distance herself, anticipating what Edward wanted to say. She was very protective of her children, and reluctant to share them with Edward.

Edward, for his part, may have been missing his own children and hoping to become more of a 'father figure' again, which may have helped him to feel an equal partner within a new relationship. He, too, may have used his slowness in accessing words to distance himself from discussing a situation that was painful and uncertain for him.

What is significant about their communication style is that it does not achieve what they hope. There are many issues which, if discussed openly, could bring them closer together. Unless their communication style improves, so that issues can be discussed without defensiveness, they are unlikely to grow closer, or to gain a deeper level of intimacy.

For the moment, this couple may prefer their separateness within the relationship, rather than risk becoming more intimate. In this way poor communication becomes a powerful defence against deepening intimacy; it also means that intimacy may dissolve when a crisis occurs in their relationship.

> Longitudinal studies indicate that the presence of negative attribution (time 1) predicts decreased marital satisfaction (time 2) suggesting a strong causal link (Fincham, 1994).

A self-fulfilling prophecy is then realised, that 'long-term relationships are impossible'. Many women and men brought up within the West, have had personal experiences of the discord generated between the sexes as a result of their own divorce or separation, or their parents' or friends' divorce or separation.

> As a result of divorce or separation, a general cynicism may develop regarding the possibility of long-term relationships.

Following divorce or separation, both women and men hesitate to commit themselves to the next relationship. They may become reluctant to enter into negotiations like Emily and Edward, because of fears that intimacy needs may not be realised (Frieze et al., 1979).

Female/male gender issues, such as the different styles of communication (4 F, 4 M), when ignored and misunderstood, contribute significantly to the current crisis in intimacy (Bradbury et al., 1996).

2.6.1.2. Example 2k, Ken and Kathleen

The next example considers another pattern that occurs in couple communication and may arise from the different genders' speed in accessing words. Ken brings the language he uses at work into their everyday communication, which infuriates Kathleen. She thinks it is sterile and unemotional. When Ken uses work-oriented language, he becomes more fluent verbally than Kathleen. He is an accountant with a familiar work-specific vocabulary.

One can assume he uses his work language to dominate the situation at home and at work, which is what Kathleen thinks. An alternative hypothesis is that he can slow down Kathleen's responses. When he gets lost in her verbal speediness he reintroduces work jargon.

> Ken (56) and Kathleen (54) have three married children and are quite well off. Having been home makers, they both find the home quiet. They now spend much of their time together

bickering. This distresses them as they have always thought of themselves as a loving couple. As Kathleen becomes increasingly depressed, Ken finds a solution to the problem and suggests they talk about selling up their four-bedroomed family home and buying a smaller flat. He feels this would give Kathleen a new focus for her life in finding and redecorating a new home.

What follows is a sample of the discussion, where the flow of communication is interrupted when Ken begins to use work-oriented jargon.

Kathleen. 'It is very quiet around here these days without the family around. Do you find that?'

Ken. 'I've been thinking; it is about time we sold this old place, and bought ourselves a smaller more modern flat.'

Kathleen. 'Why? You know this is the family home. I thought you always loved it the way the family and I do. And anyway, where would we put all of the children's things, and where would they sleep when they came to see us? I do want to be able to put them up when they are on leave, or visiting us, or when we have grandchildren.'

Ken. 'Yes, I have loved this old place, but we rattle around in it now like a pea in a drum.'

Kathleen, looking sad, and almost in tears. 'I know we will have to some day, but must we now?'

Ken. 'Well. Let's see now. Property values are going up but prices will peak soon, if we go on to the market now we could sell at the top of the market, and make a good profit if we buy smaller and keep an eye on how real estate is moving. We could invest profits in PEPS or Bonds, we could ask Alistair to give us a bit of free extra advice, but it could be a good time to go into the market and risk a bit on the stock exchange.'

Kathleen looks horrified, and does not respond.

Ken. 'So, what do you think, it might be a good time to make a killing and then invest for our future.'

Kathleen, still doesn't respond, and begins to take out a handkerchief to wipe her eyes.

Ken. 'Oh, come now, this is no time for tears. Here am I trying to look forward for us both by working out a financial strategy for our retirement, and all you can do is start crying. I thought you might like to get involved in a new project, selling this house and buying a new place. You are good at planning and decorating, you would make a good project manager.'

> Both Kathleen and Ken are rather bewildered at the way the conversation is going. Kathleen tries to bring in the children again, as a reason why the house should not be sold. Ken chides her for being so backward looking but then gets up and leaves the room. Kathleen is in tears, and Ken is in despair that he is unable to help her with what begins to feel a heavy depression. He later suggests that Kathleen should see a doctor and get some antidepressants.

There are many ways to think about the above piece of communication. In particular, both Ken and Kathleen are facing a life stage and the accompanying ageing process. Kathleen is post-menopausal, the children have left home, both sets of parents are dead and there is a vacuum in their lives. Good communication is essential at this stage to reconnect with each other, and find a creative way forward, together.

In the above example, Ken used his problem-solving skills (1 M) and his work-oriented language (4 M) to address this critical period in their relationship. However, he failed. Instead of reconnecting at a deeper level of intimacy, they were pushed further apart. They each stayed on separate sides of the invisible intimacy screen. Had he used a different language, he may have been successful, or had Kathleen understood his male-oriented approach, she may have been prepared to talk with him. Tolerance and respect for gender differences was lacking.

2.6.1.3. How to help

Wherever there are communication difficulties the therapist or counsellor can pay attention to the detail of the communication styles, both verbal and non-verbal. It is helpful to encourage the couple to talk directly to each other by decentring (2.2.4.2, iii). This makes it easier to observe the couple interaction, and to intervene to suggest ways in which they can modify their behaviour.

i. Decentre (see 2.2.4.2, iii)
ii. Draw attention to the different verbal speeds of the woman and man, and ask the couple to talk about how this affects each of them. For example, ask Ken to tell Kathleen what it is like for him that she is quick and skilled at finding words; or the opposite. Use your relationship with the couple to enable this to happen. A light touch and sense of humour are helpful. It is also important to be persistent, not allowing diversions or side-tracking.
iii. Ensure that each speaks from an 'I' position so that each may be encouraged to say 'I find that I am ...'. Be supportive and persistent to encourage each partner to speak for themselves.
iv. Help the couple to stay with the issue of their different verbal speed and find out what each feels about this.
v. Explore whether each partner has decided 'why' the other uses a particular communication style. Sometimes there are ideas that it is done deliberately to be nasty or dominate the other. If it feels helpful, introduce the idea that women are often speedier at finding words than men although men usually have a similar vocabulary. Should they be particularly interested, suggest a book to read.
vi. Help them to practise 'in session' being different; this means asking Kathleen to talk more slowly and leave a space for Ken to reply. This may enable Ken to be more responsive.
vii. Where Ken's work language is an irritation suggest that he tries to use other language.
viii. Suggest a homework task to talk together using the 'I' position with the woman speaking more slowly and giving the man more time to respond (ii and vi above). This can be a timetable for 10–20 minutes, perhaps three times a week, and at specific times.
ix. Check at the next session how they got on, practise again in session, be positive and encouraging when they change their style.
x. If the 'pattern of communicating' seems stuck it can be helpful for the couple to remind each other if the woman becomes speedy or the man slows down. A code word, which only they understand, can be used; this helps in social situations as no one else will understand. One couple chose to say, 'the radio has just come on'; another used hand signals. Such ideas help the couple support each other and bring a sense of fun, togetherness and play into the sessions and the relationship.

These are a few suggestions. With experience, creativity and good will on all sides, couples can be helped to adapt to their partner's needs, becoming aware of the impact of their own style upon their partner and enjoying the challenge of communicating across the invisible intimacy screen.

2.7. In relation to aggression (5 F, 5 M)

It is impossible to review female/male relationships without taking into account aggression (see also 6.6, 6.10).

> If we consider only the most aggressive individuals in society we would have to conclude that there are huge differences between males and females with respect to aggression, (sadistic murders, rapes, mutilations, serial killings, slasher crimes) are committed by males (US Bureau of Census 1989).....There is however, less difference in female and male aggression for 'average' people than there is for criminals' (Halpern, 1992).

Domestic violence is an aspect of female/male relationships that causes concern and distress. O'Leary and Vivian (1990) suggest that overall rates of physical aggression are approximately equal, but there may be important gender differences in the rates of severe aggression and that the consequences of physical aggression by men is greater than by women:

> and the development and maintenance of physical aggression may be gender specific (O'Leary and Vivian, 1990).

It is not clear what the man who is aggressive with his female partner is seeking from the relationship. One can hypothesise that he has learned through bitter early experiences to use physical aggression when threatened. Where a woman is in a relationship with such a man she may use her nurturing skills and her ability to put his needs before her own. In so doing she may provide him with a safe and caring environment where aggression in not necessary. However, her concern for him may not be enough to prevent outbursts of aggression when she may need to think about her own or her children's security (Goldner, 1988).

Female aggression may be expressed physically but may also be expressed verbally (Levenson and Gottman, 1985; Schaap Jansan-Nawas, 1987; Roberts and Krokoff, 1990; Gottman, 1994; Markman et al., 1994; Knedeck, 1995).

Women can often use their tongue to hurt or damage a partner in ways that are as yet unrecognised (Welldon, 1992). However, violence against women often occurs where the woman is not verbally aggressive and where the causes are difficult to establish. This is an aspect of female/male interaction that needs in-depth exploration.

Containing an aggressive interaction is difficult, and domestic violence is a serious obstacle to secure long-term intimacy. The proliferation of women's refuges suggests that many women are no longer prepared to accept physical aggression within a relationship. Additionally, society does not provide sufficient acceptable outlets for male physical aggression. Helping men contain their aggression has not yet become a priority although its expression within a long-term relationship is no longer acceptable.

A factor in the current crisis within female/male relationships may be that women are more able to insist that violence is unacceptable but men have not yet learned to take this seriously.

2.7.1. Female aggression

(See also Example 21, Larry (and Louise); 6.6.)
Female physical aggression is often ignored or understated (O'Leary and Vivian, 1990). Welldon (1992) thinks society protects the female image as being caring, nurturing and giving, and finds it hard to acknowledge that women can be aggressive and damaging within relationships.

Female aggression towards men may often be verbal aggression in which the woman demeans the man. A powerful target is the sexual prowess of her male partner – a gender specific target where the woman has no personal experience of getting-and maintaining an erection, nor of the complexities of erectile failure. She probably does know that he is vulnerable in this area.

A divorced male client who believed that sex was satisfactory with his ex-wife, sought help for impotence following the divorce. A key element in his impotence was a statement made by his ex-wife as their relationship was ending that,

> You were a terrible lover, I always faked orgasm, and you never were able to satisfy me sexually.

This may be a factual statement, but for a man, as a marriage fails, to hear this can be deeply wounding. Feminists have tended to suggest that the woman is not responsible for her partner's erection. However, such gender-specific negative statements have a powerful impact.

A woman's tongue can be as powerful as a man's fist.

Clinical experience of men who seek help for sexual difficulties suggests that early experiences of a physical sexual relationship where the female partner was derogatory or made critical comments contribute significantly to the man's sense of self-confidence, self-worth and physical sexual self-confidence. The opposite also occurs when a man undermines a woman's sense of self-worth by derogatory remarks targeted at her femaleness.

Women may need to learn to respect a man's feelings regarding his sexuality and his sexual skills.

2.7.1.1. Example 2l, Larry (and Louise)

Larry (25) was a solitary young man who had one significant relationship while at college. He fell deeply in love with an art student and began a relationship. After nine months they attempted to have penetrative sexual intercourse. Louise was already sexually experienced and spoke frequently about the sexual prowess of previous lovers. Louise was Larry's first physical sexual relationship. They had penetrative sex on several occasions but Larry found he was so anxious that he tended to ejaculate soon after penetration. Louise would laugh at him during foreplay, comparing him with other partners whom, she said, had no problem getting or maintaining an erection. She also told a few friends that he was a poor lover. After Larry learned of this, he began to lose his erection before penetration. The relationship ended.

Louise may not have intended to be hostile or aggressive, but the impact on Larry was one of criticism and aggression.

If women and men are vulnerable (see Chapter 6), particularly in relation to their sexual prowess or sexual attractiveness – a gender-specific element – both women and men may wish to think carefully before criticising to avoid jeopardising their intimacy.

2.7.2. Aggression: 'her' children, 'his' work

Another way in which a woman is often aggressive towards her partner is in relation to 'her' children and 'his' work.

Some couples divide up the roles within their partnership so that the man is seen as the main worker, even if both work, and the woman is seen as the main carer, even though both participate in the children's care. This may suit both partners. Negative consequences arise when neither respects the other's contribution to their joint lives.

In Example 2e, Jim and Susan find that they cannot understand each other when Jim discusses issues at work. Dora (Example 2f) feels neglected by Dick, who works long hours to provide a good standard of living for the family. Neither Dora nor Susan resorts to verbal violence.

2.7.2.1. Example 2m, Martha and Matt

In this example, the woman attacks the man verbally for spending too much time at work, accusing him of being a neglectful father while at the same time preventing him from spending more time with the children. This is a common pattern amongst couples who seek help for their relationship.

> Verbal violence can be subtle, often conveyed by voice tone and facial expression as much as the words used.

Martha (37) and Matt (36) have four children aged 14, 12, 8 and 6. They have a complex relationship. Matt works as a carpenter and often works evenings to complete jobs. Martha works as a dinner lady at the children's school. She is a warm-hearted enthusiastic mother and housewife. She spends much of her time badgering the children to do their homework, finish their piano practice or get to swimming on time.

She treats Matt as a fifth child. When he returns late and tired from work and drops his carpenter's bag inside the front door, she says, 'Matt, for goodness sake put your bag away, you are worse than the children.' She complains he is late, and she is tired and the two youngest still need a bath.

However, when Matt suggests that he baths the children she again scolds him and says, 'No you won't, you'll sit down and have your meal, it is already cold, and anyway I don't want you messing up the bathroom. There'd be water and clothes all over the place if I let you do that.'

This is a simple and common female/male interaction which may not seem aggressive to the reader, and may not be intended as such by Martha. However, this pattern encourages Matt to feel an outsider in his own home. Undermined and discouraged from being a caring father he retreats behind his newspaper and television. The woman's possessiveness of her children and her housewifely role, her attacks upon his lateness and his contribution to family well-being can feel very alienating and hostile. Additionally, Martha does not accept his offer to bath the children and he does not challenge her right to do this. He may feel badly done by, but finds it difficult to know what to do.

Martha in subtle and verbal ways may be experienced as hostile and aggressive and Matt feels marginalised within his own home.

2.7.2.2. How to help

i. Help the couple to take each other seriously (see 2.3.2.4).
ii. Suggest to Martha that she find out from Matt what it is like for him when she cajoles and criticises him. If necessary, help him to say more about this (Martha may be surprised to learn that she is experienced as critical). The therapist may prefer not to use the words cajoling or criticising but to suggest that Martha use more positive language, making positive requests.
iii. Ask Matt to find out from Martha what small thing he could do that would make it easier for her not to criticise him when he comes in from work. This should be small and achievable before the next session; such as hanging his bag up before she scolds.
iv. Reverse iii above: suggest that Martha ask Matt what small thing she can do to make it easier for Matt at home. It could be something like Matt being allowed to join in the bathing routine on Friday evenings when there is more time. Perhaps he can arrange to take the eldest two out on a Saturday and give mother more time for herself. In general the aim is to help the couple take each other's positions seriously, listen carefully to each other and be prepared to make some small compromises as steps towards a different relationship.
v. Pay attention to the language used, the voice tone and its impact upon the partner. It may be useful to point these out to the couple, and suggest they ask each other for any changes that would help.
vi. Where there are particular words or phrases which grate or upset the partner, see if other words or phrases can be substituted.

> Positive non-critical statements are always best.

A gentler voice tone is often easily achieved once acknowledged.

By taking small steps towards a change in the couple's relationship, a foundation of listening and taking seriously each other's positions can be built, and as time goes by they can be helped to talk about more difficult areas, such as what it is like to be the 'excluded father' or the 'housebound mother' and to listen and accept each other's perspective.

vii. A next step might be for the couple to plan a couple event together without the children.

viii. Other options which bring some lightness and fun into the relationship, such as
- saying something positive to each other each day,
- surprising each other with a 'love token' – a flower, a card on the pillow or the car windscreen,
- a specially attractive meal,
- a surprise that only the spouse understands.

These can all help to rebuild a more equal couple relationship.

These may not seem particularly gender specific. However, if each partner can take the other seriously, then respect will grow for the other's perspective. Reducing critical comment and increasing positive interchanges usually has a benign effect on a couple relationship. It may also be helpful to engage the couple in a discussion of their roles in which Martha is home based and Matt may appear to have more freedom. This may enable them to speak about resentments as well as their level of tolerance regarding gender-based issues. They can then choose new ways to give each other support.

Leff and Vaughn (1985) examined the impact of critical comments and verbal hostility upon patients diagnosed as schizophrenic and concluded that high levels of critical comments tend to increase the rate of relapse in the patient, and lower levels tend to reduce the rate of relapse. The impact of critical comments has been researched in relation to schizophrenia and depression, where it is clear that some individuals are highly sensitive to critical comments. In many studies the critical relative is a woman, often the mother.

There is some evidence that high levels of critical comment have a more general detrimental effect. Thinking about heterosexual intimacy one wonders whether women may often use critical comments, believing it to be a way of changing behaviour without understanding the detrimental effect upon the partner. It is also suggested that critical comments can be experienced as aggression disguised as caring.

2.7.3. Male aggression (5 M)

(See also 4.6, 6.10.)

Intimacy in heterosexual relationships cannot be considered without including the complex aspect of male physical aggression and violence. Male aggressiveness has for centuries been seen as heroic and essential for the preservation of family, clan, state or nation. In times of war aggressiveness has been required of all males, accompanying the parallel process of defending one's possessions, whether they be land, wealth, wife or family.

Here we are less concerned with the heroic and warlike aspects of maleness than the impact upon female/male interpersonal relationships of these attributes of masculinity which are desirable within war and protection. Men consequently may be confused that such attributes do not enamour them to their female partners within the bedchamber or the family setting.

The growing interest in marital violence is well documented by O'Leary and Vivian (1990). They assessed 272 couples, who were similar to the general public, and were surprised to find that when assessed four to six weeks prior to marriage, 31 per cent of men and 44 per cent of the women reported that they had been physically aggressive towards their partner in the past year. Even at 30 months after marriage, the self-reported rates of aggression against the partner were 24 per cent and 32 per cent for women and men respectively (O'Leary et al., 1989).

They emphasise this finding but conclude,

> although the overall rates of physical aggression are approximately equal for representative population samples, there may be important gender differences in the rates of severe aggression for groups who will not participate in population surveys by sociologists. Moreover it is generally agreed that the consequences of physical aggression by men is greater than by women, and the development and maintenance of physical aggression may be gender specific.

A study of 266 couples seeking marital therapy showed that severe husband-to-wife physical violence (14–18 on the Conflict Tactics Scale, CTS, Straus, 1979) was present in approximately 28 per cent of the couples (Vivian et al., 1989). The forms of physical aggression were pushing, shoving and slapping and were said to occur three to five times per year. Compared to non-abusive couples, verbal abuse occurred three times more frequently in couples reporting severe husband-to-wife aggression and twice as frequently in couples reporting less severe forms of husband-to-wife abuse.

Having surveyed psychological models of spousal aggression, Vivian et al. (1989) write:

> Most importantly, the evidence linking negative communication skills to interspousal physical aggression suggests that close attention needs to be given to the role of anger and hostility in promoting the shift from verbal aggression to physical aggression. In view of this escalation pattern, particular consideration is given to learning models that highlight the role of communication skills and anger in the genesis of aggression.

They go on to conclude that:

> marital discord is one of the strongest correlates of physical abuse (O'Leary 1988) and causal models of spousal aggression indicate that spouse-specific verbal aggression is the best predictor of physical aggression in couples 1 year later (O'Leary et al., 1989).

Verbal aggression, and its escalation, is associated here with physical aggression. This means that both the man and the woman use verbal aggression which escalates into physical aggression. Male physical aggression against the female because of his greater physical strength is usually the most damaging. Some feel that the man resorts to physical violence because he is losing the verbal battle.

This distressing aspect of female/male relationships is very prevalent and may be passed on to succeeding generations. That is, if violence has been experienced in the family of origin then it is more likely to reoccur in the next generation.

Virginia Goldner (1990), while being concerned that the man should take responsibility for his own violence, suggests that the woman who returns repeatedly to a violent relationship returns because of the intensity of the reconciliation period following the violence, in which the man is very contrite and loving.

Fagan et al. (1988) studied the association between alcohol use and maritally violent men. They compared the contexts and reasons for drinking of a maritally violent group as compared with three non-violent comparison groups. The maritally violent group reported higher levels of alcohol consumption in all of the drinking context items. The most significant differences were on drinking at home after work, at home while playing with the kids, at recreational activities, at home by oneself, on the job, at workday lunch, and with people after work.

They also found that the maritally violent men tended to drink to forget worries, pains, and stress in their lives more so than the non-violent groups. At least half of the maritally violent men reported that drinking accompanied abusive events at least occasionally, while about one-third reported that it often, or very often, accompanied their abuse.

> The abuse of alcohol plays a significant part within violent interactions and alcohol tends to have a disinhibiting effect on the drinker.

Additionally, the impact of the alcohol on the man and the woman can be very different. For example, a small amount of alcohol may make it easier for them to enjoy their sexual relationship, particularly if their lives are stressful. However, if the man continues to drink, he may become increasingly aroused sexually, but his sexual prowess usually diminishes. He is likely to become a clumsy lover, to smell of alcohol, to ejaculate early, and to fall heavily asleep after intercourse.

The woman is less likely to have enjoyed sexual intercourse and may not have been orgasmic. If she likes to talk after sex, his heavy sleep and general 'out for the count' behaviour is likely to breed resentment in her. She is less likely to want sex the next time he has been drinking heavily, and may refuse – a situation that can escalate into verbal and physical violence. Where an individual is already stressed and irritable and has consumed alcohol, it may take little to provoke an angry, hostile or aggressive reaction.

In summary, whilst both women and men can be violent within long-term relationships:

> it is generally agreed that the consequences of physical aggression by men is greater than that by women, and the development and maintenance of the physical aggression may be gender specific. A review of FBI reports, for example, shows that over the past decade men have killed their partners twice as frequently as women. (O'Leary and Cascardi, 1989)

It is not possible to document the many ways in which violent interactions occur. The following focuses on a life event that precipitated both jealousy and violence.

2.7.3.1. Example 2n, John and Jenny

This example is one in which Jenny knows that John had a brief affair two years ago. John is told, by his ex-wife, that Jenny is currently having a relationship with a close friend. John is beside himself with rage.

> John (36) and Jenny (37) have lived together for six years. Both are divorced. They have no children together. Jenny's 17-year-old daughter lives with her ex-husband in France. John's daughter Sophie, aged 18, lives with his ex-wife in Devon. Neither has much direct contact with their own daughter although discussions are held about major decisions. Both previous marriages ended as a result of the previous partner's affair.
>
> John and Jenny's relationship was always turbulent, with constant arguments, and intermittent bouts of violence in which both partners would hit each other and pull each other's hair. Jenny moved out for six weeks, two years ago, after she learned

of John's affair. Following their reconciliation they have occasionally talked of ending the relationship and occasionally talked of marrying; the arguments and occasional violence have continued.

John's ex-wife, Maureen, phoned to discuss financing their daughter at university. She casually suggested that Jenny may be having a relationship with a mutual friend. When Jenny returned from seeing a film with a girlfriend, John was waiting for her; he had already been drinking.

Reconstructing the situation, it went something like this.

John greets Jenny at the door with, 'Where have you been? You are late and who've you been with?'.

Jenny. 'Been drinking already, have you?'

John. 'What has that got to do with it, while you have been screwing around with my best friend.'

Jenny. 'What? You bastard, you can talk, what brought this on? Who have you been talking to anyway? Who has put you up to this?'

John. 'You are right, Maureen rang, we had a chat.'

Jenny interrupting. 'So that's it, is it? While I am out you spend your time on the phone with your ex-wife. What am I supposed to think about that then?'

John. 'Now don't bring that in, you know we have to talk sometimes about Sophie.'

Jenny. 'Oh yes, I'm supposed to believe that am I? When you went off and had an affair, two years ago, and how do I know that it is over, you still see her at work. How can I believe any thing you say?'

John tries to cool down, moves towards her, to give her a hug. Jenny pushes past him, and pushes him aside, goes into the kitchen to make some tea. John follows her pouring himself more alcohol.

A heated argument ensues, in which each accuses the other of infidelity, of lying and of being untrustworthy.

John, is by now drunk; he tries to end the argument by suggesting they have sex. Jenny is outraged, John tries to drag her clumsily towards the bedroom, when she resists he hits her several times over the head, punches her in the stomach and bruises her arms. Jenny wants to fight back but finds herself being passive.

The above interaction need not have occurred; Jenny was not having an affair. If John could have discussed his fears openly, they might have moved their relationship forward to be more trusting.

Several things got in the way; both partners had previous experience of infidelity by a loved one (see Examples 3a, 3b). They each carried anxiety about the other's fidelity from their previous relationship. John's conversation with his ex-wife reminded him of a past failed relationship. He began drinking to alleviate his stress and anxiety, but this got in the way of communicating calmly with Jenny (1 M, 4 M). Jenny, for her part, instantly becomes defensive, is not prepared to explain to John or to respond to his sexual overtures while he is under the influence of alcohol and she is upset by his accusations (3 F, 4 F). She feels that 'if he loved her, he would understand and she would not have to explain' (1 F).

Painful past experiences get tangled into the present and each gender responds from their own base. John uses his aggressive skills (5 M) while Jenny both uses her verbal skills (4 F) and feels hurt (1 F). When John suggests sex (3 M), she cannot tolerate this as a way to end the argument; she needs to feel more in harmony with him first (3 F). Neither seems able to engage any of their other skills to help them through this crisis.

2.7.3.2. How to help

i. Where the man is physically violent or where there is a dependence upon alcohol, these two aspects may need to be attended to before any couple work can be done. Specialist help should be sought.

ii. Where violence has occurred it may be necessary to develop a contract in which the man: (a)takes responsibility for his violent reactions and (b)agrees that he will undertake to control his violence.

Unless this can be entered into with some degree of trust there may be little chance of improvement within the couple relationship.

iii. After i and ii have been attended to, then it may be more possible to explore together the couple interaction. It is useful to ask the couple to describe in detail a recent interaction where violence occurred. It is necessary to find out what occurred before the violent interaction and what each did or said as the situation escalated out of hand.

iv. Once the interaction has been described and understood in sufficient detail, it is useful to ask the couple to think about their own behaviour, and suggest one thing they could each have done to make the outcome less violent. Take time to find these and be gentle in exploring the detail of the experience, but stay with the incident.

v. Find out what got in the way of each carrying out their own 'suggestions'.

vi. See if the couple feel that the next time they feel an explosion is coming on whether they can use their suggestions to defuse the situation.

vii. Discuss other alternatives to defuse the violent interactions. See if you can decide on one piece of behaviour for which each will take responsibility during any potential explosive interaction. An agreed way of cooling off may be helpful, e.g. taking the dog for a walk, leaving the scene for 5–10 minutes. It is helpful if the couple can agree what is useful so that neither takes offence later.

viii. After some time it is useful to find out whether the couple ever have times together just for 'fun'. See if time can be set aside to be together and enjoy each other's company.

ix. Sometimes it is important to check how their sexual life is experienced. This may be contaminated by the discord in their relationship and some specific suggestions to improve their sexual life may help.

x. Many couples pay so much attention to their children, dependants, work or finance that their own relationship is neglected, so that finding time to nurture their relationship, to find privacy and time together is often a big step towards diminishing the possibility of violent interactions. Violent interactions are, however, complex and it may be preferable to refer to a specialist agency if violence is an issue so that negative patterns can be altered as early as possible. The safety of the couple and therapist should be paramount in deciding whether to work with the couple or refer to a more specialist centre.

2.7.4. Alternative treatments and research

O'Leary and Vivian (1990) believe that 'there is no single effective or appropriate treatment for all cases of physical aggression in a relationship'. They share the concern that because physical aggression within relationships is so prevalent, 'it is now important to conduct systematic research in the effectiveness and maintenance of treatment'.

2.8. Summary

Chapter 2 describes heterosexual intimacy using the concept of an invisible intimacy screen containing five elements of intimacy. Each element is described separately and couple interactions are given which illustrate the separate elements. Interventions are offered that may help the couple learn about their different resources, perceptions and responses. Other interventions are designed to help the woman and man modify their own interaction and respect the resources they each bring into the relationship.

Chapters 3 and 4 describe the life cycle of traditional and less traditional couples and the impact of life events on heterosexual intimacy. The invisible intimacy screen is again used to highlight differences and make suggestions as to modifications and adjustments which could enhance the couple's intimacy.

3 Chapter

Critical Periods in the Life Cycle of Relationships and Intimacy

3.1. Introduction

In Chapter 3 the life cycles of traditional and less traditional couples are described. The invisible intimacy screen is used as a checklist to aid thinking about the couple's interaction and to identify gender differences, to consider which elements of the screen may be missing, distorted or not attended to and are causing distress. Interventions are suggested which may help to redress the balance. Discord often occurs when the needs of one gender override the intimacy needs of the other gender. Alternatively, a recognition of each other's separate needs and vulnerabilities, with a preparedness to draw on the resources of both partners, can deepen intimacy.

When working with couples in distress it may not be necessary to engage them in discussion of gender differences. It is most useful to assist the couple to acknowledge and respect their different approaches, perceptions and responses rather than blaming each other for being different.

Where the couple are very stuck in rigid attitudes and responses then it may be necessary to draw attention to gender differences and involve them in a discussion of their own perceptions and what meanings they give to gender differences (see Examples 2d, Tim and Tina; 2k, Ken and Kathleen; 3i, Harry and Helen; 4a, Stephen and Sally).

3.2. The life cycle of couples

The life cycle of a couple relationship goes through several stages, beginning at the first meeting, continuing through their first commitment until the dissolution of the relationship or death of one partner.

For heterosexual couples who follow a traditional pattern and marry for life, the cycle usually includes the stages of making a home together, having babies, the growth and development of the children – their schooling, jobs, leaving home and pairing – followed by grand-parenting, retirement, the ageing process and the loss through death of parents and of the partner.

> Being in such an expectable progression creates a visualisable future, predicated on marker events such as the birth of a child etc (Chiriboga et al., 1991).

Forty five per cent of marriages in Britain end in divorce or separation. A relationship may continue in some form, particularly where there are children. The need to continue a relationship as joint parents keeps them in an ongoing, if different and difficult, relationship.

For the less traditional couples who are divorced or prefer not to marry, one or both partners may bring a child, or children, from a previous relationship or marriage into the new relationship. There may be significant prior relationships which affect the new couple. Ex-partners may be consulted about children's welfare or finances and they may participate in family events such as christenings, birthdays or weddings (Whyte, 1990; Robinson, 1993; Gibson, 1994; Aldous, 1996).

> Being in a non-traditional family is different from being in a traditional, intact first marriage. To succeed in the face of these differences it is necessary for these families to know their experiences are normal. It is critical not to label these families as dysfunctional. (Harway, 1996)

Additionally, within traditional and less traditional couples one or both partners may have affairs during their relationship, which, if disclosed, usually become a significant life stage or event within the couple relationship.

The end of the couple's life cycle takes various forms and new relationships develop after the death of one partner or the ending of a long-term relationship, with a new cycle beginning. Previous relationships, and how they were experienced, can have a profound impact upon the individual and couple.

3.2.1. Critical periods in the life cycle of a couple

(See also Chapter 6.)

The phrase 'critical periods' is used to describe stages in the life cycle of the couple when expectations and anxieties are raised, and each gender feels under additional pressure. These critical periods are the training ground during which female/male intimacy needs are heightened and the opportunity for a deeper understanding of each other is available. However, at these times, each gender may be less in tune with the other. Their different responses and perceptions can then be experienced as a lack of understanding or concern.

Rutter and Hay (1994) reviewed individual development through the life cycle and prefer terms such as 'continuities and discontinuities' to describe patterns of relationships which change over time. They argue cogently for life stages to be thought of as 'transitions' because of social changes which have occurred since 1960.

Caspi and Bem (1990) think there is a need for studies of systematic change, not just the absence of continuity, and prefer to use 'turning point' to identify these experiences.

> Which usually involve shutting down or opening up of continuities or lasting change in the environment, or lasting effect upon people's self concept or views and expectations of other people (Caspi and Bem, 1990).

Such authors recognise that less traditional couples face new experiences which do not fit previous ideas of life stages (Lavee et al., 1987; Storaasli and Markman, 1990; Heinz, 1991).

The term 'critical period' is used here to emphasise the fact that couples' relationships are often in crisis at these times.

All crises in couple relationships are not directly attributable to life cycle or life events. Disagreements about finances, gambling, drinking, drug addiction may occur without an obvious connection with gender differences, life cycle or life events. Superficially they may result from the lifestyle of the individual. It is, however, worth taking life stage and life events into account when thinking about what has precipitated a crisis in a couple relationship. (Life events are described in Chapter 4.)

3.2.2. Critical early experiences affecting adult relationships

(See also 6.2, 6.3, 6.8)

Early childhood experiences colour how the adult responds. For some, a specific life event may carry over into the adult relationship. For example, women who have experienced abuse or known violence within their family of origin may develop a long-term relationship with a man who replicates these early experiences. There is some evidence that the violent adult male may be replicating his own earlier experiences. A direct connection between early experiences and their adult re-creation is not clearly established, but life events and life experiences can come together in the reliving of violent or abusive female/male relationship in adulthood.

Additionally, because of early abusive experiences, a women may be unable to allow herself to take pleasure in a sexual relationship, even though the partner is neither abusive nor violent (see Example 4d, Robert and Rita). The same may be true for men who have been abused, but the evidence for this is inconclusive. In these ways, life events during childhood impact upon adult relationships.

3.2.3. Individual expectations of the couple relationship

(See 6.3.2; 6.8.2)

For the individual whose parents divorced or separated or where a parent was ill or died, there may be an additional level of anxiety about the stability of the present relationship (Byng-Hall, 1982). As children of divorced or separated parents reach the age when their own parents separated, they may anticipate the break up of their own relationship. Two brief illustrations follow.

3.2.3.1. Example 3a, Rosemary

> Rosemary, whose mother was left by her father when she was 6 years old, became very anxious about her relationship with her husband Charles as their daughter became 6 years old. It was as if Rosemary carried an expectation that 'men leave women when their daughters are 6'.

3.2.3.2. Example 3b, Richard

> Richard's mother died when he was 4 years old, and he was brought up by grandparents. Richard became very anxious about his own wife's health as their child Christopher reached 4 years of age.

In these ways gender differences, hopes and fears about long-term relationships, are reinforced by personal experience. Such experiences are not always negative; some respond by being more determined to overcome any difficulties and work harder to establish and continue in a long-term relationship.

3.2.4. Shared experiences but different responses

Couples are often relieved when reminded that similar experiences are shared by others. For example, grieving for the loss of youthfulness is a process everyone faces. However, women and men face different physical changes within the ageing process and each gender is therefore presented with the problem of understanding and respecting this.

The menopause, for example, is a stage in the woman's life cycle which the man will experience as an observer. He does not participate in the physical and hormonal changes which are affecting his partner. How he makes sense of what is happening and how he responds to her during this time will affect their relationship. It will also affect how the woman feels towards him and how she feels about herself (see 6.7).

3.2.5. Continuous development

Life events and life cycle stages are two threads which are woven at intervals into the pattern of life while gender is a continuous thread though difficult to see clearly at all times. The life cycle of each couple interacts with the individual life cycle of their children, their parents, the extended family and previous significant relationships.

> It is helpful to think of couple relationships as continuously developing with a constant need for each partner to be alert to their own and their partner's changing needs.

A developmental stage for the individual may collide with a critical period in the life cycle of the couple, adding stress to the couple relationship. The pregnancy of the woman may conflict with the man's wish to be experimental sexually (see Example 3c, Douglas and Diane) or the slowing down of a man's sexual responses may conflict with his partner's renewal of sexual interest following the menopause (see 6.5, 6.7).

Where a shared sense of overcoming crises has been experienced, any new upset is likely to be faced with greater confidence by both partners (Beavers 1985). Recognising, respecting and responding to the gender needs of the other can be particularly demanding during these critical periods as each gender may feel vulnerable and stressed.

What is experienced as a critical period is not the same for all couples. Pregnancy is one of the major life stages in the development of a couple relationship which for some couples may occur in a natural and spontaneous way with no added pressures to turn a normal life stage into a crisis. During these life stages the complementary abilities of each gender enlarge a couple's repertoire of skills and perceptions, giving them an advantage when facing stressful situations.

Emerging from childhood into adulthood presents a threefold dilemma. Firstly, how to refind our own gender identity, without being overwhelmed by distorting experiences. Secondly, how to find a partner whose gender identity is not overly distorted by difficult childhood experiences. Finally, how to learn about the other gender and to trust that, although coming from very different gender bases, a satisfactory and shared sense of intimacy can develop which is not necessarily interrupted by separation or divorce, and does not involve violence or abuse.

3.3. Critical periods

3.3.1. Critical periods in traditional couple relationships

(See Chapter 6)
In presenting examples of couples during critical periods, no attempt is made to cover all possible situations. Examples of traditional couples described revolve around the following situations:

- 'getting to know you' (see 3.4)
  (Examples are 2n, 3c, 3d, 3g, 3h)
- experiencing sexuality (see 3.5)
  (Examples are 2a, 2d, 2h, 2i, 2l, 3c, 3d, 4b, 4c, 4d)
- pregnancy (see 3.6)
  (Examples are 3c, 3d, 3e, 4b)
- parenting (see 3.7)
  (Examples are 2g, 2m, 2n, 3f, 3g, 3h, 4d)
- the ageing process (see 3.10)
  (Examples are 2d, 2i, 3i, 4c).

3.3.2. Critical periods in less traditional couple relationships

Less traditional couples may also experience the above critical periods, but patterns of interaction are interrupted when separation and/or divorce occurs with ensuing layering of complexity. New relationships begin the cycle again and these new relationships may be affected by each partner's past experiences.

Critical periods for the less traditional couples are therefore less predictable. The complexity arises as few established guidelines exist. Each couple faces a unique situation according to the life story of each partner. Previous significant relationships, children, the involvement of the natural parent, who cares for the child/ren, where they live, custody and access agreements all contribute to the quality of each couple's experience, and to the less predictable nature of critical periods within their relationship. Financial arrangements, competition for finances and attention can add layers of tension for these couples (Kurdeck and Fine, 1991; Robinson, 1993; Smock, 1993; Emery, 1994; Ganong and Coleman, 1994; Lamanna and Reidman, 1997).

A further complexity derives from the multiplicity of interlocking and overlapping relationships within 'blended families'. Grandparents, in-laws, step-parents, step-children and ex-husbands or partners all belong to the network of relationships which must be reworked and reassessed as partnerships dissolve and new partnerships are made. The quality of these multiple relationships can be the seedbed for deeper levels of intimacy or heightened critical periods.

> Harmful myths also exist making life more difficult for step-families. For example, a step-family can never be as good as a family in which children live with both natural parents'. (Kurdeck and Fine, 1991)

The complexity of the situation for less traditional families means that many more occasions can become critical periods. Several authors indicate that key issues which emerge focus upon step-children and finances (Robinson, 1993; Ganong and Coleman, 1994; Harway, 1996; Lamanna and Reidman, 1997). Two examples have been specifically chosen to highlight these difficulties (see 3.8, 3.9). Harway (1996) suggests there is a great need to be creative to find new ways to be of support and assistance.

Critical periods in less traditional couple relationships which are described here through examples are:

- the impact of an earlier separation upon the present relationship (Examples are 2j, 2l, 2n, 3a, 3g, 3h)
- dealing with children from previous relationships and step-children (Examples are 2j, 2n, 3f, 3g, 3h, 4d)
- dealing with 'blended' family gatherings (see 3.8) (Example 3g)
- dealing with financial dilemmas (see 3.9) (Example 3h).

Because of changing attitudes and patterns of longer-term relationships it is not possible to give examples that represent most of these structures. However, examples are given of difficulties experienced by couples seeking help.

As society becomes more accepting of alternative lifestyles and gender orientation, a proportion of families are learning to include gay or lesbian partnerships or bisexual relationships within the family matrix. This book is about heterosexual couples and does not focus upon gay and bisexual couples. However, gay, lesbian and bisexual couples encourage the exploration of sexual intimacy and its fulfilment.

> Gay and bisexual relationships invite the question whether intimacy may be more easily achieved between same sex couples, particularly if it is acknowledged that women and men seek different elements of intimacy.

3.3.3. Separation, divorce and remarriage

The statistics of divorce or separation tend to clump around the critical periods of 'getting to know you' or the first three years of marriage; the periods when children begin school or leave home also coincide with an increase of divorces (Carter and McGoldrick, 1990; Storaasli and Markman, 1990; Family Policy Studies, 1993).

> Around one third of divorces occur within 5 years of the initiation of marriage in many European nations (examples include Austria, Hungary, England and Wales, Switzerland, Ukraine, Byelorussia, the Balkan states). This means that for many young people the process of marital breakdown has begun within three years of the wedding day. (Dormor, 1992).

Many couples who have shared a marriage for 20–30 years are also seeking divorce. There was an increase in the number of divorces in men between 45 and 59 years of age from 27,968 in 1983 to 36,668 in 1993. The equivalent numbers for women in the same age range were 20,613 rising to 27,234. Whilst older women are increasingly divorcing, more men than women are divorcing at these ages. Part of this disparity is no doubt due to the different ages of the spouses at marriage. The age of the individual or the marriage does not seem to protect the couple from divorce.

> The demographic evidence of twenty years ago suggested that some three-quarters of all divorcing couples married again. It still remains the case that the majority of spouses passing through the divorce courts will marry again, but not to the same degree as in the 1960s. The remarriage pattern of the 1980s indicates around 70% of all divorced will remarry though age, sex, social class, employment and attitude towards marriage are all factors affecting the rate of remarriage (Gibson, 1994).

Gibson writes of marriage:

> There is a growing tolerance and recognition of non-traditional family arrangements, and marriage has become a choice that an increasing proportion of younger women and men will deliberately refrain from (Gibson, 1994).

Additionally, life events such as accident, injury, illness, loss of job, home or finances may interrupt the life of a couple, placing additional strain upon the relationship. Life events are often unexpected, throwing the couple into a stressful situation. It is rare for a couple to complete a life cycle without having had to contend with a stressful and unexpected life event (see Chapter 4).

3.4. The critical period of 'getting to know you'

(See also 6.2, 6.3, 6.8)

The concept of critical periods and the impact of gender issues are examined through Example 3c, Douglas and Diane, during the critical period of 'getting to know you'.

The critical period in this example has three layers. The first is its newness, which may be the most problematic (Mansfield and Collard, 1988; OPCS, 1993). Secondly, Diane's early pregnancy; and thirdly each partner is learning to give and receive sexual pleasure with the opposite sex. Hence there is a layering of complexities which each gender experiences differently. For the less traditional couple, previous experiences will bring an extra dimension of complexity into the 'getting to know you phase'. The 'ghost' of a previous relationship can be very intrusive.

Douglas's learning how to control his ejaculation at the same time as enjoying his orgasm (3 M) becomes intertwined with Diane's uncertainty about the safety of the baby in her womb (2 F), and her own ambivalence about sexual intercourse (3 F) which accompanies her early experience of being pregnant.

3.4.1. Example 3c, Douglas and Diane

Douglas (20) and Diane (20) were immature socially and had known each other for nine months before they married. Newly married, neither was sexually experienced. They did not attempt penetrative sex before marriage, preferring to 'wait until they were man and wife'. Diane became pregnant immediately. Whilst she did not want to continue sexual intercourse, 'in case the baby was injured', she submitted to Douglas's wishes. Douglas for his part wanted to respect her concern for the baby, and usually hurried his lovemaking so that he ejaculated as early as possible. Predictably, Diane found sexual intercourse not at all pleasant and Douglas rapidly became unable to control his early ejaculation.

Fortunately this couple sought help with their sexual and relationship difficulties and were helped to take time to nurture their relationship.

They began to talk together (4 F, 4 M) and to relearn about each other sexually and how to pleasure each other by first finding out about each other's needs and responses (3 F, 3 M). Couples who have a baby early in their relationship may have little time to get to know the other's gender needs, and since the 'getting to know you' phase is already a critical period, having a baby is an obvious additional stress, as well as a pleasure.

Using the invisible intimacy screen highlights areas of difficulty. Douglas, in wanting to explore his own sexuality, finds that his ability to give and receive sexual pleasure is complicated by his own difficulty in controlling his ejaculation (3 M).

This is further compounded by the fact that Diane has got pregnant so early and by her anxiety about 'harming the baby' which she carries (2 F). Diane may also have become less interested in sex, as her womb is already engaged with the early preparation for the nurturing of the foetus (3 F).

Their wish to give and receive intimacy is entangled with their individual developmental needs, their lack of knowledge about the other, the impact on each partner of pregnancy – a 'critical period' for them both.

How each gender responds is pivotal to their sense of a shared intimate experience. Without a preparedness to respect their different gender needs and responses, Diane may soon think of Douglas as only wanting her for quick sex (3 M). Douglas may soon think of Diane as preferring to take care of the baby to being with him (2 F). Resentments build quickly in these critical and sensitive periods.

3.4.2. How to help

Douglas and Diane came for help as soon as they began to have sexual and communication difficulties and consequently were helped by a few short sessions:

- They were helped 'in session' to talk and listen to each other and to explain what was happening to them. Douglas explained that he was becoming anxious that he was unable either to control his own ejaculation, or to give Diane pleasure (3 M) (see 2.3.2.4, 2.6).
- Diane was able to explain her anxiety about hurting the baby during intercourse (2 F).
- They were both able to tell each other how much their relationship and the baby meant to each other (4 F, 4 M).
- Douglas was given the stop–start technique (3 M) (a technique which enables the man to gain understanding about, and more control over, his ejaculation).
- They were asked to stop having penetrative sex for a few weeks but to practise giving and receiving sensual and sexual pleasures to

each other, and allow themselves time to learn about each other's rhythms (3 F).

- They met, with encouragement, their general practitioner who reassured them that the baby was safe during intercourse but that they might wish to find comfortable positions during intercourse.
- In these ways, without referring directly to the invisible intimacy screen, the couple were encouraged to take seriously their different needs and abilities.
- Their ability to communicate openly and to give and receive affection rapidly improved (4 F, 4 M) (see 2.5.2.3).

3.5. The critical period of experiencing sexuality

(See also 6.5, 6.9)

Douglas and Diane were 'getting to know' each other individually at the same time as finding out about their own and their partner's sexuality and finding a way to accommodate to the practical aspects of living together. They had not expected Diane's getting pregnant so soon; nevertheless they were happy that it occurred.

Sexuality and the possibility of the woman becoming pregnant is a defining difference between the genders and causes much delight and tension for the individual and couple.

Unless both partners are equally relaxed about the woman becoming pregnant, avoidance of pregnancy with suitable contraception is of major importance. Since both female and male contraceptive devices are available both partners can take this responsibility. However, where pregnancy is undesirable, the woman is likely to feel under greater pressure since, should pregnancy occur, it is her body that provides the womb which nurtures the baby for nine months.

It would not be surprising, therefore, if her ability to relax and enjoy her own sexuality fully is moderated by worries about pregnancy. The availability of the pill reduces these anxieties even though, long term, the pill might carry some risks to her future well-being (3 F).

The man's ability to relax and enjoy his sexuality is likely to be moderated by his ability to control his own erection and ejaculation and the extent to which his partner is prepared to help him with this (3 M). Additionally, his sense of self-confidence in his own sexuality is likely to be affected by his partner's critical or supportive response should he be unable to control his ejaculation, or lose his erection at any time during foreplay or intercourse (4 F, 4 M).

An aspect of the woman's biological makeup, less easy to substantiate, may be her slower response to sexual stimuli than that of her male partner. For many women, of all ages, the ability to respond sexually and sensually depends upon two interrelated elements. Firstly, whether she is feeling resentful or preoccupied with unexpressed concerns (1F. 4F). Secondly, whether she has been adequately stimulated through touch and tenderness to reach a state of arousal whereby she is ready for her partner to penetrate her vaginally (3 F) (Kaplan, 1981).

Knowledge of the male arousal pattern suggests that, in general, the male is aroused through sight and fantasy and most young men can achieve an erection at an early stage of interaction. The younger man (as opposed to an ageing man) is less likely to require touch and tenderness or be preoccupied by thoughts which interrupt his erection (this may not be true for the male who has experienced sexual abuse). He is likely to be sensitive to criticism of his performance and, as already stated, may have an inability as yet to control the timing of his ejaculation.

In a very practical sense the woman's need to be touched and aroused may be the opposite of what the male may need in these early stages of sexual intercourse. Prolonged foreplay, which she may need, is more likely to precipitate a loss of control and premature ejaculation in the young man. This, too, may make sexual intercourse less satisfying for the female (3 F, 3 M).

Counterbalancing this is the younger man's ability to regain an erection reasonably quickly; in which case, so long as the woman is not too frustrated by the first less successful attempt at penetrative sex, at the second attempt both the female and the male may be more able both to give and receive sexual pleasure.

In reviewing the complexity of the giving and receiving of mutual sexual pleasure, one cannot but reflect with surprise that so many heterosexual couples do achieve a satisfying and lasting sexual relationship.

However, the sexual relationship can be complicated by each partner being over-sensitive to the other's needs. For the male, anxiety about his ability to satisfy his partner may lead to performance anxiety and premature ejaculation (3 M). For the female, her attention to his needs may mean that she does not allow herself to develop her pleasure in her own sexuality (2 F).

In earlier centuries, and currently in societies where mutual sexual satisfaction is not seen as a priority, premature ejaculation in the male, or inability to achieve an orgasm in the female, were not problematic. Conception and pregnancy still occurred.

Part of the change within Western long-term female/male relationships is that both partners may hope to experience something which they would each call sexual intimacy. This places new demands upon sexuality and the physical sexual relationship. For this to be achieved, both the man and the woman must be prepared to take time to learn about their own and their partner's sexual and emotional needs and to be prepared to communicate these to each other. Where a shared sense of mutual sexual pleasure is desired as part of the intimacy needs of a couple, it can usually be developed over time. It cannot be assumed to 'just happen' as a result of 'being in love'. It will also depend upon whether the other elements of the invisible intimacy screen are respected, responded to, and sufficiently satisfied to make intimacy possible.

As the couple grow old together their physical sexuality or sensuality can enhance their ageing process, where tenderness and experimentation enables a continued sexual life well into old age. Where this does not occur, the later years of a couple's life may become unnecessarily barren.

3.6. The critical period of pregnancy

(See also 6.3.4, 6.8.4)

A life cycle stage which is seen as part of the normal human cycle is that of conceiving, bearing and giving birth to a child. For the gay and lesbian couple the issue of parenting and nurturing presents a particularly stressful dilemma, emphasising a crucial biological and physical difference between the man and the woman and between the homosexual and the heterosexual couple.

When a lesbian woman conceives a child she carries that baby in her womb and society accepts her right to nurture that child. In a crude sense, her physical makeup makes it possible for her to 'lay back and think of England' during intercourse, in order to allow herself to get pregnant. She does not need to desire the man sexually to enable penetrative sex to occur. For the gay man the problem is doubly complex as he must find a willing woman and also find within himself the desire to have sexual intercourse with her or use a more clinical approach where his semen is used but there is no physical sexual relationship with the woman.

This re-emphasises two key physical differences between women and men and the vulnerability of both. Firstly, that a man cannot 'lay back and think of England'. He must first be able to get and maintain an erection before penetrative sex can occur and fertilisation becomes possible. Fertility treatments are now available which make this less of a problem, but the basic gender difference still exists. Secondly, until recent blood tests made it possible for paternity to be established, such a man could not necessarily claim even his biological rights as father to that child.

Within the context of the life cycle of the woman or man whose gender choice of partner is the same sex, the fundamental biological issue of the wish for and ability to parent children does not go away. So far, our society has been unable to find acceptable social ways of solving this problem.

3.6.1. Example 3d, Yvonne and Roger

In this example Roger's problem-solving approach (1 M) collides with Yvonne's change of feeling about herself once pregnant (1 F). Roger has difficulty in recognising this change and Yvonne is confused about what is happening to her.

> Yvonne (34) and Roger (35) had lived together for five years. Both earned large salaries, Yvonne as a personnel consultant and Roger as a market analyst. When Yvonne became pregnant, they decided together that Yvonne would stop working, they would sell their flat in Central London and move to a less expensive, larger house in South London. Superficially they pulled together to face the dilemma presented by Roger getting Yvonne pregnant.
>
> A closer understanding revealed that Yvonne was feeling vulnerable about her pregnancy, and sad to be leaving a job and a flat she had loved. Roger was excited that Yvonne was pregnant and proud to be able to support Yvonne and the baby on his salary alone.
>
> Instead of feeling supported, each was now upset by the other's reactions. Roger misunderstood Yvonne's reactions, assuming that, since she had always been very competent and a good manager, she had changed her mind about being pregnant. Her vulnerability and sadness took him by surprise, as it did her. Yvonne misunderstood Roger's excitement and pleasure as an indication that he had neither noticed nor cared that she was finding the changes difficult.
>
> Roger and Yvonne's ability to make a joint decision about moving house seems to have masked their individual responses to pregnancy. Each partner was disappointed that the other did not 'feel like I feel'.

This is a common occurrence, especially at the time of pregnancy. The man may feel that his pregnant partner is ungrateful for the practical support he is giving whilst she may feel her husband is insensitive as she does not receive emotional support (1 F, 1 M; see 2.3.1).

This apparent poor communication is particularly upsetting, when both the woman and man are 'doing their best'. Yvonne's vulnerability comes as a surprise to both of them and neither quite knows how to respond. Communication becomes skewed and each feels misunderstood (4 F, 4 M).

For others, the pregnancy may be accompanied by ill health, an absent husband or partner, unemployment, or a whole variety of other experiences which heighten the emotions surrounding pregnancy.

3.6.2. Example 3e, Peter and Paula

Peter (27) worked away from home from the fourth month of his wife Paula's first pregnancy to just before the birth of the baby. Paula (23) had no problems during her early pregnancy, but became worried by puffy ankles and tiredness after five months. Peter returned home each weekend. He spent most of the weekend clearing the spare room, decorating and preparing it for the baby's arrival. Paula told him about her tiredness and her worries about her own and the baby's health, but felt that Peter's reaction showed that he was not concerned for her or the baby's health (1 F).

He, for his part, feeling guilty that he was away during the week to support her, did his best at weekends to 'solve the problem', as he saw it, of her tiredness. He would insist that she did not help him with the spare room. He was concerned at her obvious tiredness and insisted taking over buying the cot and the preparation of the baby's room. He took Paula to collect the wallpaper, curtains and the cot (1 M).

Paula by now felt excluded from all decisions. Peter had neither talked to her nor consulted her. Because he was so busy preparing the room for the baby, she felt that he did not take seriously her worries about herself or the baby.

Peter felt that he had done his best to help and show concern for her and the baby's health, by taking care of the planning, shopping and decorating of the baby's room.

This example shows how life events add to the anxiety of each gender, and how the needs and responses of each gender can exacerbate the situation instead of solving it. Stated simply, Paula wanted emotional support through talking together and feeling listened to (1 F). Peter had heard her concerns about her tiredness and the baby's health, and was trying to solve both of these problems by helping Paula to rest (1 M). While each was trying to reach out to the other in this crisis, their responses drove them further apart (4 F, 4 M).

For the younger heterosexual couple the ability to become pregnant may not be questioned until they learn through experience that it is not happening. The question of fertility or infertility will affect their potential parenthood, which is one of the major life events within a couple's cycle. Adoption or miscarriage, a premature or a handicapped baby may be part of the couple's experience, as they face up to this stage of their own life cycle. The woman and man are likely to have different ways of approaching each of these hurdles, partly through learned experiences and partly derived from the underlying gender strengths.

Where a couple are very anxious to conceive and learn that the man is subfertile, the woman may protect her male partner by taking on the 'responsibility' for the infertility, as if she knows she can cope more easily than he (Ridley, 1994). This may be a result of social pressures. But it may be partly due to the woman's knowledge of her own strengths; her body provides sustenance for a baby for anything up to two years, while the male's role is primarily impregnation. An elemental aspect of a man's makeup may be his pride in his fecundity, and the parallel sense of shame if he is infertile. This has been called genetic death. The woman, too, may be deeply and bitterly disappointed if she is unable to have a baby; in spite of this she may protect her partner. In this way she may be recognising her own gender strengths of caring for and protecting her more vulnerable partner (see 6.4, 6.12).

The woman may have inner knowledge of coping with loss which the man may not have. She has inevitably had to cope with the monthly rhythms of the preparation of the womb for impregnation, and the monthly loss as the womb does not receive a fertilised egg. Loss and renewal may therefore be more familiar to her through personal experience of this bodily cycle (see Chapter 6).

For the couple who leave the issue of children until the woman is nearing 40, the pressure of the 'biological clock' to get pregnant before 'it is too late' highlights the gender difference between women and men and brings an additional pressure to bear upon the couple. The man, at least in theory, does not need to worry about his age and pregnancy. Should his partner not become pregnant he can choose to find a younger woman and fulfil his wish to have children.

Whatever the couple's experience of pregnancy and childbirth, whether their choice is to be childless, or through low sperm count or subfertility they are unable to have a child of their own, this is a life cycle milestone which the couple will inevitably face during their coupledom. At each of these milestones the man and the woman may have a different biological 'given' which will affect their response and perspective.

Giving birth and the quality of the experience can be formative for the woman and her ongoing relationship with her partner. Traumatic elements surrounding the birth will affect not only the woman's sense of self-worth but also her ongoing relationship with her partner.

3.6.3. How to help

The couple can be helped to understand each other's needs at this time. Areas to be aware of are:

- Recommencing a sexual relationship before wounds have healed or being insensitive to the trauma of a painful birth can be crippling to the couple's intimacy. At these times the man needs to be additionally sensitive to the birth experience and show affection and concern for her in non-sexual ways (3 F).
- Listening to her feelings, learning about the experience, touch and tenderness rather than demands for a sexual response are likely to be most effective (1 F).
- The male partner can encourage expression of the woman's negative feelings, which may be withheld; it may feel perverse to be angry with the gynaecologist or surgeon who performed the Caesarean or stitching, and the woman's ability to put others' feelings before her own may inhibit her from expressing natural anger or disappointment at being 'cut about' (5 F).
- In these ways the man can become the carer who can demonstrate his understanding of the female's experience even though he cannot fully participate.
- His ability to care for the mother as she begins the task of mothering is likely to be a crucial element in the deepening of their intimacy. Otherwise they may begin a process of drifting apart which widens as the children take up more of the couple's time. Children inevitably become a focus of concern, particularly when young, but the couple need to take care of their relationship at this time so that they do not lose touch with each other.
- Although the man may feel peripheral during the excitement of the arrival of the baby, his role as carer of mother and baby unit now becomes central to their future intimacy.

> The man's ability to be autonomous and independent may be a preparation for this time when his partner may be preoccupied with the baby and he needs to be sufficiently strong to take care of them both without feeling rejected or abandoned (1 M, 2 M, 5 M).

It is not surprising that the couple may be under stress at this time as their individual and joint abilities are being tested to the full. Stating this differently, their gender vulnerabilities, resources and abilities come into force at this time as resources or stresses to the relationship.

3.7. The critical period of parenting

(See also 3.8, 3.9)
Here step-parent is used to describe parent figures who are not the natural parent but are in a parental role to the child/ren.

Being parents in a changing world is challenging. All parents find themselves at times in conflict over the development and discipline of one or more children. Guidelines are changing as knowledge and new technologies bring greater awareness and problems for parents. Where there is one natural parent and step-parents or other parental figures the situation can be complicated by multiple roles and lack of clarity about authority and responsibility (Ganong and Coleman, 1994; Gibson, 1994; Lamanna and Reidman, 1997) (see Examples 3g, 3h, 4e).

3.7.1. Example 3f, Nora and Neil

> Nora (38) and Neil (40) sought therapy because of repeated arguments regarding their children (12, 8 and 6). Both school teachers, they each 'knew about child-rearing' and cared deeply about being good parents. Although they continued to try, things did not improve.
>
> Their difficulty arose out of different attitudes to discipline. Nora was seen by Neil to be 'too soft' on the children and Neil as 'too hard'. As often occurs with such a split between the parental attitudes, the children would complain to Nora about their father and she would occasionally keep secrets from Neil of a child's misdemeanour. She also gave them more money than Neil felt wise and generally protected them from Neil's 'harsher' treatment.

Currently the eldest child Bobby was having difficulty settling into secondary school. His teacher telephoned Nora regarding his aggressive behaviour in the school playground, which Nora did not mention to Neil. He, however, opened a letter from school which referred to this telephone conversation and was angry with Nora. A crisis was provoked which took them into therapy.

3.7.2. How to help

In general the aim of therapy with parents, whether natural parents or step-parents, is to help them cope with high levels of parental emotions and disagreement and to seek a solution in which both partners agree to give each other support in its implementation. It is not claimed that all parental disputes can be solved but, if parents can recognise their different approaches, these differences can become resources. When parents can support each other following a joint decision, much progress can be made.

It may not be necessary to speak about gender differences, what is relevant is that the therapist is able to identify and work with these differences, keeping a balance between the positive resources both bring into a situation and drawing together the positive suggestions that each offers.

A five stage process can be followed:

i. recognising different perspectives and attitudes
ii. discussing how differences affect the children in specific situations
iii. with reference to a specific piece of behaviour or situation, finding a way to support each other
iv. keeping arguments out of earshot of the children and not involving the children in arguments
v. reviewing and moving forward.

The above format can be modified for each individual situation. Where the child or children involved are step child/ren the process is more complicated. During step i, the different parental relationships to the children can be recognised, including the role of an absent natural parent. At each of the following stages the step-relationship can be kept in mind. This may be particularly helpful if the step-parental relationship is young and where the step-parent/step-child relationship is being developed. Where there is an absent natural parent figure who has also to be consulted it is important for this to be discussed openly and agreement reached as to how they, as a couple, can support each other over any final decision that is made.

It is important for the parent figures to ask each other for the support they each need, and to decide how they can continue jointly to support each other. Where step-children are concerned, the step-parent may feel isolated and ignored if excluded from any discussion. If the step-parent is a man he may find it difficult to ask for help and may tend to use his problem-solving skills (1 M) and to insist that his hierarchical position is recognised (2 M). This can lead to conflict between the natural mother and himself. At the same time, the step-parent can be helped to understand the natural parent's tendency to assume responsibility for their own child/ren. Open discussion of this dilemma can bring much needed support to both partners and give the children a feeling that their particular position is acknowledged honestly.

As children reach adolescence they can be included in step ii, so that their opinion is sought and recognition given to the fact that they are themselves moving towards adulthood. Where disagreements are not resolved, professional help should be sought before problems get too entrenched. The outsider can often identify hidden alliances and unstated resentments which get in the way of good enough negotiation.

i. Recognising different perspectives and attitudes

By the time couples come to therapy they are often at loggerheads, feeling misunderstood and isolated within the relationship. There are likely to be difficulties in listening and allowing each to express their perspective. With patience and a sense of humour the therapist can model a balanced approach by ensuring that both partners are given time to express what is happening and how they each understand what problems they face with their children. Where a step-relationship is being discussed it is important to address it openly. The natural parent may feel that her/his opinion should always carry more weight and should be supported by the partner. The absent natural parent's view may also be important and each partner may wish to express their concerns. They may need encouragement to enter into discussions of such emotive issues but it is better they are discussed than left buried, becoming reservoirs of resentment and unresolved problems.

The preferred outcome for the couple is eventually to be supportive of each other. This takes time, patience and a degree of resilience from all concerned.

When Neil and Nora were asked to talk about their different perspectives regarding Bobby, the conversation went as follows:

Neil. 'Bobby is 12 now, he is going to be a young man soon and I feel that it is time he was given more responsibility for himself, and he should be required to act responsibly' (2 M).

Nora. 'Yes, but he is very immature for his age. I don't think we can assume he can look after himself in the way that you think. You are too hard on him, and he doesn't like it' (2 F).

The couple were then asked by the therapist to think of one example where they were in disagreement about how Bobby should be treated. The topic chosen was whether he should be allowed to ride his bicycle to school on his own. They were asked to decentre, i.e. to face each other and discuss this topic together (see 2.2.4.2, iii).

In summary, Nora did not want him to ride to and from school, fearing he would have an accident (2 F). His father wanted him to ride his bicycle to and from school, but also to be responsible for its repairs, keeping it oiled and clean and to use his pocket money when necessary for this (2 M).

Bobby was torn between the two attitudes; he complained to his mother about his father's strictness regarding the bicycle but tried to persuade his mother that he should be allowed to ride his bicycle to school (2 M).

Nora blamed Neil and felt that he was inciting Bobby to rebel against her. She had always had a close relationship with her eldest son. At this point neither could accept the other's point of view (4 F, 4 M).

ii. Discussing how differences affect the children in specific situations

The couple were then asked to discuss together how their differences affected Bobby. The conversation went as follows. Each parent was able to speak about the impact upon Bobby even though so far they were not able to change their own or their partner's behaviour. Additionally, they each blamed the other.

Neil. 'I think it does make him quite upset and angry that his mother molly-coddles him. He is a tall lad, he looks older than his years and he wants to be treated as a grown-up.'

Nora. 'You are right, he is upset and angry, but that is your fault, if you were kinder to him and less severe with him he wouldn't be so upset. He comes to me and complains that you are too strict with him and his pocket money.'

They continued for some time to accuse and blame each other for Bobby's behaviour with emotions rising.

Where there is a step-relationship it is equally important to acknowledge any differences openly so that they can be addressed, rather than becoming areas of suppressed resentment.

iii. With reference to a specific piece of behaviour or situation, find a way to support each other

The therapist then intervened to say that Nora and Neil had given her a good picture of how they saw the situation and what happened if they tried to discuss it together.

Therapist. 'Let's see what happens if we try to approach this a little differently. Can you think of something you could each do differently to support each other over this issue.'

They both sat silent for a while, and the level of emotional arousal dropped. (Parents usually are prepared to make positive suggestions for their children even when they are having relationship difficulties.)

Neil, reluctantly. 'I could agree that Bobby does not take the bike to school, but I don't want to do that.'

Nora. 'I could go along with the idea that he take the bike to school occasionally, say on Wednesdays because it is sports day, but not always, and I think you are too strict about pocket money.'

These two suggestions then formed the basis for further negotiations, a balance being struck between the positive suggestion made by both partners. Eventually it was agreed that they could support each other regarding the following:

- that Bobby be allowed to take the bike to school on Wednesdays only
- that small expenditures on the bike would be covered by Bobby, but any large expenditures would be discussed by the parents and subsidised by them
- that they would tell Bobby about their decisions together and support each other if Bobby complained.

This agreement emerged slowly from the discussion, with the therapist gently but firmly encouraging them to continue to see if they could come to some agreement.

It may take a little longer for agreement to be reached where step-relationships are concerned, but the focus can still be to seek a mutual agreement which each can support. The natural parent may wish to take more responsibility and hope to be supported by her/his partner.

Open discussion is essential until each can feel ready to support the other in this joint task. The woman's need to attend to her own and others' feelings, and her desire to be protective of her children (2 F), can often collide with the man's ability to solve problems (1 M), and the importance he may place on autonomy and independence (2 M), making a joint decision difficult to achieve. The therapist may feel that speaking about their different gender approaches will help the couple understand that each is trying to be helpful rather than deliberately obstructive.

iv. Keeping arguments out of earshot of the children and not involving the children in the arguments

All parents disagree occasionally about their children's upbringing, causing heated and painful discussions. What is not helpful is for the children to be asked to take sides with either parent or to be too involved in the parental disagreements. Where step-parents are involved there is often an inbuilt bias against the step-parent, which makes it yet more important that children should not be encouraged to enter into parental squabbles. It is best if disagreements are kept away from children. This may mean choosing discussion times more carefully, taking the dog for a walk while discussing disagreements or, where space is confined, making sure that the children understand that this is 'adult business'.

Where the children are aware that the parents or parent figures have disagreed, it becomes more important that parents support each other openly when a final agreement is reached. Talking to the children together, having a united front, giving each other support in front of the children can pay rapid dividends. The children can no longer use their skills in separating the parents or step-parents, and finding the soft spot in each. For the parents, too, there is a stronger sense of being appreciated so that the couple bond is strengthened. Often during the parenting phase the mother and father get separated by concerns about the children and the couple relationship is starved of nourishment.

> Supporting each other in the difficult task of parenting helps to nurture the couple relationship.

Where the woman is the natural parent and the man is in a step-parent relationship to one or more children it may seem natural to the woman for her to consult with her own children and to share her concerns with them. She is their mother and their emotional state and general well-being are important to her (1 F, 2F). In general, it is better if she can discuss her concerns with her partner or a non-biased observer so that the children are not being asked to take sides. The same is true of the man, if he is the natural parent, though his tendency may be not to consult.

v. Reviewing and moving forward

Tasks which the parents have agreed to try at home can be reviewed in the following session. If they have been achieved, the couple can be asked to discuss what worked and how that was for them. If the task was only partly achieved, the couple can be encouraged to modify the task and try again. It is useful to find out what got in the way and how to change that. This may be a point at which the couple can acknowledge gender differences in their approaches. As the parents gain in confidence by achieving small tasks in which they support each other they can move on to more complex tasks.

Reviewing in detail is also important where one parent is in a step-parent relationship with a child. Gender differences and differences in the way each parent views his or her responsibility toward the child/ren can be teased out for discussion. It may take time, and gentle encouragement is necessary. Adjustments can be made as the couple become clearer about each partner's fears and hopes. The main aim is to enable the couple to be supportive of each other, while paying attention to the different relationships involved.

The couple relationship may be enhanced if they can do something together, without the children, which they would both enjoy. If they tend to enjoy different activities, it is possible to alternate between an activity that she would enjoy and one that he would enjoy. In these ways the couple relationship can be strengthened.

3.7.3. Choosing a recent small issue

- Work with a small issue chosen by the couple in which there is conflict about the way they jointly manage their children. The therapist can be aware of the woman's potential for wishing to focus on feelings while the man may focus on problem-solving and each feel frustrated with the other (1 F, 1 M).
- Perhaps explain that it is good to practise with a small question before moving on to the bigger more explosive issues.

- Common disagreements are bedtime, how much television, how much pocket money, late nights out, whether the parents know where the children are going and with whom.
- Work together to make the chosen issue specific and manageable before the couple are seen again, e.g. bedtime can become bedtime for one child on a Friday; television can become a disagreement about a specific programme; pocket money could be discussed in relation to one child.
- Having identified a small issue, move towards a negotiated position.
- Because of gender differences, ensure that both partners get a chance to voice their opinions and fears.
- Watch out for communication tangles such as blaming, sting in the tail, etc. (see 2.6).
- A balance between the varying perceptions can form the basis for agreement.

Gender and socialisation merge to make this a complex task. Men often feel more confident about bringing up boys, and women may feel that they know how to bring up girls. In my experience the man often defers to the woman's 'greater knowledge or experience of child-rearing' even though he does not agree with her methodology, abdicating his responsibility and not using his skills or experience. The woman may also feel that this is her area of expertise and be reluctant to listen to the man's suggestions.

Where both parents are encouraged to use their resources to pull together and consider both the emotional (1 F) and problem-solving approach (1 M), a compromise which they can both support can often be reached as a basis and model for future negotiations. In these ways the strengths of the woman and man are recognised and used for the benefit of their children.

Where intimacy needs are not being met in other areas such as the physical sexual relationship or poor communication, the focus can be moved away from the children, with the couple's agreement, on to their relationship.

> Concerns about the children can be a smokescreen for problems within the couple relationship.

The intimacy needs of both partners can then be attended to.

3.8. The critical period for less traditional couples of dealing with 'blended' family gatherings

(See also 3.3.3)

> Adjustment to the post-divorced reformed or binuclear family implies an acceptance by each formerly married partner that each of them need to develop a new social network in which their children may also become involved. (Robinson, 1993)

Robinson describes the stages of realignment and restabilisation that occur following divorce or separation and the work that has to be done by the new couple. Family gatherings such as birthdays, christenings and funerals or annual events such as Christmas provide a forum for this realignment and restabilisation of the new couple. High levels of anxiety and tension accompany these events as each member is pulled by previous alliances. Tension can be eased if the new couple can pull together and stabilise their relationship within the wider family. Gender plays its part, making it initially more difficult for the new couple to establish themselves as a couple and begin the process of realignment within the wider family.

3.8.1. Example 3g, Belinda and Ben

The following is an example where a daughter of a less traditional couple puts pressure on her mother to give her a traditional wedding, with her divorced natural parents sitting together at the top table and an outward appearance of a traditional family. The struggle which ensued to ensure that the wedding was a safe and happy occasion for all concerned, at the same time respecting the present partnership, is described.

Central gender concerns which complicated the decision-making process for Belinda were firstly, that she did not want to hurt her daughter's feelings (2 F), and secondly that her partner encouraged her to decide on her own (2 M), making her feel isolated and uncared for. This briefly affected their physical sexual relationship (3 F, 3 M) and they began to have heated arguments about the 'traditional wedding' which would have made Ben a very peripheral player (4 F, 4 M). However, with support and good communication a creative compromise was reached.

Belinda (44) and Ben (46) had lived together for four years. Both felt this relationship to be firm and strong and made up for much unhappiness each had experienced in the past.

Belinda had three grown-up children of 26, 24 and 22, none of whom lived at home. Philip, the father of the three children, had lived with Belinda for five years until the youngest was born, at which time disagreements between the parents ended in a difficult divorce. He kept in touch with his children sporadically. Now that Philip is remarried and the children grown up, a less distant relationship has developed.

Two years after her divorce Belinda developed a relationship with Peter, who became the key father figure to all three of the children until five years ago, when Belinda ended the relationship. He is also in touch with the three children, with whom he has a good relationship.

Ben has two grown-up boys who had been brought up by their mother following his divorce six years ago. He keeps in touch with their mother to discuss finances and matters to do with the boys.

Miranda (24), Belinda's middle daughter, was getting married and wanted a traditional marriage. She wanted her mother to sit together with her natural father, Philip, at the top table.

Belinda was deeply upset and agitated at this request but did not want to upset or hurt her daughter or the family into which her daughter was marrying (2 F). She did communicate this to her partner Ben, who felt that he should not interfere and left her to think this through on her own (2 M). She felt isolated and upset (1 F) and, after some encouragement from her therapist, was able to tell her partner and to discuss with him her needs (4 F).

Belinda identified for herself that she needed Ben's support and wanted him to be side-by-side with her during the wedding celebrations. She was able to ask him to do this (4 F). Ben felt this was a good solution to the problem for both Belinda and Miranda (1 M). It also established his position within the extended family as Belinda's partner (2 M).

The crunch issue became that of persuading Miranda that this was acceptable; a difficult task as she had set her heart on having her natural father and mother at a traditional top table and Ben sitting at some distance from her mother.

Belinda and Ben pulled together to persuade Miranda that a top table was not a possibility but that four circular tables could be used, with each of her 'parent figures' at a different table and the newly-weds, Miranda and Paul, having their own special table. In this way, all members of the 'blended family' could be present with the current relationships being openly acknowledged.

The celebration became a very special occasion on which all key relationships were acknowledged and enjoyed.

3.8.2. Thinking about Belinda and Ben

A central gender issue for Belinda was her wish not to hurt her daughter (2 F), but she was able to withstand the pressure from her daughter once her partner Ben gave her support rather than allowing her independence to sort it out on her own, which was how he managed his difficulties (2 M). For a brief time, while they were trying to work this out, their relationship was under immense pressure and their physical sexual relationship diminished (3 F, 3 M). They were able to work this out together because they were prepared to let each other know what they wanted and to respond to each other's needs (4 F, 4 M).

Perhaps they had learned through bitter past experiences that there was a need to respect each other, to listen to their separate needs and to respond to them. The discussions were heated and emotional, but eventually a solution was presented to Miranda in which they successfully supported each other.

3.8.3. How to help

Where gender issues are clearly getting in the way these can be discussed openly and the invisible intimacy screen used as a checklist to identify areas of discord.

- Discuss together the idea that the woman may need emotional support while the man may give practical support (1 F, 1 M).
- Discuss how they can be more attentive to the other's needs.
- The man's need to be autonomous may collide with the woman's need to be attentive to who gets hurt at these times (2 F, 2 M). This can be openly acknowledged.
- Where the couple are in distress it may be appropriate to find out if their physical sexual relationship is affected, as stress within the

relationship may cause stress within the sexual relationship (3 F, 3 M).

- Help the couple to give a clear message to the extended family that, although there are many interacting relationships, the couple cannot be separated. By giving each other support they define themselves clearly as a couple to others, particularly their children, and enhance their own intimacy.
- Good communication is essential (4 F, 4 M).
- Where couples do not support each other openly in these situations, unstated resentments and hidden alliances can resurface. Anger and hostility can then boil over into verbal or physical violence (5 F, 5 M).
- The cycle of disillusionment with heterosexual relationships can so easily re-emerge at these times.
- The couple can be helped to support each other instead of being separated by past allegiances and gender differences.

> Since there are few guidelines to go by, what the couple work out which they can both genuinely support is likely to be a 'good enough' solution.

Where a couple are in the process of realignment and restabilisation, a complex interweaving of past experience and gender dilemmas can turn family gatherings into heart-sink occasions unless the new couple work hard to support each other to overcome these difficulties.

3.9. The critical period for less traditional couples of dealing with financial dilemmas

(See also 3.3.2; 3.3.3)

Arguments over finances occur within all families. However, financial difficulties may be more severe for many less traditional families.

> Divorce entails a variety of economic challenges, as well as social and psychological changes. The most notable is the lowered standard of living, particularly for divorced women and their custodial children (Emery, 1994).

Lamanna and Reidman (1997) highlight the financial strain upon remarriages.

> Frequently, money problems arise because of obligations left over from first marriages. Remarried husbands may end up financially responsible for children from their first marriages and for their stepchildren.... Even though

> disproportionately more second wives are employed outside their homes than are first wives, remarried husbands report feeling caught between the often impossible demands of their former family and their present one. Some second wives also feel resentful about the portion of the husband's income that goes to this first wife to help support his children from that marriage. Or a second wife may feel guilty about the burden of support her own children place on their stepfather.

Many other couples choose not to marry. Financial and legal arrangements vary between couples. However, a general impression is gained that disagreements and discord about finances add a layer of distress to relationships where one or both partners have been divorced (Ganong and Coleman, 1994; Gibson, 1994; Harway, 1996; Chiriboga et al., 1991).

3.9.1. Example 3h, Zoey and Zack

The following is an example of one remarried couple where financial disagreements were not discussed but led to major problems within the relationship. The fact that Zack already had a child by his previous wife and that Zoey was unable to have children added extra strain to the marriage.

Zoey (38) and Zack (40) had been married for three years. Zack's previous marriage to Betty lasted two years during the pregnancy and birth of his daughter Katrina (now 14). Zack was extremely fond of his daughter and kept in close touch with her. She had lived with him for three years from 5 to 8 years, after which she returned to live with her mother.

Betty, now a single mother, was in a relationship with Tim, who lived nearby.

Zack and Zoey sought help for their relationship as Zoey was extremely jealous of Zack's attention to his previous wife Betty. Zoey said she was not envious of his attention to his daughter Katrina and encouraged him to keep in touch with her. Katrina came for occasional weekends with Zoey and Zack.

Zack spent many hours reassuring Zoey that he was not having a relationship with Betty, and that he contacted her only whenever there were financial problems affecting Katrina. His reassurances did not help. Their relationship deteriorated and, when they sought help, they were not having a sexual relationship. Zoey felt that this confirmed her worst fears that Zack was having a relationship with his ex-wife Betty.

During therapy it emerged that Zack was unable to keep up his full payments to Betty and that Betty would ring him constantly to complain. Zack had not told Zoey, feeling that he should solve this problem on his own (1 M, 2 M). He also felt very undermined in his ability to be a good provider and make enough money for his daughter. This may have affected his self-respect, undermining his confidence in his own sexuality and diminishing his desire for sex (3 M). Instead of communicating any of this to Zoey, he had withdrawn into himself (4 M). His reluctance to share any of this with Zoey made her feel increasingly isolated within the relationship as she was aware that Zack was unhappy. The fact that he did not share his feelings with her made her yet more suspicious (1 F).

The couple were helped to talk more openly during therapy, which seemed to be helping (4 F, 4 M). A crisis arose, however, when Zack had an unexpected financial bonus from work, and rushed to Betty's to give her most of the money. Zack neither consulted Zoey nor explained to her what he had done. Zoey learned from Katrina that Zack had sent her extra money. Zoey felt this was final evidence that Zack's real feelings were for Betty and not for her.

3.9.2. Thinking about Zoey and Zack

When unravelling this interaction, several gender issues emerge to complicate an already difficult situation. Zack wanted to provide for his daughter and felt this to be *his* problem, which he should solve on his own (1 M, 2 M). He was deeply unhappy about the constant criticism from Betty, which he had not shared with Zoey (4 M). He did not feel Zoey understood this and felt that she was jealous that he had a daughter whilst Zoey was unable to conceive and bear children. He did not feel that there was any solution to this problem and therefore did not talk with Zoey about it (1 M, 4 M).

All of these ways in which Zack responded made Zoey feel he did not care for her and did not understand her. She needed him to share feelings with her (1 F), to accept that she wanted him to have a good relationship with his daughter (2 F), to be able to talk with her about her infertility rather than withdraw from the topic (4 F). Additionally, she felt that if he could not talk with her about finances, this must mean that he put Betty's need ahead of hers since he talked with Betty about finances.

He went to see Betty and kept secret from Zoey the fact that he had a bonus from work. This meant to Zoey that he was sharing problems with Betty and therefore being closer to Betty (1 F).

When they were able to talk with each other and to listen to the meaning each gave to these interactions each was able to accept the other's perspective.

3.9.3. Some guidelines for future interactions for couples who face dilemmas because of financial responsibilities from previous relationships

- Try not to make assumptions about each other. Instead set aside time to talk together and find out how each partner would like to approach each situation.
- Men may approach financial issues as problems to be solved and be less aware of the emotional implications for partners. This may be talked about (1 F, 1 M).
- Women may attach greater emotional weight to behaviour in the same way that Zoey felt Zack must be attracted to Betty because he 'secretly' gave her money. The couple can be helped to discuss whether this fits for them (4 F, 4 M).
- The woman may feel very conflicted about attention to other children, particularly if she does not have any.
- This can be openly addressed, which is what the woman may want and the man may be reluctant to discuss (2 F)(see 6.3.4).
- Help the couple review together the aspects of their relationship, about which they have a different perspective, and see whether they can stop blaming and criticising each other for this (4 F, 4 M).
- Help the couple tell each other how they would like similar situations managed in the future.
- Find time together, away from the children, television, telephone, family, friends, etc., to talk together without being pressurised.
- Find time to be together just for fun without talking about financial or other problems. Walking together, going to the cinema, free concerts, open-air plays, feeding the ducks, can be enjoyed without being expensive.
- Doing something together, which was enjoyed before financial problems loomed, can help rekindle some sparkle within a relationship and help the couple draw together.

3.10. The critical period of the ageing process

(See Examples 3i, Harry and Helen; 4c Frank and Fiona; see also 6.7, 6.11) As couples move towards old age there are additional hurdles which require adjustments. The menopause is a natural end to the woman's reproductive period. For both partners retirement, and its accompanying life style changes, often occurs as their children are preoccupied with home-building and their parents are facing illness or death. A layering of life events can make this a stressful or lonely time.

A critical period for the older couple often occurs when they have successfully negotiated the bearing and raising of children. As the children leave home, both parents begin the period of adjustment to this, to their own ageing, the ageing and dependency of parents, and for the woman to her menopause, and for the woman and man the closing of their working lives.

For some women the menopause brings a welcome release from the constraints, or the fear, of becoming pregnant. As a result, she may undergo a renewal of interest in an active or adventurous sexual relationship. Her partner, on the other hand, may be less interested and more tired than he was as a younger man. He may now be more prone to anxiety about his own sexual prowess, and his sexual desires and sexual responses may be slowing down. His ability to get and maintain an erection may become less certain (3 M).

If the woman is finding that, although her sexual desire has increased, she is less well lubricated than when younger, she can use some easily available lubricant. For the man, however, there is no such simple solution to his more flaccid penis (although medical technology increasingly attends to this problem).

Where the woman is encouraging and non-critical her added sexual interest (4 F), if accompanied by a willingness to initiate sexual touching and experimentation (3 F), may reawaken his sexual desires and responses. Although neither may experience the intense passions of a more youthful sexual life, they are likely to develop a satisfying depth of mutual sexual pleasure.

Part of this mutuality may be that the man has been able to reveal himself as vulnerable sexually and been supported (1 F). This may mirror the woman's longing to feel a sense of shared emotion (see 2.3.1). The satisfying sexual intimacy of the older couple may contain both a depth of emotional sharing, which is often what the woman has been searching for as part of her intimacy needs (1 F), and of physical intimacy, which has been part of the male search for a trusting and supportive sexual experience (3 M) (Crowe and Ridley, 1990; Ridley, 1993).

3.10.1. Example 3i, Harry and Helen

Harry (63) and Helen (55), married for 30 years, had no children. Both were deeply disappointed and blamed each other, although they had rarely shared these feelings openly. Their physical relationship disappeared over the years and by the time they sought therapy they rarely gave each other any physical comfort.

Harry was an independent consultant who had worked hard over the years but was now looking forward to retirement and having time to be with Helen.

Helen, having recently shaken herself out of lethargy and begun a degree in French, was often out in the evenings at French conversation groups and expected to spend time in France speaking the language. She felt that her professional life was 'just beginning'.

They sought therapy since both were deeply unhappy, fearing that their relationship was under threat.

3.10.2. How to help

In the first session the couple were asked to decentre (see 2.2.4.2) and talk to each other about what was going wrong in their relationship and what they would like to change. Using the intimacy screen as a checklist to observe the couple, it did not take long to notice that Helen wanted Harry to listen to her feelings and that his approach was to problem-solve (1 F, 1 M), that Helen was sociable and Harry more independent (2 F, 2 M) and that their sexual life did not satisfy either of them (3 F, 3 M). Within their communication, Helen was speedy and verbal and Harry was slow and clumsy with words (4 F, 4 M). In relation to hostility, neither was openly hostile but both used words and phrases which hurt because of painful past associations (5 F, 5 M).

Since the motivation to improve their relationship was high, they were:

i. asked to take each other seriously
ii. given the task of finding times when they could be together
iii asked to use a talking timetable to discuss their difficulties.

3.10.3. Introduce gender differences

(See also 2.2.4.2, vi; 2.2.4.4; 2.3.2.4; 2.3.2.5; 2.4.2.3)
After a few sessions nothing was changing and they were becoming increasingly frustrated with each other and the therapist.

It seemed necessary to introduce the concept of gender differences and see, whether by understanding these, they could be helped to be more tolerant of each other.

- When introducing the concept of gender differences, time should be allowed for discussion and any reference to key gender differences can be introduced near the beginning of a session.
- The reactions of each partner can be noted carefully and time allowed for each partner to respond. Sometimes each partner believes that the other is deliberately being irritating, or is deliberately avoiding doing what the other wants or is trying to dominate or control the relationship by their behaviour.
- These issues should be taken into consideration and may contribute to a negative interaction.
- It may help to point out how gender differences are interfering with their relationship and ask both partners to comment.
- With Helen and Harry, their gender responses were most obvious regarding their disappointment that there were no children. Helen needed to speak about feelings and Harry tried to find ways of solving the problem of intense feelings.

The following is an example of an interaction in session.

Harry. 'Helen is actually very upset we were never able to have any children but I don't know what to do about it.'

Helen. 'You say I am upset, but you never want to listen to what I feel. So how can you tell me I am upset?'

Harry, turning to the therapist. 'You see what I mean, I try to find ways to help but everything I suggest gets turned down. I suggested last Thursday that we go out together to have a meal, I thought it would cheer Helen up, but she preferred her French conversation classes. I did try.'

Therapist. 'I wonder if you have ever thought that you are each being the stereotypical female and male in how you are responding to each other.'

They each turned to the therapist in surprise. 'What do you mean?'

Therapist. 'My impression is that you are both sad that you did not have any children, but you each express your sadness in different ways. Helen wants to talk about it, and Harry wants to do something to make it better for you both.'

Helen. 'I don't think that Harry is sad, but he is always trying to cheer me up.'

Therapist. 'Why not try asking Harry whether he is sad?'

Helen, aggressively. 'Well, are you sad?'

Harry. 'Yes, of course I'm sad, but I'm more concerned that I cannot help you, I do keep trying to find ways to cheer you up.'

Helen. 'Why don't you just listen to me?'

Therapist. 'Do you see that you have just done it again? Helen, as a woman, wants Harry "to listen". Harry, as a man, feels just listening won't solve the problem and tries to find something which does. Let's see what happens if Harry just listens to Helen now. Harry, what I would like you to do is to ask Helen what she now feels about the fact that you do not have children. I know it is a tender subject for you both, but see if you can help Helen to talk a little about it. Then, in reply, instead of trying to solve the problem, see if you can say in your own words what you have heard Helen say.'

Harry needed some coaching but soon began to relax and listen carefully to Helen and restate what she had said in his own words. The therapist then asked them to tell each other about the experience.

Helen. 'You have never ever done that before, just sat and let me talk to you, it was good.'

Harry. 'I felt a bit inadequate because I could not see that it would help you.'

Then turning to the therapist, he asked. 'Are you telling me that will help Helen?'

Therapist. 'Ask Helen.'

Harry. 'Well, is that what you want from me, does it help?'

Helen. 'You should know that it would help me, I have told you often enough.'

The therapist restated that many women and men have the same difficulty when faced with an emotionally arousing situation; the woman hopes to share her feelings and the man may understand the feelings but tries to find a way to make it better, or solve the problem.

- The couple were sent home to continue talking and listening three times a week for 20 minutes; Helen to talk, and Harry to be supportive, listen carefully but make no suggestions as to what Helen could do.
- Helen was asked to tell Harry at the end of these sessions how important they were for her.
- After a few weeks they were asked to share the time and see whether they could each talk about their feelings so that Harry would be given some time to talk and share his feelings with Helen. Once Harry became more confident that he was being helpful to Helen, he was more prepared to speak about his own feelings with her. He began to accept that this solved the problem by listening to her feelings and also speaking about his own.
- The other elements of the intimacy screen can be used in a similar way, by encouraging the couple to notice their differences and to see whether they can accept them, take them seriously and, where possible, respond to the other's needs.

Another aspect of ageing for many couples is the empty nest. Where couples have had children, both partners may have been preoccupied with bringing up the children and making enough money to pay the rent or mortgage and the costs of daily living. The couple relationship is often sacrificed or neglected in order to attend to the practicalities of family life.

When the children leave home each may feel they do not know their partner and wonder what old age will be like for them.

3.10.4. Other options

- For these couples, therapy often involves helping the couple find out about each other again, what each other likes, and to bring some excitement back into a relationship which may have become stale.

- This should include the sexual relationship. There are some useful books and videos which can be used for the older couple.
- A key to helping the older couple face grand old age together may be to help them talk about their hopes and fears.
- Couples who have been together for many years have often developed a ritualised way of communicating. If this has occurred, it may be helpful to set a talking timetable when the couple are asked 'not to go over old ground'. The aim is to find out about each other's interests. Individuals often pick up new interests or attitudes and rarely communicate these to partners. Finding out can renew an interest in each other.
- Choosing new activities which couples can do together, and separately, can bring renewed interest in life and in each other. Walking, swimming, dancing, taking evening classes, learning a new skill together which is of interest, to one or both partners, can help the couple rebuild.
- Paying attention to the invisible intimacy screen can help to indicate areas that are ignored and where the couple can be given help to reconnect and build a relationship for their old age.

Since each gender may approach each stage on the life cycle from a different perspective, there is ample room for misunderstandings and tensions to develop. Where couples have been together for many years, a 'crossover' of needs and interests can occur. For example, as described above, the man who was sexually very active may begin to lose interest in sex while his partner may become more enthusiastic (3 F, 3 M).

The man who feels his life's work is coming to a close and hopes to spend more time at home, may find his home-loving wife, having brought up the children, is beginning to want to get out and about (2 F, 2 M).

In these ways, the life cycle of the relationship constantly challenges both partners to stay alert to the stage and needs of the other. It is not possible to assume, 'finally, I know you'.

As couples age, some deepen their gender differences and find they have little in common and others learn from life experiences and explore attributes of the opposite gender, when a merging of female/male attributes may occur.

It is perhaps within sexuality that most changes are occurring within Western society. Women who are healthy can more easily continue an active sexual life beyond the age where men may find maintaining an erection more complicated. The advent of drugs such as Viagra may raise the hopes of many men that sexual activity can continue. Older women may be exploring the independence and separateness from both their children and their spouses as they get older, while some men are finding a renewal of interest in a relationship with a partner of a different age.

3.11. Using the intimacy screen with the couple

The intimacy screen can be used with the client in several ways:

- The concept of the invisible intimacy screen between the man and woman can be discussed with the couple and they can be encouraged to talk together, focusing upon whether they feel the concept applies to them and in what way.
- They can be asked to discuss together whether they find the idea of an invisible intimacy screen useful.
- The screen can be photocopied and each partner can be asked to rate where they would place themselves and their partner within each element on the screen.
- This can be followed by discussion between the couple as to whether change is possible.
- Should they think that change is possible it would be important to know in which specific element.
- Each partner can be asked to indicate which element on the screen is important to her/him.
- The therapist may wish to let the couple know how s/he perceives or understands their different approaches and needs.
- Where partners' responses tend to be similar to the opposite gender, the screen can be used to examine this.

Using the invisible intimacy screen involves the couple in finding out about their own gender needs and responses. Many couples will not fit the screen as outlined, and for others some elements may be more significant than others. Using the screen as a checklist with the couple may help them explore their differences in a less adversarial way and discover that they are not alone in the complex search for intimacy.

3.12. Gender responses in critical periods

It has been argued that women and men often respond from a gender base during critical periods and as a result both partners may feel out of harmony and remote from the other, their own needs and responses being uppermost. It is a simple step to feeling isolated and lonely within the relationship.

Intimacy can seem non-existent at a time when it may be most needed.

Other couples find a level of acceptance which enables respect and intimacy. Such couples tease each other about their contrasting styles. 'My wife is so soft she cannot pass by a kitten in the street without wanting to take it home', might be responded to by 'Yes, well, if I didn't watch out you would have sold the kitten for dog food', indicating through teasing an awareness of the woman's more emotional approach and the man's more problem-solving focus.

When Jenny wears an attractive dress John may make sexual overtures at an inappropriate time, and Jenny teases, 'You can't get enough of it can you?' John responds, 'You deliberately turn me on, then turn me down.' Each partner enjoys their contrasting arousal styles.

> Couples who are open to gender differences begin to learn new skills from their partner and in these ways grow more like their partner. Gender differences then become irrelevant, merge, support or complement each other.

In these ways gender differences become resources.

4 Chapter

Life Events and Intimacy

4.1. Introduction

The life cycle of a couple may be interrupted by unexpected life events such as loss of job, redundancy, accident or illness. Death, the birth of a handicapped child, infertility issues, change of home or change of circumstance are life events which have an impact on the couple relationship. Chapter 4 examines some life events where gender issues are in evidence. These are gender-specific illnesses, depression, rape, sexual abuse and marital violence.

Illnesses, such as female cancer of the womb or breast, or male cancer of the prostate gland, are gender specific because of the different physical makeup of the male and female. Other illnesses tend to occur more frequently in one gender although it is not clear why. Depression affects women more than men at a ratio of 2:1 (Beach et al., 1990), a figure questioned by Milligan and Clare (1994).

The cycle of male violence against the female partner is also discussed since, although women can be violent, there is 'general agreement that the physical damage inflicted by men is greater than that inflicted by women' (O'Leary et al., 1989) (see 6.10).

The invisible intimacy screen is used as a guide to thinking about the impact of these events on the couple to structure any intervention, ensuring that all five areas have been considered and, if appropriate, attended to. When used, the interventions should be sensitively modified for each couple.

What is important is that each of the elements of the intimacy screen be considered. If an element is being ignored this may be a clue to difficulties in that area. Alternatively, where only one element is focused upon, e.g. sexuality, it may be helpful to think through what is happening to the other elements of intimacy.

Finally, if the couple relationship is severely affected by the lack of adequate understanding and communication, it may be necessary to refer the couple for more specialist help from a relationship and sexual therapist. Referrals are best made before couple interactions have hardened into cynicism and resentment that s/he will 'never understand me'. Too many couples and professionals wait too long before seeking more skilled help.

4.2. Female illness and intimacy

The reproductive process begins as a joint venture between the female and male but the baby is carried and nurtured by the woman. The female body is very involved in the reproductive process. She has a complicated and interconnecting physical makeup, ovaries in which the egg develops, fallopian tubes which carry the sperm towards the ripening egg, a uterus or womb which nurtures the fertilised egg and sits above the cervix, or entry to the womb from the vaginal canal. She carries a vagina topped by the clitoris and surrounded by the labia minora and labia majora through which the penis penetrates to deposit sperm into the vaginal canal. If conception occurs, the uterus is then occupied with the nurturing of the foetus. During this time her breasts begin to change and prepare for the birth and suckling of the baby (see 6.3.5).

Because of her physical makeup she is susceptible to infection or cancer in all parts of her reproductive organs. Breast cancer, cancer of the vulva, cervix and uterus are common (Weijmar Schultz et al., 1995). The woman may therefore have to face surgery of any or all of these organs. Where the illness is life threatening, she and her partner then face the anxiety and fear that this arouses and the possibility that the illness is terminal and the loss through death of a partner (see 4.3.3).

Sexually transmitted diseases or urinary infections affect the female in different ways simply because of her physical makeup. Pregnancy and childbirth also carry risk for the woman and for the baby which are gender related (Pradhan et al., 1995). The menstrual cycle and the menopause have risks and difficulties for the female which the man does not experience (see Chapter 6).

No attempt is made to give examples of all of these life events. Case material is described which highlights couple interactions that have become distressed because of gender differences. In choosing these examples there is no suggestion that all couples will respond in these specific ways. However, therapists are encouraged to include gender difference within their checklist of complicating factors when working with couples in distress.

The first example (4a, Stephen and Sally) describes female/male interactions following the woman's successful mastectomy; similar responses may also follow other gender-specific illnesses. The common thread may be that it is difficult for the female or male to understand the other's experience since, for example, a man cannot experience a hysterectomy nor can a woman experience erectile dysfunction. Some work is required to find out and respect the other's needs and responses at such times.

4.2.1. Example 4a, Stephen and Sally

Stephen (45) and Sally (44) were referred by their general practitioner because of Sally's depression following a successful mastectomy and rebuilding of her left breast. They have two children (19 and 20), both working and living near the parents.

Sally's operation occurred one year previously. Stephen and Sally describe their relationship before the mastectomy as good. In particular, they always had a good and active sex life. On referral Stephen is upset that Sally is not only depressed but has gone off sex, though he constantly tries to arouse her interest.

4.2.2. How to help using the intimacy screen

i. General guidelines

(See 2.2.4.2)

ii. Decentre in order to observe the couple interaction

(See 2.2.4.2, iii)

In session it is helpful to encourage the couple to face each other and to talk together about the difficulties they face.

iii. Learn about the couple by asking them to talk together about their current difficulties

Observing Sally and Stephen's interaction, it did not take long to see that each partner used gender-specific skills to communicate, but at each stage made things worse. This frightened them as they had been very close.

> The intimacy screen obscured the needs of the other, neither being able to respond as their partner wanted.

Observing and listening to the couple discussing their present difficulties, Sally felt misunderstood, and disliked Stephen's stream of practical suggestions. She wanted him to understand how she felt (1 F). She did not feel at all intact; having had a breast removed, she felt violated and depleted as a woman and as a human being, and as such felt that all of her relationships would now alter, as others would no longer see her as a complete woman (2 F).

Stephen used many of his male skills to try to win Sally over and cheer her up. He used his problem-solving skills (1 M) to make practical suggestions each time Sally expressed feelings. He was surprised and puzzled that Sally was not overjoyed to be 'well again' and had been given back her autonomy (2 M). He became increasingly frustrated by being unable to cheer her up and became less and less verbally responsive to her (4 M). He was not physically aggressive (5 M) but was exasperated by her low mood.

iv. reviewing their sexual relationship

(See 2.5, 2.5.3, 6.5, 6.9)
An understanding of the couple relationship often includes understanding the impact of a mastectomy on their sexual relationship. This is a delicate task as each may feel embarrassed and sensitive. It may help to ask 'What has changed?'

Sally had not told Stephen previously but acknowledged during therapy that she was offended at his insensitivity in pressurising for sex when she was not feeling sensual. She wanted his understanding of her painful feelings and loss of confidence in herself as a woman (4 F). Stephen found this difficult, he responded slowly and usually suggested a new solution (1 M). After the surgery Sally did not want to be touched sexually although she longed to be held in a non-sensual way (3 F). The fact that Stephen touched her breasts made her feel worse as her breast did not feel good nor did she feel sensual. Stephen wanted to show her that she was still a very sensual and sexually attractive person by persuading her to have sexual intercourse with him (3 M).

Additionally, although Sally was tearful and depressed, she would alternate between bouts of sadness and angry verbal outbursts at Stephen, the hospital and the doctors who had 'done this thing to her' (5 F).

v. Ways to help each partner respect the gender needs of the other

In emotionally arousing situations (1 F, 1 M)
(See 2.3.1, 2.3.2, 6.12)

With the couple facing each other in a decentred position:

- suggest that Stephen listens and takes seriously Sally's distress at the loss of her breast
- suggest to Sally that she explain to Stephen what the surgery has meant to her
- encourage Stephen to ask for more detail, or to ask for clarification of anything he did not understand; help him to focus on feelings;
- encourage Sally to find out from Stephen if he has understood, and if not to go over it again
- they might be asked to read a book together about mastectomy and then discuss it in your presence at the next session.

Where there are social pressures (2 F, 2 M)
(See 2.4)

- ask Stephen to find out from Sally whether she thinks her relationships will be affected by the mastectomy
- ask Sally to find out from Stephen whether he can understand this.

Within a physical sexual relationship (3 F, 3 M)
(See 2.5, 6.5, 6.5)

- continue helping the couple to talk to each other, but move on to sexuality
- suggest to Sally that she finds out from Stephen what it means for him to have sexual intercourse with her after such an operation. See if he can explain that sex is a way of showing her that she is still attractive to him
- use massage exercises or Masters and Johnson's (1970) non-genital sensual exercises to help them explore giving and receiving touch and tenderness without penetrative sex, which will come later
- as work together progresses and it becomes possible to discuss sexuality in more detail, find out whether Sally would be prepared to stimulate Stephen to orgasm manually to show that she cares for him and understands the pressure he is under.

Within communication (4 F, 4 M)
(See 2.6, 6.4)

- Stephen can now use his slower verbal response to become more of a listener; he can be encouraged to seek more details as to how Sally

feels, what aspects of the surgery and treatment process have affected her most deeply
- he can be asked to state in his own words what he understood Sally to have said
- Sally can be encouraged to ask Stephen what it is like for him to hear about the detail of her surgery and how it has affected her
- Stephen may be encouraged to speak about his feelings of relief that Sally is alive
- their communication pattern may need to slow down, each giving the other time to think carefully about the other's interactions and to reflect upon their own
- time, gentleness and space can be part of the healing process for them both.

Where there are aggressive feelings (5 F, 5 M)
(See 2.7, 6.6, 6.10)

With Sally, any expression of angry or aggressive feelings is complicated by the fact that she may feel angry with the very person, the surgeon, who has also saved her life. But she may also feel violated and vulnerable because of this intervention. Stephen may have more experience at speaking about angry feelings:

- Stephen can then be encouraged to help Sally to express her feelings of being violated and her anger.

The above discussions may help to address the increasing isolation each feels as a result of being misunderstood. The couple might be asked to continue discussions but to widen them to include 'growing older together' and what this means to each of them. Since they are both 40+ they may be at a developmental stage where there is an inevitable reviewing of life achievements; loss and death can then be reframed as issues we must all face. Sally may be able to help Stephen understand this in greater depth as loss of youthfulness is something which he too faces. Sally will need to grieve about the losses she has encountered and in time Stephen will also have to come to terms with his advancing years.

Having given the couple experiences in session of talking together, it may be helpful to suggest that they set aside 20 to 30 minutes several times a week to continue talking together on these topics. These can be timetabled so that both partners know when they will happen. It is best to have short and regular times when the couple can get into a habit of talking about painful issues but with the knowledge that there is a time limit to each occasion.

Gender differences are addressed through helping the couple to respect each other's differences rather than by entering into a dialogue about gender differences.

vi. Acknowledging gender differences

It can be helpful to open up the question of gender differences directly by saying, for example, 'You are a very interesting couple and highlight for me just how different women and men can be. You each approach situations from very different perspectives. The task here is to help you understand and use your differences to enhance your relationship and deepen your intimacy.'

The couple could be helped to understand the invisible intimacy screen or specific elements of the screen, particularly that of female/male responses to emotionally arousing situations such as a mastectomy (see 2.2.4.2, iv; 2.2.4.4; 2.3.2.4; 2.3.2.5; 3.10.3)

4.2.3. Vulvectomy

An interesting piece of research highlights female/male responses following severely disfiguring surgery for cancer of the vulva. Vulvectomy is one of the more radical operations because of invasive cancer of the vulva.

> Invasive cancer of the vulva, nowadays accounting for approximately 8% of all gynaecological cancers, means confrontation with severely disfiguring surgery requiring vulvectomy. This surgery implies the loss of labia majora and minora, removal of the clitoris, mons veneris, surrounding tissues and frequently extensive lymphenode dissection. In advanced disease additional radiation therapy is given. Sexual functioning is usually affected as a result of the disease and treatment. (Van De Weil et al., 1990)

Van De Weil et al. conducted research into women who had experienced vulvectomy and the impact upon their marital relationship and came up with a surprising result. In spite of the fact that the women experienced severe or moderately severe negative changes in relation to experience of sexual arousal and orgasm, they continued to have intercourse with their partner. When compared with a control group of couples where vulvectomy had not occurred there was no significant difference in sexual behaviour.

> In fact, with regard to the main aspects of sexual functioning, i.e. sexual satisfaction, sexual behaviour and sexual motivation hardly any difference between the two groups do occur. Only significant differences are experienced in sexual arousal and orgasm can be noticed.

They conclude:

> Our impression of the interviews is that the meaning of sexuality seems to be located elsewhere. Our impression of the meaning of sexuality and the wish for sexual interaction is mainly determined by the desire to please the partner to get harmony in the relationship.

A fragment from one interview illustrates this:

> Well I really have to force myself to it. I think to myself, come on, you have to do something for someone else now again, I don't feel like it anymore.

This research leaves many questions unanswered, but shows that some couples can overcome radical and disfiguring surgery without professional help. It also indicates that women and men may place different emphasis upon sexual intercourse and the meaning of penetrative sex within a couple relationship. The women, in this research, put their partner's need for penetrative sex ahead of their own lack of sexual arousal and orgasm (see 2.5, 2.5.3).

4.3. Male illness and intimacy

The male reproductive organs are also vulnerable to infection or to cancer. Enlargement or cancer of the prostate gland is increasingly common and, like cancer of the penis or scrotum, can have significant implications for the man and for his relationships (Absoe and Thin, 1996; Champion, 1996).

> There is very little realisation of and research on the damage to sexual health consequent on specific male cancers such as prostatic and testicular cancers, and very little information on the repercussions for sexual health in men. It is well realised that clients seeking advice are predominantly female. In the first two years of operation of the national cancer information service run by the British Association of Cancer United Patients, 80% of enquiries were from women. (Slevin et al., 1988)

However, it is known that anxiety about the future and the impact of the illness upon sexuality, anger, depression, concern about becoming dependent upon others, issues of income and mortgages, the stigma of uncleanliness and worries about passing on infection all begin to affect the individual who is diagnosed with cancer.

Erectile impotence, or the inability to achieve and maintain an erection, often accompanies pelvic surgery for some invasive cancers of the bladder or lower rectal tumours. Following surgery of this nature, erectile problems and ejaculatory difficulties may ensue. It is reported that there is no increased incidence of divorce and that marital difficulties occur only where couples were already in conflict (Schover, 1991; Schover et al., 1987).

The following is an example where erectile difficulties occur in the absence of complications such as cancer. The man had erectile impotence and the woman was concerned to start a family. Erectile difficulties can present couples with major hurdles to overcome, and very powerful female/male issues at particular times in the life cycle.

4.3.1. Example 4b, Catherine and Claude

Catherine (38) and Claude (40) had been married for 12 years with no children. The earlier part of their marriage was stormy, causing them to consider splitting up on two or three occasions. They were referred by the general practitioner because of Claude's erectile failure and Catherine's growing concern about getting pregnant. They both felt their relationship was sufficiently stable to contemplate having a child, and both took this issue seriously.

At the initial session they agreed that Claude's ability to get and maintain an erection had deteriorated; they had enjoyed penetrative sex during the early years of marriage. Claude was able to satisfy Catherine by manual stimulation but was deeply disappointed that he was unable to satisfy her through penetrative sex. He believed that he had a low sex drive but wanted to get Catherine pregnant and therefore wanted penetrative sex. Theirs was a complicated relationship which contained layers of pressure and counter-pressure.

Within their communication pattern (4 F, 4 M) Catherine was the more fluent. Although she would say that she was being supportive of him, and encouraging by cajoling and scolding him, he felt 'put down' by her constant reminders that he was unable to get and maintain an erection sufficient to penetrate her and possibly give her a child. One could say she was verbally aggressive, though she would dispute this (see 6.6).

Sexually, Catherine was satisfied with non-penetrative sex (3 F), except that it did not allow the possibility of conception. She did need Claude to show her affection by touching and holding her. Within their relationship Claude felt pretty inadequate and vulnerable as a man and as a husband (2 M).

4.3.2. How to help using the intimacy screen

- In therapy they were encouraged to move slowly through the stages of non-genital and genital massage, with sexual intercourse forbidden, to see whether a non-pressurising situation would enable Claude to regain an erection. This did not occur, nor did he have morning erections or erections during sleep, though he could occasionally get a slight erection while watching 'blue' movies.
- After tests which suggested there was no organic or physical cause for his erectile difficulties, it was felt that he should encouraged to use papaverine.

> 'An injection into the corpus cavernosum of the penis of either alpha-adrenoceptor blocking agents or smooth muscle relaxants, which, given the correct dose, in the correct place, encourages a firm erection thus enabling the couple to have penetrative sex no more than twice a week at a time chosen by the couple' (Crowe and Qureshi, 1991).

- Following discussion with both partners, it was agreed that Claude would be taught how to inject himself and thus get an erection sufficiently firm to allow penetration. At this stage Catherine was somewhat apprehensive but agreed to experiment with this approach as she felt anything was helpful towards getting pregnant. Claude was more relaxed and confident that he would now be able to penetrate and possibly enable Catherine to conceive a child (3 M).
- As soon as Claude was able to get an erection by using papaverine injections, Catherine decided that she did not want to co-operate with this approach to sexual intercourse. From her perspective, if Claude was only able to get and maintain an erection through artificial means, rather than desiring her and therefore being sufficiently sexually aroused to achieve an erection, she did not feel that she could make love to him in spite of her deep desire to have a baby.

> The solution to the 'problem' for her had to be an emotional one (1 F), whereas for him if the problem could be solved (1 M) by technical means, that was acceptable, even if he had to put himself through the indignity of injecting his penis.

Of course, this is simplifying the relationship. There were strong feelings on both sides about their readiness to be parents, the stability of their relationship, and their ability to be 'good enough' parents. There was also a covert issue about who was dominant within the relationship. However, it seemed that their desire to have children was equally strong and the reason for seeking treatment. The treatment on offer was unacceptable to Catherine, even though it may have helped her with her desire to get pregnant, because it was neither spontaneous nor an emotional response. The treatment was acceptable to Claude as a solution to his erectile problem. He also seemed able to accept with greater equanimity Catherine's decision that they would not have penetrative sex, perhaps because he no longer felt so inadequate, knowing that he could, if necessary, achieve an erection by injection.

Following this decision, the work within session was to help the couple to grieve for the losses involved in giving up the hope that they would have a family. At the end of treatment neither felt they wanted to use other approaches to enable Catherine to get pregnant. They were sad but able to face the future together without children.

4.3.3. How to help with male illnesses and loss

Where a man has treatment for cancer of the penis or scrotum, prostate cancer or invasive cancers of the bladder and lower rectal tumours, much useful work can be done with the couple to ameliorate the individual and relationship repercussions. The different gender responses can be discussed with the couple so that they do not fall into the trap of assuming that s/he is 'like me'. The following suggestions may also help couples when other illness affects the man's sense of self-esteem or his sexuality.

i. Information-gathering and mutual sharing

- It is helpful if the couple can talk together about what is known about the illness, so that both partners are equally aware of issues such as fatigue or nausea following chemotherapy or concern about body image for the ill partner. This is important because the man may need to understand the nature of the problem (1 M) and the woman may want to understand the emotional impact of the illness or the treatment (1 F).
- Both are likely to want to understand its impact upon their social relationships (2 M, 2 F)
- and their sexual life (3 M, 3 F).
- It is helpful if both can attend clinics, or at least share as much information as is available, together.

- Both partners can be encouraged to talk together, but ensure that the woman does not take on too much of a caring role and turn the man into a dependent child, and that he is encouraged to develop his autonomy as much as is possible within the illness. In her wish to be caring she may be over-protective, and the man may try too hard to maintain his independence and autonomy so that his partner feels rejected (2 F, 2 M).
- Issues such as the impact upon the man's ability to continue to work and the couple's financial stability will depend upon the nature of the illness, but these issues will need to be addressed by the couple (4 M, 4 F).
- Both partners may need to find ways to express their anger without hurting the other (5 F, 5 M).
- Each partner may wish to talk about their anger with someone outside of their relationship.

ii. Within the physical sexual relationship (3 F, 3 M)

(See 2.5, 6.5, 6.9)

- The woman may need to be particularly understanding of the man's deep disappointment at any loss of sexual prowess, and be more prepared than Catherine to accept a clinical approach to penetrative sex if sexual aids or penile injections are required for penetrative sex to occur (3 M, 3 F).
- Many couples are able to accept the lack of spontaneity involved in using penile injections to facilitate penetrative sex, and of course there are other fertility treatments which can be sought if fertility becomes problematic.
- Catherine and Claude were prepared to accept that they would not have children and so additional work was required to help them grieve.
- The man can be helped to find an outlet for his aggression (5 M) otherwise he may frighten both himself and his partner.
- The woman can recognise that concern and cajoling can be experienced as hostile or unhelpful (5 F).

iii. Helping couples grieve

This section is placed here to think about the management of losses and grief, including death. Grieving and grief work is universal. It is as important for the separating couple to grieve at the loss of their dreams as it is for the others to grieve at the loss of a job or a limb. It is necessary to grieve for the loss of youthfulness or sexual prowess.

Each couple will face slightly different problems depending upon their life stage and life circumstances. The details of each situation, illness or death will be different, but the principles are similar (Kübler-Ross, 1970; Hinton, 1967; Murray Parkes, 1987).

- Each gender may respond differently; the man may prefer to seek solace more privately, and the woman may wish to share her feelings (1 F, 1 M).
- Over time they can be encouraged to share together their feelings about the loss of self-esteem, self-confidence and some of their dreams and hopes (4 F, 4 M).
- Where a professional carer is working with the couple, help the couple start the process in which both participate. Often one partner speaks and the other is a listener, or one is too probing while the other withdraws. Try to ensure that both partners get a chance to speak about their feelings of loss or anxiety (see 2.2.4.2).
- Be aware of communication styles, and help each to respect the other's style (4 F, 4 M).
- Intervene gently and consistently to point out ways in which they can modify their approach to enable both to participate.
- Cancers of the penis, scrotum or surgeries which affect the man's potency or their treatments bring with them many disappointments, anxieties and a sense of loss which over time can be shared, even if the man may initially prefer to maintain his separateness and autonomy through silence (2 M).
- Cancers of the female reproductive organs, her womb, cervix, breast or ovaries bring with them similar disappointments, anxieties and a sense of loss which may need to be expressed (1 F, 4 F).
- Most illnesses threaten the individual's or couple's sense of security in themselves and their future. This sense of insecurity can be discussed and each helped to support the other (4 F, 4 M).
- Grieving for 'what might have been', or the loss of a future which they had both looked forward to, can be shared.

iv. Setting a timetable for talking

- Because illness, or loss, can be experienced as all-consuming, a timetable for discussion can bring a greater feeling of being in control. Half an hour a day may be sufficient unless there an urgent life-threatening illness which requires immediate attention.

Couples are helped if the time and day can be agreed, taking stress out of an already fraught situation.

- Timetables can help contain gender differences. For example, where the woman seeks constant reassurances from the man and he finds it stressful to talk for long periods, setting regular 30-minute timetables can reassure both partners. She knows that she will get the chance to talk (4 F) and he knows that it is time limited (4 M).
- Where one partner may dominate these talking sessions, each partner can be encouraged to use half of the allocated time, e.g. 10 minutes each. Subjects of loss are not always easy to discuss, and a time limit can help.

v. Planning forward

- As time goes by and the couple have been able to share their joint sense of loss, it is useful to help the couple discuss what the future may hold for them.
- Where there is anxiety about the future, each anxiety can be identified and ways of coping considered. Sharing of concerns can bring a renewal of commitment to each other.
- Couples can be very creative if encouraged to do so, and it is at times of crisis within a couple relationship that the rich resources that are available within the joint female/male spectrum become most valuable.
- At such times there is likely to be a tension between the various elements of intimacy: the need to express feelings and to problem-solve may be at its height (1 F, 1 M), and the social pressures (2 F, 2 M) and the ability to give and receive sensual and sexual pleasure will be deeply affected (3 F, 3 M).
- In such circumstances the temptation to resort to anger or aggression (5 F, 5 M) may also be great so that there is intense pressure upon the couple relationship and an increased need to find ways to communicate across the gender divide (4 F, 4 M).
- For others, where the illness is life threatening the issue of loss and anxiety about the future can be very intense.

vi. Facing the death of one partner

It is not easy for couples to face the immanent death of one partner and there is an understandable tendency to avoid facing such a possibility. Each couple will choose their own particular approach. Experience indicates that many couples find it helpful to talk and plan together how to manage this painful time, and think through some of the practical problems raised by the illness and death of one partner. This is particularly necessary where there are children and dependants. During such times, the ability to respect and respond to the gender needs of the partner is essential; at the same time, paradoxically, each is likely to feel vulnerable, causing tension.

- In relation to social pressures, the breadwinner may feel very responsible or guilty for being unable to continue supporting the partner and family (2 M) and may therefore welcome the chance to plan forward as much as possible. This may apply regardless of whether the breadwinner is male or female.
- Where the man is ill, the woman may find herself well supported by family and friends and go to them rather than the partner to share feelings and worries (2 F). While this may be natural and helpful, it is also important that she is supported to share with her partner, otherwise he may feel increasingly isolated.
- The man may focus more than the woman feels appropriate upon his sexual prowess and she may find it quite difficult to respond to his requests for sex when she is feeling deeply upset (3 F, 3 M). He may turn to sex as a way of expressing his feelings and a reassurance that he is alive. Or the opposite may happen and cause dismay if the woman would have preferred to continue with touch and tenderness even if full sexual intercourse is inappropriate or difficult (3 F). The couple can be helped to talk through these differences.
- The various phases of grief work can be attended to if couples can acknowledge their gender differences in communicating (4 F, 4 M).
- Taking time, allowing space and being available to each other at a non-verbal level may make it much easier to participate in ways that feel empathic for both. Again, the gender balance between different communication styles needs to be constantly kept in mind (4 F, 4 M).
- Both partners may feel angry and hostile at times and there may be occasional outbursts of aggression (5 F, 5 M). Sometimes it is useful for the carer to find other outlets for bouts of anger and hostility which are natural responses to the loss of a partner but can be too much for the ill person to bear.

vii. Review and remember

> Reviewing and remembering the good and not-so-good times together is also important for separating and divorcing couples.

If there is time, it is essential to:

- review and remember the good times that have been experienced as a couple
- look at photographs, play nostalgic records, revisit special places
- review and remember the good times with family and friends
- review and remember the difficult times, and how you survived them
- review and remember illness of children, major rows, social situations that went wrong, and those that went well
- review and remember the ways difficulties were overcome and the times of fun and pulling together in spite of problems;
- think together about the loss of an ideal and unfinished business, which can help to alleviate some of the pain of separation.

viii. Coping with terminal illness

Again, this will vary from individual to individual, and some couples may wish to attend to this privately. Sensitive issues such as whether the patient wants to be cared for at home, and how this can occur, will require attention if the couple can accept help. 'Time off' for the carer, and other support, should be included. Planning practical details may be easier for the man than for the woman, because it may fit into his problem-solving mode (1 M), and help him to feel more responsible (2 M). The carer may also feel resentful (1 F, 1 M, 5 F, 5 M) and can be encouraged to speak about feelings with the patient or seek additional individual help, either through counselling or through friends, to cope with feelings of being left behind.

ix. Planning forward

It may seem bizarre to plan the funeral together, but couples do find this reassuring. The music, flowers, who will be there, what can be said, can be discussed and bring a greater sense of being in control and purposive.

x. Keeping memories alive

Where there are young children it can be helpful to discuss together:

- future birthdays, family celebrations, where the patient can write a letter or buy gift/s for these occasions. In particular, 18th or 21st birthdays, weddings, christenings, can be discussed and plans made which will help both partners to feel more prepared for the death of one partner.

xi. Finances

Finances can be complex; the wage earner may feel guilty about deserting her/his role, the partner may feel aggrieved and abandoned (2 F, 2 M). Difficult feelings can be expressed and overcome if the couple pull together and plan forward. In spite of intense feelings, it can help to share together concerns over insurance, bank accounts, pensions, selling the house, moving home (4 F, 4 M).

Touch and tenderness, showing each other affection in non-sexual ways, become increasingly important. Touching, massaging, bathing, may all help the couple to both give and receive bodily comfort at this crisis point in their relationship (3 F, 3 M).

Many women and men have experienced the loss of a partner through illness and found separate resources to deal with this painful experience. Others have been left feeling scarred and abandoned. Nothing can replace the presence of a well loved partner, but attending to the grieving process can develop a greater sense of a shared intimacy. The memory of this deeper intimacy can help the bereaved partner to overcome the loneliness s/he will experience in the days after the funeral and will also give a greater sense of completeness to a relationship which otherwise may always feel incomplete.

4.4. Depression

Milligan and Clare (1994) write of depression:

> It is one of the most commonly occurring disorders – and also one of the most distressing. At any one time about three million people in Britain are suffering from it.

Milligan suffered from manic depression throughout his life. His waves of depression and mania are well documented (Milligan and Clare, 1994). Milligan has been courageous in using his illness to explain to the public the torment which depression brings to the individual and those immediately concerned. Milligan's first marriage ended in divorce but continued to be significant to him. Milligan and Clare acknowledge the impact of depression upon relationships and aim to publicise depression and the treatments available for all sufferers regardless of gender. Paykel's figures indicate that 'depression in treatment samples shows an approximately 2:1 female preponderance' (1991) but Milligan and Clare think that when forms of depression such as bipolar depression are taken into account, the incidence of depression averages out at 0.9:1 female to male.

They consider that the preponderance of mild to moderate depression in the female population may be more psychosocial in origin.

Jack (1991) accepts the psychosocial origins of depression and suggests that women are relationship oriented and become depressed over disruption or conflict in close relationships, whereas men, who are autonomy and achievement oriented, become depressed in response to the loss of an ideal or achievement-related goal, or over performance issues.

It is not the purpose of this section to enter into debate regarding the origin and aetiology of depression; instead the aim is to draw attention to gender differences that affect depression. Suggestions are made to improve the quality of the relationship towards a 'confiding' relationship that can be protective against depression.

Brown and Harris (1978) drew attention to a 'confiding relationship' being instrumental in protecting women from depression, a finding that has not yet been replicated. However, much research has focused upon marital discord and depression.

> Marital discord is the most common life stressor that is a precursor to depression. (Paykel et al., 1969) Relapse of depression following acute depressive episodes and following pharmacological treatment of depression are often precipitated by marital disruption. (Hooley et al., 1986; Rounsaville et al., 1979) In more than 50% of maritally discordant couples at least one spouse is depressed. (Beach et al., 1985; O'Leary and Beach, 1990)

This section draws attention to intimacy needs and depression.

4.4.1. Example 4c, Frank and Fiona

> Frank (68) and Fiona (60), happily married for 38 years, had four grown-up children and five grandchildren. Frank was a successful businessman and Fiona a successful senior civil servant. Soon after her retirement Fiona became depressed and was referred by her doctor for depression. She was invited to attend therapy with Frank.
>
> During the assessment Frank was most concerned about his wife. He felt she was giving in by being depressed, and that she should have approached retirement, as he had five years previously, by making herself busy.
>
> Frank had retired two years early and set about rebuilding his life around early morning walks, keep fit classes and a regular timetable of events such as visits to museums and stately homes. He was fit, slim and young looking.

Fiona, for her part, was sad to retire and missed the companionship of her colleagues. She was disappointed in herself that she was finding life a burden. Additionally, she had suddenly become arthritic; getting up in the morning was particularly painful. Frank was concerned about her because she had started drinking 'heavily', though Fiona disputed this; she felt that the occasional gin and tonic was acceptable.

Frank was particularly disappointed that Fiona was depressed as he had been waiting for her to retire so that they could do things together. He also found her attitude to retirement upsetting. He had hoped she would look forward to sharing his activities, which would mean getting up early in the morning, planning the day's activities, and getting on with them. Fiona had other hopes for retirement. Having lived a very busy life first as a mother and later as a civil servant, she expected a slower, more relaxed time, particularly in the early morning. She was also very disappointed to find that she was becoming arthritic, while Frank doubted her arthritis and thought it was an excuse for laziness.

Thinking about Frank and Fiona without considering gender issues, one might say that each is trying to find their own individual way to adjust to retirement and growing old together, and gender is therefore irrelevant. Additionally, they had always enjoyed a rather different life style, she being less organised and he being a good organiser.

If one considers gender issues, as described in the intimacy screen, retirement is thought of as a major adjustment for both women and men. Frank approached it as a 'problem to be solved' (1 M), whereas Fiona approached it as a loss of her friends and support network (2 F), as well as a sign of advancing age. Frank was happy to get on and develop his individual approach to retirement (2 M) and Fiona was regretting having left behind a network of friends and colleagues (2 F). As far as their sexual relationship was concerned, this had ceased some years ago, although Fiona would have liked it better if Frank had been more prepared to be physically demonstrative and exchanged touch and hugs (3 F, 3 M).

With regard to their communication (4 F, 4 M), Frank spent much of the day cajoling and criticising Fiona, in an attempt to chivvy her into activity, believing that this would help her feel better. He had good verbal skills and used them to spur her to activity. This is a common response to depression, whether by a man or a woman. Frank seemed determined to stay young by being active, and Fiona was sad about the loss of her youth, but they found it difficult to respect each other's different approaches to retirement. They did become quite angry and irritated with each other, although neither would have said they were aggressive (5 F, 5 M).

4.4.2. How to help using the intimacy screen

i. In emotionally arousing situations (1 F, 1 M)

(See 2.3.1, 2.4.1)
Fiona was aware that one phase of her life – her working professional life – was over. It is as if she thought of retirement rather as the menopause, bringing to an end a creative and productive part of her life. It has been suggested that women gain much experience of the rhythms and cycles of life (see 6.3). Fiona was aware and sad about the ending of her working life (1 F). Frank, on the contrary, had entered retirement with a workmanlike attitude to retirement, as if one job was over and another was beginning (1 M). In doing so, he did not grieve for the ending of his professional life but got on with the new job, retirement.

By being depressed, Fiona was bringing the reality of retirement into focus within their relationship (1 F). Frank was verbally skilled, he had no problem in responding quickly to Fiona; however, he did not like to speak about feelings (1 M). He did not acknowledge his own feelings although he was upset to see Fiona so sad. He was also very upset that she was now arthritic.

- In therapy they can be helped to talk together about what it felt like to be growing older and for Fiona to be handicapped by arthritis (4 F, 4 M).
- Where illness has occurred it can be important to share feelings of disappointment and anxiety regarding the meaning of the illness (see 4.3.3). Frank was able to say that he was very fearful in case Fiona would die before himself. He had always assumed that he would die first, as he was eight years her senior. The fact that she suddenly became arthritic reminded him of their frailty and of how alone he would feel if she died first (4 F, 4 M). He was also quite afraid of illness and uncertain as to how he would cope if Fiona were to become increasingly immobilised(1 M).

As they talked, over several sessions, about their disappointments and shared concerns about ageing and its handicaps so Fiona's depression began to lift. By Frank admitting to his own fears and need for Fiona emotionally, rather than just as a busy companion, it is possible that some of their joint needs for intimacy were being met (1 F, 1 M).

ii. Encouraging touch and tenderness

(See 2.5.2)
This couple were a very verbal couple; sexuality or sensuality had ceased to be part of their relationship as soon as Frank retired.

- They were encouraged to give and receive affection through touch and massage. This helped Fiona cope with arthritic pains but also helped them both reconnect with the more physical and less verbal aspect of their relationship (3 F, 3 M).

iii. Encouraging positive non-critical language

(See 2.7, 6.6, 6.10)

- During therapy they were asked to use positive non-critical language with each other and speak more about feelings than doing. This was more difficult for Frank than for Fiona (4 F, 4 M).

Frank never expressed himself through physical aggression but perhaps did use aggression through the use of criticism and scolding (5 F, 5 M).

iv. Planning joint activities

- They were also encouraged to plan together to 'do things together' which both would enjoy and Fiona could manage. This meant planning for later in the day and also seeking some extra help in the house. This attended to Frank's need for a more problem-focused and activity-based solution to retirement (1 M).
- Where couples have very different interests it is possible to encourage them to plan alternative activities – her choice and then his choice. In this way each gets one activity they like, either separately or together, and go with the partner to another event or activity with the partner (2 F, 2 M).

By attending to how each gender approaches such difficult times as retirement or illness, intimacy can be deepened, even where ageing is unwelcome or illness is debilitating, as it was for Fiona and Frank.

A pattern which often occurs is that the non-depressed partner becomes the manager of the household business, is competent and caring in a distant unemotional way. The depressed partner becomes dependent, needy and is emotionally expressive.

If the depression, or sadness, can be shared more equally between both partners, then both can express their vulnerability and each can be cared for by the other (see 6.12).

During critical periods, where one partner is depressed, specific aspects of the intimacy screen may be absent or ignored. Frank and Fiona had completely ignored the sexuality/sensuality aspect of their relationship (3 F, 3 M) but were reminded of this in treatment when touch and tenderness became an important healing agent.

Talking about feelings was also ignored by both partners, though Fiona showed her feelings through her depression.

> Intimacy can be heightened if all the elements of intimacy can be engaged.

Emotional sharing, being respectful of each other's social sensitivities and sensual or sexual needs, talking together at a speed and pace that the other can cope with, as well as being non-critical and non-aggressive all assist in a deepening of intimacy.

Where these elements can be more equally shared, the depression may lift or be modified and adjustments can be made to make life easier for both partners.

Where the dynamics of the relationship have become rigid, or where the depression is seen as the main problem, it may be sensible to seek specialist professional help. There is growing evidence that specialist relationship therapy can help to moderate the depression (Beach et al., 1990, 1994; Crowe and Ridley, 1990). The therapist can use cognitive, structural or systemic skills to work with couples within a clinic setting.

4.5. Sexual abuse and rape and their impact upon intimacy

(See 6.3.2, 6.5, 6.6, 6.8.2, 6.9, 6.10)

> The pain, suffering, misfortunes, and other problems of sexual victimisation of both adults and children are harsh realities that we have witnessed all too often in our professional practise. The victims of rape, incest, and other forms of sexual molestation come from all social strata, all racial and ethnic groups, and all geographic areas. We still do not know the extent of the problem. (Thomas, 1988)

It is not the purpose of this section to consider the causation or extent of the problem of sexual victimisation such as rape or sexual abuse, but to focus upon the impact of the experience of rape or sexual abuse upon the current relationship of a couple and their intimacy. There is a growing awareness that men as well as women have been victims of rape and sexual abuse, and a reluctance on the part of men to report or discuss their victimisation. There is probably much under-reporting of sexual abuse throughout society.

> Part of the difficulty in understanding and treating victims of sexual abuse is clinicians' failure to inquire about a past history of sexual abuse along with the patient's difficulty in discussing it. The taboos against rape, incest, and child molestation are so great and accompanied by so much shame that it has been difficult for victims and their families to receive proper care. (Gise and Paddison, 1988)

Not all victims of sexual abuse or rape report negative consequences; about one-third of all victims report no enduring adverse consequences (Kendall-Tackett et al., 1993). This may be because of a reparative good relationship with a partner or for reasons not yet understood.

For those victims who do experience negative consequences, the common factors seem to be abuse by stepfather/father, bizarre or violent abuse, actual penetration, lack of support or disbelief when disclosure occurs, and the victim's general personal circumstances.

Some evidence indicates that where a man has been abused as a child he is more likely to go on, as an adult, to abuse, and may also form an abusive relationship with his partner (Burgess et al., 1988; Stanko, 1985; Revitch and Schlesinger, 1988). A similar pattern may not occur for women.

The focus here is the couple's interaction following an experience of sexual abuse and the contrasting nature of female and male intimacy needs (see 6.3, 6.3.2, 6.8, 6.8.2).

4.5.1. Example 4d, Robert and Rita

Robert (43) and Rita (41) had two children, a boy (8) a girl (10). Both partners worked as full-time, well trained professional carers. With a busy family life they worked hard at being good parents. They tended to disagree about bringing up the children, but did their best to overcome this.

They had been married for 12 years before Robert learned that Rita had been sexually abused by her father from about 10 years to 19 years of age. It would seem that Rita had suppressed the memory of this experience, or had felt she could not talk about it, until she began to have powerful flashbacks after witnessing an accident. Up until this time their relationship had been good, if argumentative. Following the disclosure of the abuse, their relationship deteriorated and they sought help from a relationship and sexual therapy clinic.

At the assessment, their sexual relationship had deteriorated so much that Rita could not accept any sexual advances and Robert did not feel he could approach Rita for sex. They had also stopped any physical touching. During the previous months sexual intercourse became a battlefield as Robert was pressuring for penetrative sex, and Rita felt she should be able to accept it. Penetrative sex occasionally occurred with neither enjoying it.

Robert was deeply upset on learning about the abuse, and in particular that he had been meeting the abusing father-in-law, although he had never liked him, and was now very worried in case his children were in danger of being abused when visiting the grandparents.

He was equally devastated that his wife, whom he had believed to be a virgin on marriage, was in fact 'soiled goods'. This offended his self-respect as if his own autonomy or separateness had been violated (2 M).

Rita was overwhelmed by the power of her flashbacks and devastated that she seemed to have 'forgotten' about these abusive experiences until after observing an accident in which a child ran into the street and was badly injured by an oncoming truck. She became moody, irritable and defensive; Robert became critical of her ability to be a good parent, and preoccupied with the detail of her abusive experience.

4.5.2. Thinking about the couple interaction using the intimacy screen

Using the intimacy/gender screen (see 2.2.1) as a tool to analyse the couple relationship, one can see that all five areas of intimacy have been severely affected for both partners following the disclosure of the abuse (Douglas et al., 1989; Firth, 1997).

i. In emotionally arousing situations (1 F, 1 M)

(See 2.3.1, 2.3.2)
The emotionally arousing situation for Robert and Rita is the disclosure of her sexual abuse, which was unknown to Robert. Robert became intensely interested in the detail of what occurred between Rita and her father and wanted Rita to describe her experiences. Rita found this extremely painful but, because she felt she had let him down by not revealing this earlier in their relationship, she tried to respond. Robert did not seem to notice the pain this caused Rita and she began to think of him as insensitive to her feelings.

Robert seems to be trying to understand the problem in detail while Rita wants only to express her feelings (1 M, 1 F). Both become increasingly upset and Robert is insistent that he learn about the abuse, which further upsets Rita.

ii. Where there are social pressures (2 F, 2 M)

(See 2.4.)
Following the abuse, Rita did not attempt to break off relationships with her father; on the contrary, she tried to keep her network of relationships within the family intact. Her stated aim was to protect her mother and ensure that her children had a continuing relationship with their grandparents.

Robert, on the other hand, was very upset about the relationship with the abusing father-in-law and wanted an immediate cessation of all contact with Rita's family. He was ashamed to have been placed in this situation and tried to ensure that he, and his family, regained their autonomy and independence.

A deep rift developed between Robert and Rita, neither understanding the other's perspective. Rita wanted Robert to understand and support her to maintain relationships with her family, and Robert was outraged that Rita should ask this.

iii. Within a physical sexual relationship (3 F, 3 M)

(See 2.5, 2.5.3, 6.5, 6.9)
During therapy, when discussing their sexual relationship, Rita indicated that she would prefer Robert to hold her tenderly and not seek to have sexual intercourse. Rita did not allow Robert to touch her as she feared he would want penetrative sex. Robert was hurt and bewildered to find that Rita had turned against him sexually and felt she was blaming him for her father's abuse. He occasionally insisted upon sexual intercourse and Rita submitted to him, without any enjoyment, as she felt a good wife would respond in this way. Sexuality became increasingly difficult

for both Roger and Rita, and she began to have flashbacks during penetrative sex. Her father had occasionally penetrated her during the abusive experiences. Sexuality and sensuality became a battleground, and neither partner was able to give or receive what they each needed at this time.

Thinking about physical sexuality, a good sexual relationship for the woman may often require emotional sharing, touch and tenderness with the whole body engaged in the process. The man may need to feel confident that he can seek penetrative sex. For Rita and Roger these aspects of sexuality have been severely affected by their experience of sexual abuse. Roger has become the 'second victim' of sexual abuse and their intimacy is in crisis. In a rather tragic repetition of the initial abuse, he is occasionally experienced as abusing by Rita. He is aware of this but cannot understand or accept it.

iv. Within communication (4 F, 4 M)

(See 2.6, 6.4, 6.5, 6.10)
Roger and Rita tried to use their communication skills to overcome their relationship dilemma. Rita found it difficult to talk about her experience and Roger, who normally found Rita very able to share her feelings and experiences, did not understand her reluctance. He felt that she was deliberately withholding information from him.

Rita was so caught up in re-experiencing her own traumatic experiences that she could not use her ability to read non-verbal cues or reach across the gender divide to understand or console Roger. Consequently, there were periods when communication became angry, with both partners shouting and blaming each other. This aspect of their communication was deeply painful to both partners as neither understood why they were attacking each other. They each wanted to be supportive.

v. Where there are aggressive feelings (5 F, 5 M)

(See 2.7, 6.6, 6.10)
Both partners were occasionally verbally aggressive then apologetic, and Roger was occasionally sexually aggressive in seeking penetrative sex. Rita tried to understand his needs and wanted to have a good caring sexual relationship with Roger. She knew rationally that he was not the abuser and genuinely wanted to continue a sexual relationship with Roger.

There are other ways to think about the impact of a sexual violation upon an adult relationship, and the invisible intimacy screen is an additional tool in the therapist's repertoire. By using these guidelines to examine the detail of the couple relationship, the overwhelming impact of the abuse upon the couple's intimacy is revealed.

In-depth knowledge is necessary if such couples are to be helped to recover from the trauma of sexual victimisation and its disclosure, and to renew and deepen an intimate heterosexual relationship. Each can be helped to be sensitive to the gender responses and needs of the partner. Otherwise, the relationship may end in crisis and separation.

4.5.3. How to help using the intimacy screen

These guidelines should be carefully modified to suit each couple and do not necessarily apply to all couples.

i. In emotionally arousing situations (1 F, 1 M)

(See 2.3.1, 2.3.2)

- The man will need to learn to be very gentle in asking questions or listening to the woman's experiences.
- He will help his partner most if he can listen to her feelings, even if they are very painful for him.
- He may also be wise not to pry too closely into the detail of the abuse, and remind himself that his relationship is happening in the present, whilst the abusive relationship, however beastly, was in the past.

Clinical experience suggests that they are best helped as a couple if there is not too much joint exploration of the abuse, but this is done with another therapist who has specialist skills in working with abusive experiences. The man may also need to see a separate therapist in order to offload some of his anger and his need to know about the detail of the abuse.

ii. Where there are social pressures (2 F, 2 M)

(See 2.4, 2.4.1, 2.4.2)
This is a complicated area in which each partner feels misunderstood by the other.

- The woman will need to understand and respect that her male partner also feels abused and victimised by her abuse, and for a time will find it extremely painful that she did not tell him.
- She will also need to understand his outrage that she has kept contact with her family, and his determination to cut himself off.

- These issues can be talked about, although his anger and her hurt can often get in the way. The therapist can help them pace their discussions so that they do not hurt each other further by going too quickly.
- It is helpful if the couple can timetable talking sessions to perhaps half an hour each day (with a day off) so that the anger and hurt can be contained, but the discussions can go on over time.
- It is important to end these difficult discussion times with some way of showing they each care for the other. A hug, a cup of tea together, walking the dog, sharing a glass of wine together, can all help contain the powerful emotions that disclosure arouses.

The couple will need time to work slowly through these experiences together.

iii. Within a physical sexual relationship (3 F, 3 M)

(See 2.5, 6.5, 6.9)
Sexuality is often deeply affected. Each needs to take time to reconnect sensually.

- It is helpful if the woman can let the partner know how she would like to be touched and held, and if he can be persuaded, for the moment, to be patient with himself and her regarding when and how to resume sexual intercourse.
- For a time, both partners may need to avoid situations which remind the abused partner of the abusive experience. Small reminders, such as a smell, a light behind the head, touching a specific part of the body, can be a reminder of the abuse.
- It can be useful to help the couple to remind each other of their presence, using their first names; looking at each other and talking to each other can help the abused partner stay 'in the present' rather than constantly being reminded of the past abuse.

Where sexuality has been severely affected, it may be necessary to seek the help of a specialist in relationship and sexual therapy.

iv. Within communication (4 F, 4 M)

(See 2.6, 6.4, 6.6, 6.10)
Communication has been called the facilitating dimension (Lewis, 1985). However, too much or too little can also be crucial at times of crisis.

Following the disclosure of sexual victimisation, the couple feel under immense pressure to talk, each partner wanting to sort it out in their own way. Being patient and taking time seems essential. Therefore regular timetabled talking sessions can be very helpful (see above, 'Where there are social pressures').

- This means choosing times when the couple can be private, without pressure, to talk together. It also means deciding how long to talk on each occasion (20–30 minutes is likely to be sufficient on each occasion); and agreeing to continue talking at the next session.
- It is also necessary to agree to set the topic down in the meantime.
- Each partner may need to respect the difficulty each has in facing this situation and give each other time, without being pressurised, to think and feel it through.
- Additionally, while they will want to talk things over together, consideration should be given to individual sessions with a professionally trained person with whom they can share their feelings; otherwise, the partnership may become overburdened. She may need to talk about her distress at the experience (1 F), and he about his anger and hostility (5 M).
- Talking about the life they share and the things they enjoy together needs to be encouraged; otherwise the 'abusive experiences' can swamp a once healthy relationship.
- Making positive requests, turning complaints into requests, and making requests specific and realistic, all tend to help the couple unsnarl a complex interaction.

v. Where there are aggressive feelings (5 F, 5 M)

(See 2.7, 6.6, 6.10)
Robert and Rita's relationship did not escalate into significant violence, though his wish for penetrative sex could be understood as aggressive. There are many elements which contribute to an escalation of frustration, hurt and hostility. Where a couple are less determined to overcome such a crisis, or where previous experience has undermined the confidence of the individual, then physical or verbal violence may well ensue.

Where possible, attending to the central aspects of communication and sexuality, as above, should help defuse a potentially violent interaction.

- It is important to help the couple understand that negative statements or criticisms are experienced by the recipient at times of crisis as deeply wounding, and the verbal violence should therefore be kept in check.

- Strategies may need to be discussed to avoid aggressive interactions. Cooling off strategies such as taking the dog for a walk, going out of the room, seeing a good film together, doing some exercises together, watching a favourite comedy on video together, can help to bring back some lightness and sense of humour into a situation.
- Other strategies, such as identifying the 'triggers' that make each partner angry for example a tone of voice, a facial expression or a particular physical stance – can be helpful.
- Once the 'triggers' have been identified, a code word or message can be used to let one partner know that they are irritating the other. A raised hand, a phrase, such as 'it is happening now' or 'King Kong's around', although simplistic, can help add lightness to a situation, but more usefully lets each know about the other's sensitivity. These signals can be used to shortcut painful interactions and to let each other know that there is a willingness to modify behaviour that offends.

Two central elements of intimacy that are usually severely affected are how the woman and man react to this emotionally arousing situation (1 F, 1 M), and sexuality (3 F, 3 M). Initially, the non-abused partner may need to hang on to his anger (5 M) and his wish to focus on the cause of the problem (1 M). He will need to be prepared to listen to the abused partner's feelings (1 F), and be sensitive about renewal of sexual intercourse (3 F). In particular, it may be helpful to avoid sexual contact which is similar to the initial abusing behaviour, at least in the early stages.

This is not an easy task for either the couple or the therapist. Patience and an empathic understanding of how each gender is affected is essential, and as time goes by the couple can develop a deeper intimacy based upon greater understanding of female and male needs. However, unless time is taken to be respectful of each other's intimacy, the abused partner can begin to doubt that female/male intimacy can ever be found, and the non-abused partner can develop a deep cynicism about relationships. Each gender may then become more suspicious and less trusting of the other and the relationship becomes a hostile arena.

4.6. Domestic violence and its impact on intimacy

(See also 2.7, 6.6, 6.10)

Male aggression is reviewed in detail (see 6.10). Statistics suggest that most serious domestic violence is perpetrated by men against women, although recent studies question assumptions previously held (O'Leary et al., 1989).

The case presented is one in which violence by the man against a woman occurred in the presence of verbal violence from both partners. This pattern does occur; however, there is no attempt here to blame the woman for the violent response of the man. He must take responsibility for his physical violence whatever the circumstances that surround it. Also not all domestic violence occurs in the presence of female verbal aggression. Detailed research is urgently needed.

4.6.1. Example 4e, Eustace and Elly

Eustace (41) and Elly (39) have known each other for four years. Elly is divorced from her previous husband with whom she had two boys (11) and (15). Eustace was married to an American when he was 21 but has not seen her for 10 years. He is still officially married. Eustace is an Afro-American and Elly is Irish. Both have led unconventional lives. Eustace is a musician, who has made his livelihood singing at gigs, busking and occasionally more formal concerts; he describes himself as a 'down and out singer'. Elly has travelled widely, knows Africa well and now works as the manager of a hostel for the homeless. They live together in Elly's house in North London and have a passionate and conflictual life together.

Financially they have insufficient money to support the life style they would like; the two boys' schooling, two cars and the mortgage consume the available finances. Elly has a more reliable income than Eustace and they both contribute to the joint budget. Occasionally Eustace makes a lot of money, which they spend immediately.

Elly's two boys enjoy Eustace's presence and have a good time together. However, many of the rows focus on the two boys and Eustace's 'interference' or 'slackness' with the boys. He is seen as either too disciplinarian or too soft. Rows quickly escalate until they are both hitting each other, Eustace is bigger and stronger and his blows bruise Elly. She has twice had to attend her GP with suspected fractures of the arm.

Drinking is an attractive aspect of social relationships and can help couples relax and enjoy each other's company. Many couples enjoy a glass of wine as a preliminary to sexual intercourse. Both women and men may use alcohol to help them forget or to numb difficult feelings, and alcoholism, which was once thought of as more prevalent amongst men, is increasingly a woman's issue too. It is a sad fact that too much alcohol can damage the health of the individual and the relationship. Heavy drinking or binge drinking is often part of marital violence. Drinking is not part of Eustace and Elly's relationship and in this respect they may be atypical.

4.6.2. How to help using the intimacy screen

i. in emotionally arousing situations (1 F, 1 M)

(See 2.3.1, 2.3.2)
Elly and Eustace's arguments would often begin with Elly talking about her anxieties regarding her two boys, particularly the 15-year-old, who wanted to stay out late and go to gigs. Elly worried for his safety but also because finances were tight. Eustace knew Elly had been an adventurous young woman and was surprised at her protectiveness towards the boys.

The following is an example where the interaction escalates into violence. A major contributor to the violence is that instead of listening to her fears and worries (1 F), Eustace 'problem-solves' and suggests ways of helping Peter (1 M).

Eustace. 'Well, let him start a paper round, or he could do some car washing and make some money.'

Elly, now upset. 'That is no good, he would be tired at school and he has his GCSE exams coming up' (1 F). You know that he has been told he has to concentrate on his school work this year.'

Eustace, still trying to problem-solve, tries several additional suggestions. 'Peter could do the paper round each morning, and the car wash on Saturdays, he would still have plenty time for homework in the evening.'

Elly, now angry and attacking. 'You haven't a clue about how to bring up children, you are always indulging their whims, and never seem to be able to take their school work seriously.'

Eustace, also angry. 'Oh, so you are so great with them, how come they are always asking me to help them with mending their bikes. Your problem is you don't want any help from me, unless it suits you. Why don't you just tell me to get out as you usually do when you don't agree with me, and then come apologising when you want me for something?'

Insults flow, each topping the other's criticism until eventually physical force is used. Elly was hurt physically and felt deeply misunderstood, while Eustace felt provoked and misunderstood (5 F, 5 M).

Examine the interaction and how it escalates

- by examining the interaction, it becomes possible to think of alternatives to the negative pattern
- each partner can be asked to think of one way to behave differently during such an escalation
- ideas such as Eustace listening to Elly's worries and making no suggestions
- or Elly listening to what it is like for Eustace to be part of this family but unable to make suggestions that are acceptable
- after examining the interaction, each can be asked to repeat what the other has said before replying so that it is clear s/he understands, and also takes more time before replying (see 2.4.1.3, 2.6.2.1).
- by examining the interaction, one can consider voice tone, body language, and aspects of the interaction which upset the other; a change of voice tone, or pace of responding, can turn negative interactions into more empathic exchanges;
- small behavioural changes which are practical, positive, balanced between the couple and achievable in the immediate future, although simple, can improve a seemingly intractable situation.

Making a non-violent contract

Where the violence is regular and severe it may be necessary to ask the violent partner, usually the man, to enter into a contract in which s/he agrees that s/he will not resort to violence for a designated period.

- In order to achieve this it may be necessary to help the violent partner to think through what s/he will need to do to avoid violence.
- Avoiding alcohol may be essential, but complex to achieve.
- Taking time out, walking away from the situation, counting to 200.
- Finding a useful thought which can be memorised and repeated to oneself at such times, e.g. ' take your time, things can be sorted out without being angry' or 'life will be better if I don't respond now'.
- Finding what will be helpful for each individual may take time, but will be well worth the effort.

- The non-violent partner can be included in the contract setting, but it is essential that the violent partner accept his/her responsible for his/her violence by taking responsibility for the contract of non-violence.

Elly and Eustace both agreed to try to listen to what the other said, and also use a softer voice tone. It was interesting and reassuring that when eventually they used a softer tone of voice, each giggled and became playful with each other. It was as if being 'playful' and gentle was good fun and violence was not necessary.

ii. Where there are social pressures (2 F, 2 M)

(See 2.4)

- In their discussion of the boys, gender differences were in evidence. Elly was concerned about her boys' schooling and Peter's safety if he went to gigs, since he was only 15 years old (2 F). Eustace was prepared to allow Peter to test out his independence and autonomy by doing a paper round or car washing to fund his own social life (2 M). In these ways they stress very different aspects of social pressures.
- Elly and Eustace can be encouraged to discuss what is appropriate behaviour for a 15-year-old, until they can come to a compromise which both can support (see 3.7).
- A complication is that Eustace is not the natural father. Elly, having spent several years bringing up the boys on her own, is uncertain about including Eustace in their discipline.
- Such a discussion can help them to face up to the issue of pulling together regarding the children, and may help Elly to appreciate Eustace's contribution to their upbringing (see 3F, Nora and Neil).
- It is a very good rule for couples who share the upbringing of children, even though one partner is not the natural parent, to discuss what the approach to the children shall be, and then ensure that they back up each other in its implementation.
- Eustace can bring issues of autonomy and independence into the discussion and Elly can bring concerns about their social network and responsibilities. A joint approach helps the children to develop in these ways.

iii. Within a physical sexual relationship (3 F, 3 M)

(See 2.5, 6.5, 6.9)
Eustace and Elly had a good and passionate sexual relationship which was interrupted by withdrawal and moodiness following these violent

interchanges. Although their sex life was good, they worried that it could not continue in the presence of violence.

With other couples where alcohol plays a significant part in the violent interaction, the sexual relationship can become fraught and unsatisfactory, particularly for the woman. If the man has drunk a great deal, he probably feels highly aroused, but is an inadequate lover, smelling of alcohol, ejaculating early, and falling heavily asleep immediately afterwards. If he is a regular heavy drinker he may lose his ability to gain an adequate erection, which may make him anxious or angry. He may then blame his partner for being unhelpful sexually and violence may occur.

If the woman is full of resentment she is unlikely to experience sex as satisfying. Even when sexual intercourse is satisfactory she may be disappointed if he falls asleep and is unavailable for conversation or tenderness.

- Such couples need specialist help to rebuild a more satisfactory relationship which can encompass emotional sharing, touch and tenderness, as well as safe penetrative sex which is satisfying for both partners.
- The banning of sexual intercourse, and the use of non-genital touching can help couples begin to reconnect with sensuality.
- Using good educational videos can remind couples of alternative ways of making love.
- There are many good books available which describe the different sexual needs of women and men and can be recommended reading.
- Setting aside regular private unhurried times together when they can nurture their relationship can help to bring back some romance and sensuality into a trouble sexual relationship.
- The violent interaction will usually need attention for the sexual relationship to remain satisfying.

iv. Within communication (4 F, 4 M)

(See 2.6, 6.4, 6.6. 6.10)
Where there is domestic violence the couple communication is likely to be severely affected and will need detailed attention. It is likely that hidden resentments and fears are rarely stated but erupt during a violent interaction and there may be little mutual trust.

- Observing the detail of the couple interaction should make it possible to observe what is getting in the way of good communication.

- Voice tone, non-verbal interaction and the meaning each gives to gesture, facial expression and voice tone are usually significant and may need attention.
- After gaining the couple's trust, the therapist may need to comment upon their different styles and over time help the couple to let each other know what is intimidating or irritating in the other's behaviour.
- It may be necessary to slow down their communication.
- Various options are available, such as providing a book with the 'rule' that the person holding the book can speak and the other listens. The book is passed across to the partner, who can then speak while the other listens.
- It is helpful to suggest for how long each partner can speak; one sentence, one minute, or one subject only can become a 'rule' to which each agrees.
- Bringing some lightness and humour into the interaction in session can help the couple learn to 'play' at finding a different way to talk with each other.
- Patience, being well boundaried and clear, is necessary if such couples are to improve their communication styles.
- If the man is slow to find words it can be very helpful to let the couple know that many men have a similar characteristic.
- If the woman finds words speedily they can both be helped to understand that many women have a similar skill.
- She can be encouraged to slow down and allow the man more time to respond.

The way they communicate may be central to their difficulties but may also be difficult to change, and referral to a specialist therapist may be necessary.

v. Where there are aggressive feelings (5 F 5 M)

(See 2.7, 6.6, 6.10)
For Eustace and Elly the aggression was mainly in their voice tone, the speed with which they moved from discussion into anger and hostility, and the uncertainty of their commitment to each other. When these issues were attended to, the aggression became more containable.

For many couples, all of the elements of the invisible intimacy screen may require attention before aggressive interactions can be modified, and specialist help may be necessary.

4.7. Summary

Chapter 4 has indicated some ways in which life events impact upon the couple relationship and influence their intimacy. The intimacy screen was used as a checklist to examine couple relationships where gender-specific illnesses or where depression, sexual abuse or a violent interaction affected the couple. The intimacy screen was also used as a guide to thinking through alternative interventions that may help couples deepen their intimacy.

Part II

5 Chapter

A Realistic Approach to Gender

5.1. Introduction

Part II considers the development of femaleness and maleness, giving references for further reading in areas lightly touched upon here. Chapter 5 introduces alternative approaches to gender and outlines the approach used throughout this book in greater detail. Chapter 6 describes the individual development of the female and male and indicates periods when each is vulnerable.

Reviewing current research into distressed couples, Halford and Markman (1997) conclude:

> From a prevention and intervention point of view, we think that couples who are made aware that divergent gender traits and divergent social roles put them at higher risk for communication problems may come to understand the social and situational roots of their communication problems.

5.2. Gender differences

Gender difference is an emotive and controversial arena. In the search for a realistic approach to gender one cannot but be fascinated by the variety of ways in which maleness and femaleness are viewed. Alternative approaches often focus on similar phenomena, occasionally supporting each other or arriving at opposite conclusions.

There are those who take an extreme position.

> Women not only seem to be more able to maintain intimate relationships, we tend to be more attuned than men to the cyclical nature of the universe and

> ourselves. In our search for healthy models for relationships, we might do well to look at lesbian relationships. (Van Arsdall, 1996)

Moir and Jessel (1991) think:

> Women are simply better equipped to notice things to which men are comparatively blind and deaf. Women are better at picking up social cues, picking up important nuances of meaning from tones of voice or intensity of expression.

Others take the view that most gender differences can be attributed to social and political conditioning (Lips, 1997). A United Nations Development Project suggested that gender differences vary according to each cultural setting.

> Gender is the social construction of men's and women's roles in a given cultural location. Gender roles are distinguished from sex roles, which are biologically determined. (UNDP, 1994)

Cairns and Kroll (1994) define gender as:

> referring to those psychological characteristics, behaviours, attitudes and beliefs believed to be differentially associated with females or males.

Using this definition they review gender differences from a developmental perspective described as:

> A new synthesis across disciplines that have evolved over the past two decades to guide research in behaviour and biology.

This synthesis emphasises the dynamic interplay between processes across time frames and contexts. Cairns and Kroll describe four areas relevant to the development of sex-related differences: (i) personal integration, (ii) time-relativity of socio-behavioural mechanisms, (iii) relevance and irrelevance of biology, and (iv) universality of developmental processes.

Their detailed study of current research identifies 'myths' of gender difference and suggests they arise because of a non-developmental bias in research designs. They conclude:

> The information currently available indicates that certain key gender differences are not stable over the lifespan. (Cairns and Kroll, 1994)

However, they also think some key differences emerge at adolescence and begin to converge in later maturity (Cohn, 1991).

Rutter and Hay (1994) and Cairns and Kroll (1994) prefer a developmental synthesis across disciplines; others view gender through their own theoretical orientations. Rice (1995) examines the major theories of human development under five categories: psychoanalytic theories, learning theories, humanistic theories, cognitive theories and ethological theories. Having described these perspectives, he adds, 'no one theory completely explains human developmental processes or behaviour'. Rice (1995) prefers an eclectic orientation in which no one theory has a monopoly on the truth though it may have contributed significantly to the understanding of human development.

Among the theoretical orientations there are many contrary and divergent views which cannot all be described here (Chodorow, 1978; Oxnard, 1987; Bate, 1988; Buss, 1989, 1994; Tiger and Fox, 1989; Ory and Warner, 1990; Chiriboga et al., 1991; Halpern, 1992; Rancour-Laferriere, 1992; Ward, 1992; Hatfield, 1993, 1996; Cairns and Kroll, 1994; Rutter and Hay, 1994; Anderson, 1996; Lips, 1990, 1997; Johnson, 1994).

Ward (1992) is amongst those who prefer to think in terms of 'perinatal hormonal and pre-pubertal social factors' and in so doing links biological and social factors together at crucial periods of development. He draws upon research into the impact of social isolation on such diverse animals as guinea pigs, rats, dogs, rhesus monkeys and chimpanzees and suggests that both the *in utero* environment and the prepubertal social influences can be shown to have a direct impact upon adult sexual behaviour.

> The wealth of accumulated data leaves little doubt perinatal hormonal events and pre-pubertal socialisation influence the expression of sexually dimorphic behaviours at all stages of the life cycle.

(Here he is referring to animal studies.) He describes the interaction between these two critical periods of development, underlining the fact that there is likely to be a profound interaction between the inherited characteristics and experiences during critical periods of development.

Buss (1989, 1994) advances an evolutionary-based model of conflict between women and men. His evolutionary-based approach focuses upon the reproductive strategy of each gender and the notion that women need monogamous relationships in order to protect their offspring, while the male does not. Hence there is a rather basic divergence of need between the female and male which leads to tension or conflict.

Chodorow (1978) offered a social learning explanation for the different roles and personalities of women and men. She argues cogently that girls are raised by mothers who are physically like them, and that social learning takes place within the mother/daughter relationship, in which there is a tendency for fusion to occur. Boys, on the other hand, also primarily raised by mothers in early life, develop their maleness by actively separating from the mother. Chodorow (1978) re-evaluated women's development as different from male development but of equal value; while she saw the male development based upon separation, she understood female development to be based upon attachment, and not deficient by comparison to male development.

Gilligan (1982) also criticised the traditional developmental model which saw women as deficient in moral development and as striving for connection and the maintenance of relationships. She described women as viewing moral choices as dependent on a network of relationships within a context, whereas men see moral choices based upon consideration of absolute alternatives of right and wrong.

Lips (1997), on the other hand, holds that socialisation alone can explain many of the gender differences experienced within interpersonal relationships.

> The influence of gender on peer and family relationships is rooted in our socialization into feminine and masculine patterns of behaviour and maintained by social arrangements that favor these patterns.

She writes:

> Women are supposed to bc naturally interested in and good at parenting, by virtue of their sex. The motherhood mystique encourages them to feel guilty if they find motherhood uninteresting or problematic, or if they try to combine it with other goals. Men, by contrast, are not expected to be particularly interested or involved in child care, although there is some evidence that these expectations are slowly changing.

Kerber (1996) acknowledges the superior nurturing skills of women but is concerned that too much emphasis upon these skills will create an oversimplification of womanhood which would maintain her subordinate status and undermine her self-esteem.

Bate (1988) develops the thesis that communication creates gender while Ridgeway and Diekema (1992) present a robust defence of the theory that gender differences, in how women and men interact socially, emerge as a result of status differences experienced between women and men during their lifetime, not as a result of any basic biological or physical differences. They also review theories which revolve around the social expectations placed upon women and men in task-oriented groups; the cultural approach which suggests that people learn rules for interaction with peers; and they compare Eagly's (1987) role approach with theories about the impact of the dynamics of power and prestige (Bales, 1950; Fisek and Ofshe, 1970; Anderson and Blanchard, 1982;). They conclude:

> Despite recent criticism, a status approach to gender difference in interaction continues to provide more theoretical insight into gender inequality and more predictive power over behaviour than other available approaches.

The view that cognitive or intellectual differences exist between males and females is often challenged. Social or cultural attitudes or experiences during the maturing of the individual are said to create these differences (Rowbotham, 1983; Ardener, 1987; Caplan, 1987; Weeks, 1987; Evans, 1993).

5.3. Psychoanalytic approach to gender

Within the field of psychotherapy and counselling there is an influential psychoanalytical school, or schools, which have their own distinct view of gender and its development. Their ideas are often taken up and explored within literature and the arts and to some extent have become part of our cultural heritage. As such, they continue to have a major impact upon professionals within psychiatry, psychology, social work, counselling and therapy, often dividing otherwise close colleagues. They provide a rich source of alternative hypotheses about the development of maleness and femaleness. Many statements are reassessed as research evidence challenges early Freudian theory.

The psychoanalytic school/s are concerned to understand the internal worlds of the female and male. Concepts such as the female being an incomplete or inadequate male, who is filled with penis envy as a result of her discovery that she is penisless, derive from early Freudian thinking. The inadequacy of the clitoris as a replacement for the penis was thought to add to her sense of inferiority and lead her to suppress any hostility towards the father into a more passive and masochistic stance; in order to suppress her penis envy she seeks to become pregnant. Freud seemed to see a woman's wish to become pregnant as a direct result of her need to manage her penis envy, rather than a purposeful identification with the mother or a fulfilment of her own biological needs.

Paralleling the concept of the female's penis envy is that of castration anxiety, which Freud felt affected men more than women (since women were already castrated), and that the male development depended upon his ability to manage or come to terms with his castration anxiety. According to Freud, in order to overcome his castration anxiety, he learns to identify with the father rather than wishing to kill him off in his desire for the mother.

For the boy, rivalry with the father for the mother, and for the girl, rivalry with the mother for the father, as part of the oedipal conflict, are central concepts within psychoanalysis.

A creative debate continues within psychoanalysis following Freud's early contributions (Samuels, 1989; Breen, 1990).

Within psychoanalysis, 'primacy of the penis' in the development of gender identity has been challenged (Jackson, 1987) and alternative theories have been developed. Helene Deutsch (1946) introduced the idea that the early relationship between the mother/daughter was fundamental in the development of the girl. She also:

> recognised the clitoris as a primary sexual organ, not merely an inferior analog of the penis which a woman must later renounce. (Bernstein and Warner, 1984)

Horney (1932) tipped the balance again by suggesting that men valued the penis as a direct reaction to their fear of castrated women as part of their own castration anxieties. She developed the theory that men envy the female her breast and her ability to bear children.

Kestenberg (1956) takes this aspect of femaleness further and describes the girl's 'productive inside' and her interest in her reproductive abilities. Kestenberg (1956) also suggested that pregnancy could be a major integrating force and a significant stage in the development of a woman. She thought that the pregnant woman may go through a re-evaluation of and a 'rapprochement' with her mother (see 3.6).

Melanie Klein (1952) and Margaret Mahler (Mahler et al., 1975) were both interested in the development of the child in the first year, and focused upon the mother/child relationship as central to female and male development. Klein viewed the girl child, or the boy child, as being able to distinguish themselves from birth. She did not postulate an inner knowledge derived from her biological makeup, rather that the girl child understood that she did not have a penis and that her father had a penis. This the girl developed through her fantasy life. Many see Klein's contribution as a major modification of Freud's theory, which stressed the early stages of development.

Whilst both Klein and Mahler continue to accept the oedipal conflict as central to the development of the girl or boy, they place additional emphasis upon the availability of a good enough mother figure during the early months of the child's life. In their view, the mother figure provides the secure environment, or container, which allows the individual child to proceed through the various developmental stages.

The debates within the field of psychoanalysis continue to generate refinements to an understanding of the development of maleness and femaleness. The presence or absence of a penis, castration anxiety, envy of a penis, womb or breast continue as focus for debate or insight. The role of the father is being considered in more detail (Samuels, 1985, 1989) and paralleling this is the importance of separation or individuation of the individual from the mother figure, and the question as to what constitutes 'good enough' mothering of the boy child or girl child continues to be asked (Winnicott, 1965).

5.4. Early sexual identity

(See also 3.2.2, 6.3.2, 6.8.2)

Other researchers have approached the issue of gender through the establishment of early sexual identity, (Stoller, 1968, 1974; Money and Ehrhardt, 1972). They identified the second half of the second year as a critical period for establishing gender identity. Roiphe and Galenson (1981) also suggest that:

> The second half of the second year of life is a critical period for the development of the sense of sexual identity for boys and girls.

Although these authors approach the development of gender identity from very different theoretical orientations, they agree that by the second half of the second year the core gender identity is formed.

Stoller (1968, 1974), Money (1986) and Ehrhardt and Baker (1974) place emphasis upon the decisive influence of early parental rearing for boys. Stoller studied a group of men who were transsexuals, and he concluded that the mothers had treated the boys in a way which interfered with their development of 'core gender identity as boys'. For girls, Stoller (1974) felt that there were two phases within this two-and-a-half year period; the first, the primary recognition of femaleness, which is added to at a later stage as a defensive response to her growing awareness of the fact of her different genitalia. The role of the mother or mother figure is seen as crucial to the development of both genders.

The importance of the father is emphasised by Roiphe and Galenson (1981).

> The importance of paternal availability and support for the boy's growing sense of his male identity during the second part of the second year of life cannot be too strongly stressed. We believe it is a crucial factor in providing the boy with the confirmation of his own phallic body image.

Cairns and Kroll (1994) reviewed the research, taking a developmental perspective. They challenge the primacy of parental influence and suggest that:

> Males and females in both Western and Asian societies tend to affiliate in same-sex groups. This phenomenon is observed across ontogeny, from pre-school period to early adulthood. The simplicity and ubiquity of this phenomenon may have blinded researchers to its powerful implications for social and sexual development.

They think that 'differences – in mortality rates, social behaviour, sensorimotor capabilities and cognition – emerge at adolescence', and suggest that there is a convergence of behaviour patterns and attitudes in later maturity.

Rutter (1980), on the other hand, describes normal development of gender identity in the following way:

> Children soon learn whether they are a girl or a boy. Gesell (1940) found that two-thirds of 3 year-olds knew their own sex. (whereas most 2 1/2 year olds did not). Rabbon (1950) found much the same and showed that correct sex awareness was almost complete by age 4 years .... Children often do not recognise other people's gender except by hair or clothes, and it is not until 11 years that there is a full awareness that the genital difference is the dominant characteristic differentiating boys and girls.

He concludes:

> A child's gender identity is well developed before he or she has a proper appreciation of sex differences generally.

Rutter (1980) also thinks that most children accept the discovery of anatomical differences between boys and girls as natural. About one-third of children had thought that girls may have had a penis which had grown small or got cut off. Not all of this third were in any way perturbed by this thought. However, Rutter (1980) suggests that evidence collected by Conn and Kanner (1974) and Levy (1940) seems to support the view that perhaps one-third of children (more boys than girls) may experience some form of anxiety about castration.

5.5. A 'working hypothesis'

(See 1.3)

Daniel Stern (1985) explores the relationship between psychoanalytic theories developed from recalled material of patients and the experimental approach, and questions many of the psychoanalytic hypotheses. He describes his own material as a:

> working hypothesis which remains to be proved, and even its status as a hypothesis remains to be explored.

He thus underlines the need to be hesitant and exploratory when considering human development.

This book draws upon his thinking in several key areas. Firstly, that there are 'sensitive periods' during which the experiences of the child are of utmost importance. These are not seen as age specific, and are not tied to the oral, anal and genital phases of more traditional Freudian thinking. Hence the notion of becoming fixated around one of these phases is challenged. They are seen more as ways in which the 'emerging self' makes sense of the experiences.

> From the point of view taken here, the actual point of origin of any pathogenic events, could be anywhere along their continuous developmental line.

Stern sees the infant as going through four phases as the sense of self develops; these are an emergent self, a core self, a subjective self and a verbal self.

Secondly, he suggests the life task of the individual is to move from a position of separateness towards a sense of connectedness. This is opposed to traditional psychoanalytic theories. Stern challenges the theory that separation/individuation is a central organising principle of development and also challenges the concept of an 'undifferentiated' or 'symbiotic' period during which the baby does not know that it is a separate individual, but experiences itself as part of the mother.

Rather than seeing the baby as needing to work towards separation, Stern (1985) sees the baby as inherently having the psychic equipment (through perception, touch, and ability to learn and differentiate), to develop the ability to connect with others as a result of inherent separateness.

Applying this concept to maleness and femaleness, the task of the male or female becomes that of learning about the other from an inherent position of separateness and difference (Benjamin, 1988; Keller, 1985; Sheinberg and Penn, 1991).

5.6. A realistic approach to each gender

(See 1.3, 1.4, 1.5)

Faced with alternative theories regarding the existence or non-existence of gender differences, how can professionals think about gender when working with couples in distress? It is argued here that taking seriously Stern's (1985) hypothesis that the emergent child has the potential to experience itself as a separate entity and Rutter's (1980) view that a child's gender identity is well developed before he or she has a proper appreciation of sex differences generally, one can think of each gender as containing a separate and distinct understanding of either their own maleness or their own femaleness.

This shift in thinking about female–male interrelationships begins with the premiss that each gender has shared knowledge about its own gender but not of the opposite gender. A life task, therefore, may be to move from a position of separateness to one of connectedness. A basic error we may be making in our relationship with the opposite gender is to assume that she/he is similar to me. Each gender may, at times, perceive, feel and make sense of the world in gender-specific ways, and a life task for women and men may be to learn about the other gender.

Gender-specific differences may arise out of basic biological needs (Money, 1986) or 'through socialisation alone' (Lips, 1997) or as a 'dynamic interplay among processes that operate across time frames, levels of analysis, and contexts' (Cairns et al., 1995).

> Clinical experience suggests that a realistic approach for couples who struggle with the question 'why does s/he not behave like me?' may be to understand that in very simple ways s/he is not like me.

5.7. Defining gender

(See 1.3)

When using the word gender it is not intended to make a clear separation between physical sexuality and gender. While acknowledging that gender differences are not absolute, it is suggested that the physical and biological inheritance of women and men is inextricably interwoven with the fabric of each man's or each woman's sense of self within the social and cultural setting.

For this purpose the term gender is used to include a complex matrix of physical, biological, sexual, social and cultural aspects that together define some essential aspect of maleness or femaleness. Halpern (1992) neatly encapsulates the interconnection between the biological and the social.

> Nature and nurture are like Siamese twins who share a common heart and nervous system. The technology has not yet been developed that will allow them to be separated.

Gender is used to describe sexual and social attributes that may be derived initially from a physical and biological inheritance, which are built upon or modified by life cycle experiences and life events, but an essence of gender deeply affects our search for intimacy. Contained within the socially and culturally determined aspects of maleness and femaleness there are specific and essential ways in which women and men are physically and biologically different and can approach the same event from alternative perspectives and with different perceptions. A change in social and cultural attitudes may, over time, affect some of these attributes while physical and biological aspects of gender remain constant.

Brown and Harris (1986, 1989) draw attention to the interaction between the internal world of the individual and the social and cultural pressures on the individual. They use the term 'life structure':

> to tackle the way the internal and external meet in an individual, and to reflect the fact that, despite great complexity at any point in time, there is some structure – and some regularity.

Having spent many years studying the structure of life and the contribution of life events to illness, Brown and Harris believe it is too easy to forget the complex interplay between the internal world of the individual and external pressures upon the individual. A two-strand perspective is outlined: strand one factors impinging on the individual from the external environment are contrasted with factors in strand two, which are internal and psychological.

This interdependent and interactive model is helpful, although it ignores the question of gender throughout the life cycle. To include gender would necessitate adding a third strand – the development of the female and male and their interaction throughout the life cycle of the couple.

Others divide gender into gender identity and gender roles, describing gender identity as a subjective sense that I am a male, or I am a female, and separating out gender roles as:

> society dictates a set of behaviours that are considered normal and appropriate for each sex. These standards are typically labelled gender roles or sex roles. (Crooks and Stein, 1988)

Influential authors (Chodorow, 1978; Caplan, 1987; Bem and Bem, 1976; UNDP, 1994) have defined gender as a social construct in which physical sexuality can, and must, be separated from the social and cultural role and position of female and male within any society.

> Gender difference is not absolute, abstract or irreducible, it does not involve an essence of gender. Gender differences, and the experience of the differences, are socially and psychologically created and situated just as are differences among women. (Chodorow, 1978)

The perspective of this book is that there are gender differences which, unless understood and taken seriously, can get in the way of female/male intimacy.

5.8. Satisfactory heterosexual relationships

(See 1.2.2, 1.4, 2.2.1)

The question arises why gender differences do not affect all couples detrimentally (Weiss, 1980; Heider, 1958). Weiss developed the idea that couples within satisfactory relationships are able to process their partner's behaviour and to edit incoming negative behaviour in a way that does not lead to a negative interaction, whereas distressed spouses are less able to do this. This has been called 'sentiment override'.

Bradbury and Fincham (1988, 1989, 1993) investigated this factor in depth and conclude that attribution, or the explanations that spouses give for events in their marriage, should be taken into account. They think that spouses go through a private process in which decisions are made about their partner's behaviour. Where the behaviour is seen 'as negative, unexpected, and self-significant', a second process begins in which attribution of 'responsibility or blame may be made'.

They hypothesise that:

> to the extent that an attribution reflects a pervasive explanatory style it is likely to relate more strongly to long-term satisfaction ... a specific attribution may affect long-term satisfaction directly when it pertains to an event that is highly significant to the spouse and his or her appraisal of the marriage (e.g. an extramarital affair). (Bradbury and Fincham, 1993)

In other words, if a spouse explains a behaviour by deciding that the partner is, for example, insensitive, this is likely to affect long-term satisfaction. If the behaviour is in relation to an event which is important to that spouse, the impact upon feelings about the relationship will be significant.

Where spouses are unable to recognise and respect gender differences, the accumulated experiences of unsatisfactory responses may encourage couples to blame each other. One often hears couples in distress saying, 'she doesn't understand me', 'if he loved me he would not behave like this', 'if s/he loved me s/he would know what I need'.

Although not discussing gender differences, Bradbury and Fincham (1990) suggest that:

> Happily married wives may reciprocate negative behaviours less because they make attributions that are more benign or because they are able to separate a negative evaluation of the partner from a judgement that is self-relevant.

The hypothesis of 'sentiment override' in relation to gender differences may explain both distressed and non-distressed relationships. The distressed couples may lose their feelings of affection for the partner because of experiences where s/he feels misunderstood, while the non-distressed couples may make an adjustment to the gender needs of the other, enabling them to continue with feelings of respect and affection.

Bradbury and Fincham (1989) think that:

> Happily married spouses are somehow able to process, or edit, incoming negative behaviour in a way that does not lead to reciprocation, whereas distressed spouses possess this ability to a lesser degree.

Where gender differences occur, the task of the therapist may be to help the couple translate gender differences. Five areas are identified as part of an invisible intimacy screen (see 2.2.1) through which the man and woman may respond from a different perspective, with differing needs and aims.

5.9. Summary

While thinking about gender it may be practical and realistic to assume that each gender knows its own but not the other gender. Such an acceptance may be a necessary step towards helping couples in distress develop deeper levels of intimacy within a long-term relationship.

6 CHAPTER

Critical Periods and Vulnerability

6.1. Introduction

This book is about relationships between women and men. However, to understand gender differences it is necessary to recognise how differences emerge during the physical and emotional development of the individual female and male. Chapter 6 describes the development of these differences. Sections 6.3 to 6.7 focus on the female and 6.8 to 6.11 on the male.

A concept of critical periods is used to identify times when physical changes occur that affect the self-confidence, perceptions and needs of each gender. Critical periods include the in utero environment of the foetus, the early experiences, puberty, pregnancy, breastfeeding, the menopause and ageing.

Sexuality, aggression and potential cognitive differences are also reviewed. Finally, the vulnerability of the female and male is discussed as a backdrop to an understanding of female/male relationships (see 3.2, 4.2, 4.3).

This overview of the physical development of the female and male does not dwell in detail upon each period, each of which is a specialist subject. The material presented is therefore inevitably simplified. References are given to enable the reader to follow up areas of interest.

6.2. Critical periods

(See also Chapters 3 and 4.)

A theme that emerges in the development of the foetus in the womb is that of a 'critical period' during which there are environmental prerequisites for the satisfactory development of each gender. For the boy baby there may be a critical period for satisfactory masculinisation of the foetus. Money (1986) thinks much of the adult male's sense of security in himself, as physically and psychologically male, may depend upon this early environment.

Money's concept of the 'critical period' is used here to include stages in the individual's development when maleness and femaleness may be threatened or vulnerable; unless the environment is 'good enough' the adult may feel insecure and anxious about his or her maleness or femaleness.

6.2.1. Critical periods in the development of the female

For the girl, the in utero environment may be less crucial to the establishment of her femaleness. Early experiences, puberty and the onset of the menstrual cycle with the accompanying bodily changes are critical periods in her development. Pregnancy, childbirth and breastfeeding, the first sexual intercourse, experiences of sexual abuse, rape or violence each contain elements of a critical period when the essential femaleness is vulnerable.

The female's journey towards femininity lasts until her adjustment to the menopause as she reaches 50 or so. Once her adult body begins to develop during puberty she is constantly reminded of her physical femaleness through the rhythms of her periods, pregnancy and breastfeeding. This need to respond to the demands and rhythms of her body is absent before the onset of her periods and after the menopause.

6.2.2. Critical periods in the development of the male

Critical periods for male gender development include the in utero environment, early experiences, particularly from 18 months to 36 months (Money and Ehrhardt, 1972; Fagot and Leinbach, 1993), puberty and the earliest sexual experiences, whether abusive or affirming, and – within the context of a relationship – pregnancy, childbirth and breastfeeding. Finally, the response of the male to the natural ageing process may be a 'critical period' when he is vulnerable to the changes experienced in his physical and emotional self.

6.2.3. Critical periods and the couple

(See 3.3.1, 3.3.2, 4.2, 4.3, 4.4, 4.5, 4.6)

As described in Chapter 3, 'critical periods' occur during the development of the couple relationship, when emotions and anxieties are raised and gender issues may increase tension. For the couple, critical periods can be the training ground during which female/male intimacy needs are heightened and the opportunity for a deeper understanding is available. However, each gender may be less in tune with the other at these times and differing approaches or perceptions may be experienced as a lack of understanding or concern for the other (see Chapters 2, 3 and 4).

6.3. Critical periods and female vulnerability

Although each gender has periods of vulnerability, the female may begin life, in utero, less vulnerable than the male. Her later development is subject to changes and rhythms which require her to make constant readjustments throughout her adult life.

Her vulnerability focuses around these demanding periods when her physical self may be at variance with her intellectual self and where the demands upon her emotions and nurturing skills are great. Pregnancy and breastfeeding can be a time of change in the woman's sense of self and self-confidence (see Examples 3c, Douglas and Diane; 3d, Yvonne and Roger; 3e, Peter and Paula). Many women find that their earlier independence gives way to a sense of being dependent and an awareness of their nurturing needs and skills. For those who were previously independent and autonomous, this can come as a shock and disappointment. Not all women have this experience and doubts about 'mothering' abilities haunt women who feel pressurised to be nurturers (see 6.3.4).

After the menopause the demands upon her body are lessened as her fertile period ends, and her experience of herself may become similar to the male experience when the burden of pregnancy is absent (see 6.7).

6.3.1. The in-utero environment

For the female, the in utero environment is important, but, as far as we know, the stability of the female is not at risk in the same way that the masculinisation of the male may be in utero. Current thinking indicates that if the in utero environment is inadequate to promote the masculinisation of the male foetus, the child is more likely to develop some feminine physical or personality traits (see 6.8.1).

Setting aside much of the negative social and cultural attitudes to the birth of a girl, at this stage of development the female is less vulnerable than the male. Through infertility treatment it is known that the female sperm is able to swim faster, and is stronger, than the male sperm.

> This added vulnerability (of the male) can be seen even before birth. For every 100 female embryos, there are around 130 male, but as the male foetus is far more prone to spontaneous abortion and stillbirth than the female, only 106 of those will ever see the light of day as live births. ... Finally then, when the angel of death has made his last circuit of the lying-in hospitals, delivery rooms and nurseries, only 95 boys survive every 100 girls. (Miles, 1992; see also Austin et al., 1981.)

Recent medical advances have begun to level the ratio of boy:girl births.

The greater physical resilience of the girl may be essential because of the greater physical burden that will be placed upon the female body through multiple pregnancies, childbirth and breastfeeding (Watson, 1995).

6.3.2. Early experiences in the search for intimacy (female)

(See 3.2.2)

The biological and physical inheritance of the female and male interacts with the social environment and upon each gender's search for and need for intimacy. Many clinicians and research workers have drawn parallels between the early mother/child or caregiver/child relationship and the adult's behaviour during courtship or when 'in love' (Winnicott, 1965, 1971; Papousek and Papousek, 1974; Stern, 1983).

Scharff (1982) writes:

> The adult need for kissing, smiling and physical caring or lovemaking have their origins in the shared gaze, touch, holding and vocal 'conversations' of infant and mother.

Pines (1989) uses the term 'mental state sharing' to describe moments during the mother/child relationship where there is a sense of shared pleasure.

> In mental state-sharing, the infant and the mother share similar experiences. State-sharing covers such events as vocalising together, games such as pat-a-cake, interactional synchrony, mutual gazing, and interaction between mother and infant such as smiling, where the smile of one evokes the smile of the other, which in turn increases the pleasure and the intensity of the smiling response, acting as a positive feedback loop.

Whether the adult state of 'being in love' is an attempt to recreate the mother/child shared mental state can only be hypothesised. However, it may help us to understand the somewhat irrational nature of 'being in love' and it may also give a hint of what the adult may be searching for in an intimate relationship (see 1.2.2).

Where the infant, whether male of female, has not experienced 'good enough' levels of nurturing or of satisfying 'state sharing', the adult's ability to relate at a more intimate level is likely to be affected.

Benjamin (1988) makes an important contribution to the study of human behaviour in her discussion of 'intersubjectivity'. She believes there is a need to develop a new theory of human development in which:

> the individual subject no longer reigns absolute must confront the difficulty that each subject has in recognizing the other as an equivalent centre of experience. (See 5.6)

By emphasising the intersubjective nature of human development, Benjamin (1988) makes a link with Chodorow (1978) who thinks that:

> We cannot understand gender differences apart from this relational construct.

Attachment research demonstrates how early experiences of the mother/child relationship have a remarkably stable impact upon the development of that child over time (Grossmann and Grossmann, 1991).

> What subsequent work by the Grossmanns and other researchers has emphasised is that an infant's communication patterns develop, or fail to develop, in parallel with those of his mother .... Thus at 6 years of age, mother–child pairs who were communicating freely and effectively at 12 months are continuing to do so, in contrast to the limited and inadequate communication patterns that are found to be still characteristic of pairs in which the child was earlier assessed as insecurely attached. (Bowlby, 1991)

Whatever genetic and biological inheritance the boy or girl is born with is affected by the security or insecurity he or she experiences in relation to the significant caregiver.

> Both the psychoanalytic and the interactional studies make it clear that the intensity of relationship needed to promote good bonding of the baby to the parent is considerable. (Elton, 1982)

The child's gender security is also affected by parental attitudes to her/his gender. A couple who wanted a boy may have treated their girl baby as a boy, having a powerful impact upon her development.

Bancroft (1990) asks the question:

> What would happen if, quite arbitrarily, an anatomical female was brought up as a male or vice-versa? Would the effects of rearing determine the psychological gender of the child? A few such attempts have been described (Diamond, 1965) each apparently failed.

Where women and men have anxieties about their gender orientation, inadequate nurturing or inadequate support during sensitive phases may help explain this anxiety. At the same time the in utero environment may have a particular influence upon the male (see 6.8.1).

6.3.3. Puberty and female vulnerability

Puberty is an important and perhaps defining critical period when the girl's body begins to develop its adult potential. At this time the development of the breasts, the onset of the monthly periods, the rounding out of the figure, and the development of pubic and underarm hair are occurring. These outward signs indicate that she is female.

The onset of the menstrual cycle is the signal that her womb is maturing and she may soon be physically capable of conceiving and bearing a child. These physical changes and their meaning for the girl bring with them the question of how to protect herself from, or respond to, her ability to conceive and bear children.

6.3.3.1. Unseen and mysterious

(See also Example 2d; 2.5)
The maturation of the girl physically and sexually is an unseen and often unexplored aspect of her physical self. Her dormant womb, Fallopian tubes and vaginal canal are internal, mysterious and secret. The girl child may carry within her 'knowledge' that she is to be a carer and nurturer of future generations, but her body hides the symbols internally.

Contrast this with the boy child whose penis is available to touch, fondle and to see. For him, though mysterious, his symbol of masculinity is worn outside his body. Bancroft (1990) writes:

> The anatomical sexual differences between boys and girls contribute in a variety of ways to differences in their sexual development. The obviousness of the boy's external genitalia results in a definite vocabulary for their description. Interest and curiosity about genitalia amongst boys is common and facilitates peer group learning as well as homosexual play. Girls, by contrast, are strikingly unaware of their genitalia, a fact reflected in the almost complete absence of a suitable vocabulary for these parts. Not surprisingly, the clitoris, vagina and urethral opening remain, for many girls, uncharted territory and not a matter for mutual discussion or exploration.

The development of the female breast, as she reaches puberty (between 8 and 16 years), is the first outward and socially observable sign that she is female. From birth, her 'brother' can parade his observable penis as a sign of his masculinity but she has had to wait at least eight years for her more visible sign. This may be one reason why the size and shape of the bosom and penis are focused upon, even though size and shape of a woman's breast does not affect her ability to breastfeed nor does the size and shape of the penis affect the man's ability to give and receive sexual pleasure.

These basic physical differences have an impact upon how each gender makes sense of themselves and their perception of the world. Within psychoanalysis much is said about the meaning of the female 'injury' and 'penis envy' (Maguire, 1995). Tyson discusses the girl's preoccupation with her mother's breasts and suggests that 'breast envy may equal or be greater than penis envy' (Tyson, 1989). This ongoing dialogue conveys a fascination with femaleness and maleness.

6.3.3.2. The female at risk during puberty

From the moment a girl begins to menstruate (menarche) until she reaches the menopause and periods cease, she experiences a monthly rhythm which is out of her control, and which is not experienced by men. She must learn to live with and accommodate to the rhythms of her body, to the cramps and premenstrual tension or restlessness which may anticipate the onset of her period. In general (unless she is subfertile, or has conception difficulties), she must learn to adjust her lifestyle to the fact that she can now conceive and carry a child for nine months, that she has the physical capability to suckle and nurture that child for a further nine months or more, and that she, and not the male, has this physical ability.

These physical and biological realities can be modified by the availability of tampons, contraceptives and bottle-feeding. However, the woman, unless she is anorexic, must learn to adjust to these rhythms which can affect her mood, her cognition, her sense of her own physical well-being, and her total life style.

Tyson and Tyson (1990) write:

> A woman's eventual ability to find a satisfying and narcissistically valued femininity and to experience sexual pleasure is largely influenced by her response to the developmental tasks heralded by menarche. (See also Ritvo, 1976; Kestenberg, 1961.)

A woman's mood and ability to make decisions can be affected at different points on the menstrual cycle. There may be a boost to her general sense of well-being immediately prior to ovulation, and a possible increase in emotionality premenstrually.

With regard to spatial ability, manual dexterity, articulation and verbal fluency, Hampson (1990) writes:

> Many people, particularly women, may not be happy to hear that science has found that all of these abilities vary in women according to the point in their menstrual cycle.

Lips challenges these findings and thinks there have been many assumptions that these are 'women's problems'.

> Much more research on both women and men is needed before the myths about 'raging hormones', pregnancy, postpartum depression, and menopause can be replaced with facts. (Lips, 1997)

When a woman becomes pregnant she enters a nine-month phase which has its own rhythms and demands upon her body. Unless she has an abortion or an early miscarriage, she must learn to accept the changing demands upon her body, her emotional and physical well-being, her intellectual self and her self-esteem. These physical and biological demands upon her have no parallel for a man.

Psychoanalytical theory explores male 'envy of the womb' in response to criticism of the concept of 'penis envy', again indicating a fascination with female/male differences.

6.3.3.3. Anorexia and the vulnerable female

There is no consensus about the causation of anorexia. It often occurs at the onset of puberty when all of the physical and biological changes are occurring. An explanation for the emergence of this illness as a modern Western phenomenon may be that the girl is in conflict with herself about her femaleness, and that the girl child is reluctant to accept the heavy responsibilities of allowing her body to develop its adult potential.

An interesting consequence of extreme and prolonged loss of weight for the anorexic girl is the delaying of the menstrual cycle and the ability to conceive a child. In some cases not only is puberty delayed but an early onset of the menopause occurs and the menstrual cycle, the possibility of conception, pregnancy and childbirth are bypassed (Crisp, 1990; Dare et al., 1990; Dare, 1997).

6.3.4. Pregnancy and female dependency needs

(See 3.6; Examples 3d, Yvonne and Roger; 3e, Peter and Paula.)
Pregnancy is a 'critical period'. Ainsworth (1991) explores women's vulnerability and attachment needs at this time. She wonders whether women may be genetically more predisposed towards becoming attached and relying more on attachment figures than do males. She thinks a predisposition may be triggered during pregnancy, childbirth and the early child rearing period. Ainsworth suggests these are times of greater vulnerability for the female, when a need to rely on another person would be genetically useful.

> It is fairly certain that a genetic bias for females to be more attachment-oriented than males is not evident in infancy. Indeed this makes sense biologically, for in infancy females and males are equally in need of nurturance and protection. (Ainsworth, 1991)

Whilst cautioning that more research is needed into 'normative changes that take place throughout the life cycle', she thinks that pregnancy and childbirth may encourage a shift in the woman, making her more vulnerable and therefore seeking out attachment figures to protect her and her infants during this vulnerable period.

> The shift with clear biological underpinnings which takes place in the case of women in the course of pregnancy, childbirth, and the period during which infants and young children are being reared.

Ainsworth concludes:

> In this we must be alert to the fact that key changes in the nature of attachment may be occasioned by hormonal, neurophysiological, and cognitive changes and not merely by socio-economic experience.

This particular aspect of femaleness deserves further detailed research. Many women are surprised at the changes that occur in their attitude to themselves and their careers as they experience pregnancy, breastfeeding and nurturing the baby. Women who have been trained to develop their academic and management skills for the active world of work can find it extremely disturbing to feel needy or emotionally labile, at this time. Some women are prone to depression during or after pregnancy and it would be helpful to understand in more detail the impact of pregnancy and breastfeeding on the woman's sense of self (Kestenberg, 1956, 1976). Where this occurs for the couple the man may not understand the changes in his partner and may find it difficult to support her.

The woman yet again finds she must adjust to what her body and hormones are telling her. She may feel torn between the intellectual and creative part of her which finds satisfaction in work and involvement outside the home, and the nurturing and dependent part of her which may be triggered by pregnancy, childbirth and breastfeeding. This struggle does not seem to have a parallel in the development of the male.

6.3.4.1. *The female at risk during pregnancy*

Pregnancy carries with it not only emotional and physical changes to which the woman must adjust, but also a degree of risk.

> The World Health Organisation (WHO) has estimated that about half a million women a year die, because of complications during pregnancy or childbirth. Ninety-nine percent of these deaths occur in the developing world. (Pradhan et al., 1995)

Pradhan thinks that poverty and ignorance are the major factors that lead to malnourished girls getting pregnant, 50% of whom are anaemic.

> Anaemia contributes to many maternal deaths. Anaemic women, besides being of poor operative risk, are also more vulnerable to infections, which in turn may lead to pre-term labour, low birth weight, ante-partum and post-partum haemorrhage. They are even unable to withstand the blood loss of a normal delivery, while a normal woman can tolerate blood loss up to about one litre.

Here we see a complicated interaction between the biological and physical aspect of being female and the social and cultural aspects of poverty and ignorance which add to the risk factors for the female when pregnant.

In the developed world, which accounts for only 1per cent of maternal deaths due to complications of pregnancy or childbirth, the five main causes of maternal deaths are unsafe abortions, hypertensive disease of pregnancy, haemorrhage, obstructed labour and infection.

Unsafe abortions account for 13 per cent of these deaths. Additionally, unsafe abortions increase the risks of complications such as infection, haemorrhage, internal injuries and long-term complications such as infertility (Pradhan et al., 1995).

Add to this heavy task that of breastfeeding the infant, one begins to define a fundamental differences between the male and the female. The woman's body has been designed in such a way that she is the container for the fertilisation and gestation of the human infant for nine months, and is given the ability to suckle the infant for several months, or years if necessary – a 'critical period' in the life of the baby.

The health of the mother is important for the health of the baby in her womb. Smoking, drinking, and the use of some drugs can detrimentally affect the health of the baby, as well as her own health. Should she have German measles during a critical period early on in the pregnancy, the baby may be severely defective at birth. Should she have contracted AIDS there is a 30 per cent chance that this will be passed on to her baby.

For the woman who becomes pregnant and wishes to give the baby a reasonable chance of survival, it is her body and her physical condition which is of supreme importance to the health of the unborn child. Better social, economic and political conditions may ameliorate the burden upon the woman, but they cannot take it away. An awareness of the nature of the burden may be one reason why about one fifth of Western women are choosing not to have children.

6.3.5. Breastfeeding and femaleness

As women seek greater equality with men, this aspect of physical and biological inheritance is often given up. By not using the ability to breastfeed her infant, the woman can demonstrate a greater physical similarity with the man.

Assuming that a woman breastfeeds her baby, another complex biological and physical cycle takes place. As the baby sucks on the mother's nipple, the act of sucking encourages the milk to form in the breast. At the same time the woman feels contractions as the womb begins to shrink. An interactive relationship develops between the offering of the nipple to the baby and the sucking of the baby. The baby's sucking helps the mother get back into shape, and/or begins to prepare the mother's body for its next pregnancy.

This interactive relationship defines the mother/child relationship as uniquely different from the father/child relationship. Once breastfeeding is established, if the mother is preoccupied with other things when her baby cries she may experience her breasts filling with milk. Intellectually or practically she may prefer to complete her writing or her telephone call, but her body is responding to the baby's cry for nurturing. Many women find this a reassuring aspect of mothering whilst others resent the 'hold' the baby has over their bodily rhythms.

Breastfeeding is usually advantageous for the baby but a demand on the mother to be available even though there are other demands may make this difficult. Breastfeeding provides the baby with some immunity from illnesses which otherwise could have serious consequences for the baby. Immunity to measles, mumps, chickenpox and German measles for several months may be passed on to the baby through breast milk. For the severely premature baby, breast milk may be the only food tolerated that may be protective for the baby.

These can be life or death needs. Observing photographs of starving women holding starving children to empty breasts demonstrate graphically these pressures. It is possible that if a woman gives up her right to breastfeed she may be sacrificing the development and fine-tuning of her more intuitive skills as well as setting down a demanding task.

6.3.6. Mother/daughter likeness

The growing girl may initially have a gender advantage. She is physically 'like her mother'. One can hypothesise a close physical understanding between the mother and daughter which is easily transmitted non-verbally (Chodorow, 1978).

For the mother/daughter, there may be little reason to speak about the physical self as the mother and daughter are physically/biologically a replication and reflection of each other. This physical twinning or sameness may explain an intensity of the bonding, mirroring, dependency and difficulty in separation that girls are said to experience between themselves and the mother (Klein, 1932a, 1932b, 1952; Deutsch, 1946; Bernstein, 1979, 1989, 1990).

Because of the close physical/biological matching of mother/daughter, girls and women may gain more practice in using the senses that make up non-verbal communication. Such early experiences may explain why girls seem to have a greater sensitivity to non-verbal cues than do many men (see 6.4).

Several authors suggest the mother passes on to the girl her own acquired attitudes of subservience, and her sense that a woman's destiny is to become a carer of others, modelling or conditioning the woman to be less powerful and submissive in a home-based caring role (Chodorow, 1978; Rowbotham, 1983; Eichenbaum and Orbach, 1983, 1990). Women have been dominated by the needs of a male-oriented society and for many, social, political and economic reasons have encouraged passivity and acceptance in women, especially their daughters.

As a therapist, one experiences female clients who have learned from their mother a sense of being of little value. Many potentially suicidal clients can speak with feeling of having been rejected by mother (and father) and hence develop a deep inner sense of hopelessness and worthlessness.

Both mothers and fathers have encouraged submission in their daughters. Foot binding and genital mutilation are extreme examples of cultural/religious practices used by society, practised by mothers and women, and supported by fathers. Such practices bring pain, physical and sexual restrictions, as well as illness and infections, and mar the lives of women (Watson, 1995).

Women have played their part in protecting men, rather than their daughters, from the effects of rape or sexual abuse. Women are not excluded from being the abuser of their children (Welldon, 1992).

Another factor may also be involved. The girl baby 'knows' that she, like her mother, and her mother's, mother's, mother's, mother ... throughout the lifetime of the species has had the physical potential to bear a totally dependent offspring, to be the container and nurturer for nine months of the next generation.

In a physical and biological sense, the child whom she bears lives within her body and is nurtured from her blood supply. To the extent that she is fit and healthy, the baby is likely to be fit and healthy. If she smokes, her baby may be light for dates; if she drinks alcohol or takes drugs these may affect the health of the baby. If she is anaemic the baby will continue taking the iron out of her body at the expense of her own health. If she contracts German measles, or carries the AIDS virus, the impact upon the child can be very serious.

If she sings to the baby she may encourage it to be more musical or more intelligent. If she keeps herself physically and mentally fit during and after childbirth she may help her child to be physically and mentally fit.

These fundamental physical/biological links cannot be ignored in any attempt to understand the nature of femaleness. It would be surprising if the girl child does not have inner knowledge of her capacity to conceive, carry and be the seedbed for the future generation of human animals. Given this knowledge, it is not surprising that she begins to exercise and develop this ability when she plays as a child. Play is often understood as a preparation for adult life, in which the child is creative while exploring his/her potential (Winnicott, 1971).

6.3.7. Providing an egalitarian environment

Feminists and educationists, anxious to provide an egalitarian environment, have discouraged the practice of giving girls dolls and boys tractors to play with. The assumption has been that the girl child is conditioned to be forever a 'mother' and the boy a 'tractor driver'.

Research tends to show that girls choose to 'play with dolls' as if they are following some inner knowledge (Berenbaum and Hines, 1992), rather as the salmon 'knows' its way to the river where it was spawned, or the swift returns yearly to its nest in the eaves.

The social and intellectual development of the girl and boy depends to a large extent upon the emotional security of the child and the provision of the appropriate educational building blocks (Piaget, 1955; Rutter, 1981; Bowlby, 1969; Ainsworth, 1991). Girls are proving themselves in academic and practical areas once undreamed of. This push towards developing the potential of the girl is exciting.

In the process, it is hoped that her different strengths are not ignored. These strengths may be her non-verbal skill, her ability to understand nuances of interpersonal relationships, the ability to consider alternative options simultaneously, to think and act within a network of relationships, to use her verbal skills to develop interpersonal relationships, her awareness of the impact of decisions upon the lives and feelings of others. These female skills are often neglected or seen as inadequacies within the work world.

At present the emphasis is upon equality of treatment and opportunity. Perhaps in the future specific female and male skills can also be valued and developed.

6.4. Female/male moral, communication and cognitive differences.

(See 2.4, 2.6)

Gilligan (1982, 1987) and Tannen (1990) researched how boys and girls make moral choices, and the ways in which adults communicate. Their findings emphasise current significant differences between women and men.

Maccoby and Jacklin (1975), both feminist authors, were initially sceptical of biological differences. Having reviewed the available research they found support for some claims. These are that girls may have greater verbal ability than boys, which becomes more evident after 11 years, and that boys tend to be superior in visual/spatial tasks. At a similar age, boys' mathematical skills tend to grow faster than girls' and in particular boys tend to be more aggressive than girls from an early age.

Halpern's (1992) exhaustive study of differences in cognitive abilities found that conflicting research methodologies make it difficult to draw clear conclusions. At the same time she writes:

> There are real, and in some cases sizable, sex differences with respect to some cognitive abilities. Socialisation practices are undoubtedly important, but there is good evidence that biological sex differences play a role in establishing and maintaining cognitive sex differences. A conclusion that I was not prepared to make when I began reviewing the relevant literature.

Regarding verbal abilities she writes:

> Most readers want a simple answer. Unfortunately simple answers are not possible. The best conclusion that we can make to date is that many types of verbal abilities show no sex differences, but there are some consistent sex differences. Females outperform males in fluent speech production, anagrams, and general mixed tests of verbal ability; males outperform females on solving analogies, with a small advantage on the verbal portion of the SATs (Scholastic Aptitude Test) (see 2J, Edward and Emily 2 K, Ken and Kathleen).

An important aspect of maleness is his focus on problem-solving skill. As with many skills, it is difficult to determine from where the skills originate. Pool (1994) thinks that women and men may approach problem-solving from very different routes. He suggests that men may approach problems from a mathematical perspective and women from a verbal perspective. Halpern (1992) doubts a significant difference between female/male mathematical skills and wonders whether the different ways in which women and men use their mathematical skills is due to confidence rather than gender differences. Tannen (1990) found that men often turn to their problem-solving skills when faced with situations which are emotionally arousing for the woman, and that the woman may turn to her verbal skills. Pool (1994) seems to agree with Tannen (1990):

> In trying to solve problems for example, females may take a more verbal approach, trying to reason them out with words, whereas males may quickly resort to numbers. Since a numerical approach is usually more efficient for solving problems, this could explain the male advantage in tests of this type.

Johnson and Jacob (1997) examined the communication styles of 50 couples with a depressed husband and 41 couples with a depressed wife, and 50 non-depressed control couples. An interesting finding, relevant to the different way women and men approach problem-solving, is that 'wives are less likely to withdraw from problem-solving interactions than are the husbands' (Christensen and Heavy, 1990; Heavy et al., 1993).

Does this mean that the woman continues to rely upon her verbal skills to solve a relationship difficulty when the man has given up or withdrawn from any attempt to solve the problem (See 2.3.1, 2.3.2)?

There is no overall consensus regarding female/male differences and their origins within the genetic and physical makeup of each gender. Wallace (1991) predicted accurately that some cognitive differences would disappear as educational opportunities become available to girls.

> Educationally in the UK in the 80's there is a steady trend towards girls gaining more qualifications at 16 (O level and CSE) than boys and 'catching up' with them at 18 with A levels. It is conceivable that there will be as many girls as boys entering at all levels of the education system.

Having reviewed recent research findings, Pool (1994) feels able to say the following:

> The idea of the brain as a 'neural sexual mosaic' fits perfectly with what we know about people. Women and men are blends of masculine and feminine traits, a little of this, a lot of that. As a group, women have better verbal skills and better dexterity, are more nurturing and more interested in people, and look for solutions to problems that take everyone's interests into account. As a group, men have better spatial ability, are more aggressive, competitive and prone to violence, are interested in objects and facts more than people and tend to think in solutions more in terms of right and wrong. But to see women and men as members of these two mutually exclusive groups is to create an artificial distinction, one that is true on average but not necessarily true for any given man or woman.

In spite of the healthy debate to understand female/male relationships, it is wise to keep in mind that where gender differences occur they can be a source of relationship tension, distress or excitement.

6.5. Female sexuality

(See 2.5.2)

Sexuality is a complex aspect of the female. The female body can develop its adult shape and potential (unless affected by illness, hormonal deficiency, infertility or anorexia, see 6.3.3.3), and the women can become pregnant, give birth and breastfeed her infants without enjoying her own sexuality. The woman's pleasure and confidence in her own sexuality is interwoven and interactive with the totality of her life experiences. Because of this, some women do not learn to enjoy their own sexuality for many years.

Much has been written about the modern Western woman's search for sexual fulfilment. She is encouraged to free herself from the myths and ignorance of the past regarding female sexuality (Kitzinger, 1985; Walsh, 1987; Dickson, 1989; Greer, 1991; Swift, 1993). Her sexuality can remain a mysterious and unseen aspect of herself for many years.

Changing attitudes to virginity and the availability of contraception bring with them a greater freedom to explore sexuality. The woman's virginity is no longer protected until marriage within Western societies, although virginity is still highly prized in some cultural traditions and the cruel practice of genital mutilation is considered necessary to ensure the woman's virginity and consequent marriageability.

In Britain boys and girls are becoming sexually active at younger ages.

> The median age of first intercourse for the youngest birth cohort, those aged 16–24 and born between 1966 and 1975 was 17. (Wellings et al., 1994)

This was four years younger than those born four decades earlier. Also:

> A sizeable proportion of young people are now sexually active before the age of 16. 18.7% of women aged 16–19 had experienced sexual intercourse before the age of 16 compared with fewer than 1% of those aged 55–59. (Wellings et al., 1994)

Since the 1980s the number of children born outside of marriage has increased dramatically and represented three in ten of all births in 1991. The proportion of babies born outside marriage to teenage mothers has actually decreased over the period 1971 to 1990 from 39 per cent to 28 per cent (Wellings et al., 1994). This latter figure may result from easier availability of abortion since the Abortion Law Reform Act of April 1968, which came into force in 1969.

In spite of greater knowledge and freedom surrounding female sexuality, her sexuality remains complex and mysterious. Complex because the female's pleasure in her own sexuality is interactive with how her partner treats her, her feelings about herself and what is happening to her and those she cares for. It is also interactive with the rhythms of her body, whether she is having a period, is pregnant, has had an abortion, is nursing a baby, or has children or dependants for whom she is responsible.

Female sexuality is mysterious, because the experience of penetrative sex and orgasm is within her body. She cannot see her orgasm, she can only feel it within her. Until recently little was known about the mechanisms of the female orgasm, unlike the male erection and orgasm which can be witnessed by both partners during masturbation.

The woman can experience sexual intercourse without much pleasure, whilst for the man if he is able to ejaculate he usually experiences the pleasure of ejaculation and orgasm. The woman's arousal pattern, in addition to what feelings and worries are preoccupying her, is often slower than the man's and is often dependent upon appropriate bodily contact, touch and stimulation. She may need to be stroked and touched in a mounting sequence, beginning with general body massage, through touching of her breasts and nipples to eventual touching of the clitoris, or the clitoral area.

This preparatory touching stimulates the female sexual arousal and responsiveness including lubricating the vaginal canal. Unless she is lubricated the woman may not feel ready for penetrative sex, which may be painful. For the male, once he is erect, the appropriate next step may be penetration. This potential time lag between the readiness of the female and male for penetration can be a cause of misery for couples.

For the male, thrusting the penis within the vagina is usually sufficient to stimulate orgasm and ejaculation. The experience of the movement of the penis within the vagina, though satisfying, may not lead to orgasm for the female. Many couples learn that stimulating the clitoris adds to the enjoyment of intercourse for the woman. Not all women experience orgasm during penetrative sex, some may only experience an orgasm during masturbation or mutual masturbation with a partner.

A woman's sexuality is intertwined with the totality of her life experience. Consequently she can have difficulties in concentrating upon her own sexual pleasures if she is upset, resentful or anxious. (See Examples 2a, Alan and Amy; 2h, Janice and Roy; 3c, Douglas and Diane; 3d, Yvonne and Roger; 3e, Peter and Paula.)

Elizabeth Stanley (1981) developed the 'ladder concept' to help couples to satisfy each other sexually. During intercourse each partner assesses their own arousal on a scale 0–6. Using the 'ground level' as 0, 'feeling no interest or pleasure in physical contact'; at rung 1 the feeling state is 'physical and emotional pleasure while cuddling without genital sensation'; as each partner rises through the ladder so the feelings become more aroused until rung 6 is described as 'orgasm occurring'. Each partner can ask which rung the other has reached. This is a crude but effective tool which acknowledges that the woman and man may become aroused at different rates.

> The ladder is also useful because it provides the couple with a common language which facilitates clear communication. (Stanley, 1981)

It also encourages the couple to take pleasure in each other at each rung of the ladder so that sexual enjoyment can be satisfying even where both partners do not achieve an orgasm.

The woman is not always slower to become aroused. There are many women who respond to or initiate sex because of their easy and speedy arousal pattern. Whenever a disparity occurs in their arousal the ladder concept can help both partners to learn about each other's pace and rhythms.

A woman's sexuality can be severely affected by difficulties experienced in giving birth. Since the birth canal is also the vaginal opening, any tearing, stretching, stitching or infections can temporarily, or for a prolonged period, affect the woman's pleasure in sexual intercourse. Where the birth was painful this can make the woman apprehensive about sexual contact or penetrative intercourse.

Too often, within clinical experience, sexual intercourse is resumed before the woman has adequately healed or has regained confidence in her ability to relax and enjoy her own sexuality. She may be reluctant to speak about her needs and find it difficult to understand the extent of any scarring, because it is internal and unseen. The man, in his eagerness to show his affection by resuming penetrative sex, can seem insensitive to her needs. These gender differences are ordinary and obvious, yet much relationship discord originates from such simple sources.

Another aspect of femaleness that is insufficiently recognised, is the multiple demands placed upon her body, making it difficult for her to be fully present during sexual intercourse. For example, with the woman who is breastfeeding, her breasts are available to the baby at feeding times, and to her husband sensually during foreplay. If she is pregnant her womb is occupied by a growing baby, at the same time as her partner may wish to have penetrative sex, or she may be experiencing her period at the same time as her partner hopes for sexual intercourse. In these different ways the woman's body is being asked to respond to demands which may be in tension with each other.

The impact on female sexuality of mastectomy and hysterectomy is discussed in Chapter 4. It is sufficient here to draw attention to the fact that cancers of the breast, uterus, womb, Fallopian tubes or vagina are by their very nature gender-specific cancers. The age and stage of the woman's life cycle when these occur will affect her response to the illness and to the possibility of surgery. For a time her confidence in her femininity and sexuality may be deeply affected.

Bancroft's research (1990) into females presenting at sexual dysfunction clinics showed that 35 per cent of females presented with low sexual interest and 12 per cent with lack of enjoyment. Dyspareunia (painful intercourse) and vaginismus (inability to accept penetration) were 11 per cent and 13 per cent respectively. The complexity of the interaction between a woman's emotional and relationship needs should be understood when assisting her in overcoming sexual difficulties. The invisible intimacy screen highlights some of these interactions (see 2.2.1).

6.6. Female aggression

(See 2.7; Examples 2m, Martha and Matt; 2n, John and Jenny.)

It is customary to think of the male as more aggressive and the female as more nurturing. Statistics of criminal offences tend to bear this out. Roughly 85 per cent of all homicides in the United States are committed by men and 15 per cent are committed by women (Wilson, 1993).

> In an analysis of data from the Uniform Crime Reports, Murphy and Meyer (1991) found that twice as many husbands killed their wives as wives killed their husbands.

Whilst men are most often the perpetrators and the victims of homicide in the United States (Stout and Brown, 1995), women are most often the victims of partner homicide. Browne (1987) reported that of the 2,000 victims of partner homicide studied in 1984, two-thirds were women.

There are currently highly publicised examples of female physical aggression, and some indication that women may be learning or allowing themselves to be more aggressive and assertive in their work or family life.

The question of female aggression becomes cloudy for two main reasons. Firstly, a woman's aggression may be linked to her monthly cycle, in particular to premenstrual tension.

> Whilst pre-menstrual syndrome (PMS) is still a controversial topic, at least two cases have been established in law in which the plea of PMS has successfully reduced murder charges to manslaughter. (Ridley, 1993)

(See also Sommer, 1983; Dalton, 1987; Colby and Damon, 1987.)

Secondly, her aggression may be linked to provocation and fear, and is felt to be defensive. Stout and Brown (1995) compared 23 men and 18 women who were incarcerated for manslaughter, murder or capital murder. Responding to questions related to physical abuse by their male partner, 16 of the 18 women reported physical abuse by their partner. Nine of these women stated that they had been injured by the physical abuse and all of these had sought medical attention for their injuries.

> Some of the injuries requiring medical attention were concussion, broken ribs, cuts from knives, a split ear, black eyes, a fractured skull, a broken hand, a miscarriage from having been pushed down stairs while pregnant, stitches to the face and hands, cigarette burns, and a fractured back. Twelve of the 23 men reported that their partners had battered them, but none had been injured by their partners. (Stout and Brown, 1995)

This study considers the level of fear at the time of the aggression. Of the 22 respondents who reported 'absolutely no fear', 18 were men and four were women. Of the 19 who reported experiencing fear, 14 were women and five were men.

This research was described as 'beginning data to promote discussion of and scholarly attention to legal and social differences between women and men who kill intimate partners'. It supports earlier findings that suggest women kill in self-defence, defending themselves against:

> physical abuse that increases in frequency and severity over time (Dobash and Dobash 1979, Pagelow 1981), continues after efforts to involve the police, and escalates at times of separation (Lindsey 1978, Browne, 1987; Martin 1976; Walker 1984). (Saunders, 1988)

Research into female and male aggression is in its infancy and attention needs to be paid to the issue of self-defence on the part of the woman.

A complex aspect of female/male aggression is whether aggression can be defined only as physical abuse. Green (1998) suggests that 'women may be no less aggressive than men in non-physical ways, such as verbal aggression'. He goes on to suggest that women and men may express a differential preference for verbal and physical aggression respectively (Shupe et al., 1987).

Within the context of therapy one has met many women who use their verbal agility to great effect and it would be useful to have more research data on verbal aggression (see 2.7.1).

> Evidence from a variety of sources supports the finding that, on the average females have better verbal abilities than males. (Halpern, 1992)

Although there is evidence that women have more verbal fluency – the ability to come up with words or sentences quickly – this does not mean that women use their verbal fluency aggressively.

Halpern (1992) comments that:

> despite the finding that females score higher on most tests of verbal ability, the overwhelming majority of critically acclaimed writers are male. A fact which demonstrates just how complicated it is to compare female and male abilities in any realistic way.

Halpern (1992) and Pool (1994) reviewed research into female and male verbal abilities and came to similar conclusions that boys figure more prominently at the lower end of verbal abilities. Stuttering is overwhelmingly a male problem with three to four times more male stutterers than female. Dyslexia is found in mild forms five times more frequently in males than in females, and in more severe forms, ten times more frequently than in females.

Pool (1994), discussing Hines' (1990) research, writes:

> It is not that men have smaller vocabularies – many studies have shown that females and males know the same number of words – but rather that men were somehow less efficient in accessing their vocabulary.

Knowledge of the impact of high levels of expressed emotion and critical comment may be relevant to the issue of female aggression. Research carried out at the London University Institute of Psychiatry identified high levels of critical comment as predictive of relapse in schizophrenia. When identifying critical comment, attention is paid to the quality of words used, their repetitive and critical nature and voice tone, which may be out of the awareness of the critical person (Leff and Vaughn, 1985).

The majority of those using high levels of critical comment in these studies were women, usually mothers or wives. Where the criticism can be modified to a lower level of expressed emotion, the patient is less likely to relapse and experience another schizophrenic episode.

In thinking about female aggression, the question arises whether women may sometimes use their verbal dexterity and critical skills as unacknowledged aggression. This is an under-researched area but clinical practice suggests that some women are unaware of the power of their verbal skills. Verbal aggression can be intensely hurtful if difficult to identify, while physical aggression is more easily noticed as it can result in bruising or broken bones. A factor well described by Welldon (1992) is an unwillingness within society to acknowledge that women and mothers can be attacking and non-caring in their relationships, both physically and verbally.

6.7. The menopause and its impact upon femaleness

(See also Examples 4a, 4c; 6.3.3.3)

A further stage in a woman's physical development is the menopause. While the menstrual cycle is sometimes called 'the curse' the ending of the menstrual cycle is often called 'the change'.

During the menopause a significant change occurs within the woman's body which impacts upon her attitude to herself, her hopes and her dreams.

> Women, by comparison, have a relatively abrupt cessation of fertility around the menopause ... This is however a gradual process. The most discrete marker is the last menstrual bleed (literally the menopause) ... This last menstruation is preceded by a gradual slowing down of ovarian responsiveness over a variable number of years, a process which continues for a time after the last menses, before the woman reaches a stable post-menopausal state. (Bancroft, 1990)

Menopause is a controversial aspect of the woman's development, but what is clear is that the natural potential for conceiving and carrying a baby within her womb ends. Whatever her circumstances or attitude to her own physical and biological inheritance, she now faces another bodily change that once more requires a readjustment. This critical period of a woman's life contains within it the need to accept the inevitability of the ageing process.

The menopause signals a huge change in the woman's life, the ending of her fertile cycle which, up to this moment, has been a central aspect of her physical self. The menopause confronts the female with her own ageing, the loss of her youthfulness and the onset of the slowing down of her total abilities. In making an adjustment to the menopause the woman is of necessity making an adjustment to her own mortality.

This is another obvious physical difference between the female and male. While the male experiences a generalised ageing process, the female has a specific physical experience which marks her ageing and the movement into a new life stage.

For some women, the menopause brings few physical symptoms and is experienced as a relief from the burden of pregnancy and the fear of conception. For others, hot flushes, nightly hot sweats, dizziness and a general feeling of nausea and faintness can be very distressing. The permutations of responses to the menopause may lie in the woman's life situation; if she has had no children she may now experience a deep sense of loss that the 'potential' to have children has gone. If getting pregnant was always a recurrent fear making sexual intercourse full of anxiety, the menopause may be liberating, freeing the woman to enjoy her own and her partner's sexuality. She may become more spontaneous and adventurous in her sexual advances.

At the same time physical changes do occur; the vaginal wall thins with a reduction in vaginal lubrication, causing pain on penetration unless a lubricant is used. There may be a slowing of the desire and arousal phases and the orgasm may be experienced as less intense. These are a natural consequence of the life stage. Once through the menopause, her body stabilises around a more consistent base. The woman's body no longer responds to the rhythms of periods, pregnancy or breastfeeding and she is once again like the pre-pubescent girl.

Accompanying the menopause may be an urge to review life and its achievements. Some women reconnect with aspects of themselves lost during the middle years of childbearing and rearing. She may remember earlier aspirations and resources which, if realised in some measure, may be satisfactory. Should her earlier aspirations and her present situation have little in common, she may be disillusioned and resentful.

Many women find they are healthy and active beyond the menopause, and instead of settling down to grandparenting and gentle old age, which may previously have been expected, take the opportunity to catch up with opportunities unavailable during child-rearing days. After the menopause women are physically more like men without the demands and rhythms of the monthly cycle and may wish to explore this new self.

> The positive side of aging is coming to terms with new horizons and a different body. Adjustment is not the same as restriction. (Dickson, 1989)

For other women, the menopause is accompanied by painful physical and psychological experiences, which make it difficult to see the menopause as an entry-point into a new era of challenge and opportunity.

Men are not pressurised by the rhythmic changes within their body in the way that women are. By the very nature of her development, a woman must learn to adjust firstly to the onset of the menstrual cycle; then if she becomes pregnant, to the nine months of pregnancy perhaps followed by five or more months of the breastfeeding cycle; and finally as she reaches her 40s or 50s, to the ending of the menstrual cycle and of her fertility. All of these bodily changes have accompanying physical and emotional responses over which the woman may have little or no control. Initially, she may not understand the changes that are developing within her. She has little choice except to learn to adapt to and understand her feelings, and over time to learn to live with them.

6.8. Critical periods and male vulnerability

In contrast to the woman, a man's masculinity once established is not interrupted by the rhythms of other physical and biological changes, such as the menstrual cycle, pregnancy or breastfeeding; nor is his body required to cope with other demands, such as an occupied womb or breasts suckling an infant.

The physical development of the male is more linear than the that of the female. Once established, the male's gender orientation tends to focus on his penis and how it performs, a focus reinforced by social pressures and sexual myths. While the woman has a complex series of physical reminders of her femaleness, for the man the cycle of production of semen, the need to ejaculate through either masturbation, wet dreams or penetrative sex, is the most significant physical reminder of his maleness.

The male has a paradoxical and contradictory inheritance, often being the stronger physically, more prone to aggressive behaviour and to seeking sexual outlets, yet at the same time his sense of confidence in his sexual prowess is easily undermined. Physical strength and aggression may cover an anxiety and vulnerability about his physical sexuality and his maleness.

The in utero environment, early childhood experiences, puberty, pregnancy, childbirth and breastfeeding, sexual experiences, aggression and the ageing process offer situations in which his concept of himself as a confident male are formed or are threatened.

6.8.1. The in utero environment: impact on gender development

It is necessary to begin with the development of the child before birth in utero. Ethical, moral and practical dilemmas place constraints upon observation of, or experimentation on, the baby in the womb and conclusions are therefore tentative. Many hypotheses are based upon observations of animals (rats, birds or monkeys) and parallels drawn regarding the human animal. Their accuracy cannot be tested, leading to a realistic hesitancy to accept such findings as valid.

The material of Money (1986), Moir and Jessel (1991) and Pool (1994), is particularly interesting for the diligence with which they search for 'the biological roots of sex differences' and their overlapping findings. Central to the debate is the physical development of maleness and femaleness within the womb. Moir and Jessel (1991) write:

> women and men are different but complementary ... The hormones, as we shall see, determine the distinct male or female organisation of the brain as it develops in the womb. We share the same sexual identity for only the first few weeks after conception. Thereafter, in the womb, the very structure and pattern of the brain begins to take a specifically male or female form ...

> During the eighth week the foetus chooses between two paths: masculine or feminine. If the foetus is genetically male – if it has a Y chromosome – then a 'master switch' on the Y chromosome clicks on at the same time .... The flipping of this switch is the key step. The testis-determining factor signals the embryonic gonads to form into testes, which then begin to produce male hormones, and the hormones take it from there.

Focusing on the same issue of masculinisation or feminisation of the brain, Pool (1994) concludes:

> The general pattern is clear. Sex hormones influence the developing brain, shaping various mental and psychological traits as well as the physical body. That influence may be modified by events later in life, but later echoes of it can still be heard.

Money (1986) takes the discussion furthest by suggesting that the stability of the sexual orientation of the male may depend upon the in utero environment.

> From conception onwards, there is evidence of the greater vulnerability of the male as compared with the female.

Similarly,

> The risk of being male may well be a spin-off of the 'Adam principle' namely that the embryo will develop as Eve, unless something extra is added. For the reproductive organs, the additive is chiefly testosterone, which is also the hormone important to the prenatal masculinisation of the sexual brain.

Money (1986), Moir and Jessel (1991) and Pool (1994) share a common view best summarised by Moir and Jessel (1991):

> The way our brains are made affects how we think, learn, see, smell, feel, communicate, love, make love, fight, succeed, or fail.

They go on to define female intuition as the sum of women's greater sensitivity to touch, smell, sound sight, etc.

> Women are simply better equipped to notice things to which men are comparatively blind and deaf. Women are better at picking up social cues, picking up important nuances of meaning from tones of voice or intensity of expression.

These views are not shared by all researchers (see Chapter 5 and 6.4).

6.8.2. Early experiences in the search for intimacy (male)

The boy child's first relationship is with a female. Even if his natural mother does not rear him, he is nurtured for nine months within her womb. His mother is likely to breastfeed or bottle-feed him, change and bathe him. Psychoanalytic theory sees this early relationship as central to his development, with resolution of the oedipal conflict being the key to forming relationships with women later in his development.

Regardless through which theoretical perspective one views female/male development, this early symbiotic relationship is significant as it is a man's sole physical experience of being totally cared for within another's body. Additionally, this bodily and intimate relationship is lodged in the pre-verbal, pre-memory period of development.

For the rest of his life he knows only the separate and independent existence of maleness. He cannot know the pleasure and pain of carrying within his body another human who is totally dependent upon his physical self. He can only observe, from a distance, the woman who carries his child. He cannot always be sure that the child she bears is his.

Separateness, independence, autonomy – these are states of being that are familiar to him. Society also seems to feel obliged to condition the boy towards being tough, and in control of his feelings. A life task for the male may be to impregnate the woman and to protect her if she bears his child; but his experience is as an observer and support to the woman whose body nurtures his child.

At the same time his separateness may already provide him with a greater ability than the woman to feel less intensely, to observe from a distance, to be available to provide for and, where necessary, use his aggressive abilities to protect the mother and child.

Stern thinks that a life task may be to move from a position of separateness to a position of connectedness (Stern, 1985) or, as Benjamin (1988) suggests, to develop intersubjectivity. In this regard, apart from his in utero experience, the male begins from a more separate position than the woman (see 5.6, 5.7).

Little emphasis has so far been placed upon the male child's experience of sexual abuse and his sense of confidence in his own sexuality, although many young boys have been sexually abused. Evidence is slowly emerging that the developing male's sense of confidence in his own sexuality, orientation and enjoyment may be impaired by abusive experiences. Whilst sexual abuse is common, it is not treated here as part of the developmental stages that apply to all male children, except to recognise the damaging effect of childhood sexual abuse.

Coates and Wolfe (1995), studying gender identity disorder in boys, consider the possibility of a sensitive period in the development of these boys, which occurs between 18 and 36 months.

> Gender identity disorder of childhood is brought about by complex multiple factors – biological, interpersonal, and intrapsychic – that interact during a vulnerable stage of development in a temperamentally predisposed child.

The 'temperamentally predisposed child' is a boy child who has a sensitive and inhibited temperament.

Regardless of disagreement as to whether a constitutional predisposition, psychodynamic, or familial factors are most significant in the emergence of gender identity disorder, a cross-discipline agreement exists that the period from 18 to 36 months is a vulnerable one in the development of the child (Bancroft, 1990; Bowlby, 1991; Elton, 1982; Rutter, 1980), and that temperamentally predisposed boys may be particularly vulnerable (see also 6.3.2).

6.8.3. Puberty and its contribution to male vulnerability

The onset of puberty for the boy is a critical period during which he achieves the adult male's physique. Bancroft (1990) thinks the length of time it takes for a boy to develop into a fully adult male has a significant impact upon his sense of security.

> In the male it is not until a bone age of approximately 12 years is reached that there is any increase in testosterone production. Thereafter it rises steeply until the age of 15–17 years after which there is a further slight rise to adult levels by the early or mid 20's. (Bancroft, 1990)

Boys vary in the pace of their maturation physically and the physical changes may take several years.

> Beginning with the accelerated growth of the testes and scrotum (9.5–13.5 years). Shortly after this pubic hairs begin to appear. About a year later the penis starts to grow (10.5-14.5 years) accompanied by development of the internal structures, the seminal vesicles and prostate. About a year after the start of penile growth the first ejaculation occurs. The growth spurt in boys starts between 10.5 and 16 years with deceleration of growth starting about 18 months later. The voice starts to break and deepen towards the end of the growth spurt. About one-third of boys show noticeable enlargement of the breasts around the middle of puberty which normally recedes after about a year. The considerable difference in timing and speed of these pubertal changes contributes to the uncertainty about body image that adds to the adolescent's problems. (Bancroft, 1990)

In addition to his physical development, concern is often expressed about the impact of social conditioning and pressures on the boy to become a 'macho-man' physically, to excel in sport or associated activities such as competitive beer drinking, or to have 'laid' as many females as possible – a pressure that has not changed in spite of the threat of HIV and AIDS. Adolescence can be a painfully slow progression towards mature male physical attributes which is experienced as an uncertain and vulnerable time.

6.8.3.1. External and obvious

The male child's physical structure is more external and obvious than the female's and the little boy easily becomes aware that his penis defines his maleness. The ability to gain an erection, to masturbate and ejaculate are all physical attributes which are external and obvious. They can be compared with peers, generating anxiety for the boy who is a late developer, who is shy, or small in stature. Comparisons of sexual prowess or experimentation with masturbation are all part of his development that can cause concern. If he is uninterested in sport or physical strength this can set him apart from other boys and make him feel inadequate as a male. His voice tone and the 'breaking of his voice', the growth of facial hairs are all external and obvious and available for comment from family and peers. Adolescence is one of those critical periods in a boy's (or girl's) life when the interaction between the physical self and social expectations are at their height.

6.8.3.2. The male at risk during puberty

The considerable difference in timing and speed of these pubertal changes contributes to the uncertainty about body image that adds to the adolescent's problems (Bancroft, 1990; Rutter, 1980). Bancroft does not subscribe to Money's hypothesis of male vulnerability, but places emphasis upon the boy's anxiety about his body image and the length of time it may take for his body to take on the adult male attributes.

Issues of gender orientation tend to emerge during early adolescence and it may be that about 1–3.5 per cent of all males are exclusively homosexual (Pietropinto and Simenauer, 1977; Brecher, 1984); for women the number may be half of that. Men also seem to figure more prominently in other forms of sexual 'deviance' or 'dysphoria' such as fetishism, sadomasochism, transvestism and transsexualism, as well as a small number who seek gender re-assignment. Estimates of the incidence of people seeking sex re-assignment range from 1 in 100,000 for males to 1 in 400,000 for females (Pauly, 1974). A more recent study (Ross et al., 1981) estimates a prevalence of 1 in 37,000 in Sweden and 1 in 24,000 in Australia for biological males, and 1 in 103,000 in Sweden and 1 in 150,000 in Australia for biological females.

It is unwise to draw conclusions from these figures, since for religious, moral and social reasons reliable data are not available. However, the preponderance of males to females who are concerned about their gender identity suggests the vulnerability of the male.

This vulnerability, coupled with the elongated maturational span, may increase anxiety about gender. Rutter (1980) draws attention to the different pace of the maturational process during puberty and the anxiety caused to the individual.

> The Fels longitudinal study suggested that the adolescent boys with non-masculine interests during early childhood tended later to be anxious about sexuality and to have less heterosexual activity (Kagan and Moss 1962). The possible reasons for this are not hard to find. Manliness and sexual vigour are highly regarded attributes among adolescent males, and boys who have still not reached puberty by 16 years or so may well begin to doubt their masculinity and become anxious and introspective about their development.

Rutter (1980) thinks that since late maturity is not a handicap in all cultures, the disadvantages are largely due to society's reaction to continuing physical immaturity (Mussen and Bouterline-Young, 1964).

Puberty is not all anxiety. For many young boys puberty is experienced as a time of excitement and growing independence. The development of his physical ability to penetrate and impregnate a female is a marker along his journey to maturity which signals his growing independence from his family of origin. He may have a renewed sense of confidence and purposiveness.

> The days of my late youth were the best times of my life and it was an exciting time, full of eager plans for the future, excessive idealism, and great hope. (Crooks and Stein, 1988)

6.8.4. The male at risk during pregnancy

(See Examples 3c, Douglas and Diane; 3d, Yvonne and Roger; 3e, Peter and Paula.)

Pregnancy is a time during which the man is vulnerable. His vulnerability may be because his sexual partner is preoccupied, or because he is envious of the attention lavished upon the expectant mother. He may no longer feel central to his partner's needs, and taken for granted as the provider of money and sustenance. Her body, which was once available to him for sexual satisfaction, is now changing shape and announcing the pregnancy to the world. This may be a source of pride for the man demonstrating his fertility, or her shape and obvious pregnancy may deter him from feeling sexual towards her. The male is also vulnerable during pregnancy as he cannot be sure that the child carried by his partner is his (unless DNA tests are sought). This anxiety contributed to the insistence, in the past, upon the woman's virginity and fidelity.

During pregnancy he becomes a 'provider object' often taken for granted. He may experience a duality within himself, partly feeling proud of his ability to fertilise a woman, and to provide for her, partly feeling ignored and pushed out. The expectation of being the provider may make it difficult for him to acknowledge his needs for emotional, sensual and sexual support and the woman, who can usually be relied upon to be aware of his needs, is preoccupied.

The man often seeks other sexual outlets at this time (Hunt, 1964), and when questioned about his marital satisfaction may express disappointment that pregnancy has altered the relationship in ways he had not anticipated (Mansfield, 1993).

The man may also have a deep longing for a child but learn that his sperm count is low or he is infertile. This is extremely upsetting, causing grief and, for some, lifelong concern at their 'genetic death' (Ridley, 1994). Fertility difficulties may occur for either or both partners, making them feel deeply vulnerable. Couples who embark upon infertility treatment may undergo years of heart rending treatment. For such couples there may be intense pain in the knowledge of the infertility and an overwhelming desire to become parents (Read, 1997). There is some evidence that women protect men at these times by themselves assuming the responsibility for the infertility (Ridley, 1994)

6.8.5. Breastfeeding and maleness

A significant physical difference between the male and the female is the female's ability to breastfeed her offspring. In many parts of the world, if the woman does not, or cannot, breastfeed, her infant does not survive. Bottle feeding, whilst a good substitute, can have tragic consequences where water is impure or sterilising is difficult. Breastfeeding is also a bonding relationship during which the mother and child make bodily contact and the woman's body responds to the baby's request to be fed. Eye gazing, touch, smell are all engaged in a mother/child developing relationship.

The man cannot ever feel the bodily responses when the baby cries and the breast begins to fill with milk, nor can he experience the intensity of the love/hate relationship the mother may feel when the baby demands to be fed and she would prefer to be left in peace. He cannot experience, at that deeply personal level, the woman's fear that she may not have enough milk.

The man is outside of this relationship. He can nurture the child in other ways, providing the child with a less emotional haven when mother is tired or in need of care herself, but his own body is not available to provide food for the baby. The consequences of this important difference between the two genders are rarely discussed, as if, by avoiding any discussion, the differences can disappear.

His vulnerability and his strength lie in these very areas, that he is not narcissistically drawn into the mother/child intersubjectivity. His task is to support the mother from a more remote and objective position, providing her with relief from the baby and comfort when she is distressed. His greater ability to problem-solve, and to make decisions from a position of separateness and objectivity, adds a dimension to child rearing which the woman may lack. She is too absorbed with the daily task of understanding this non-verbal creature.

Together, the woman and man provide a rich spectrum of resources for the growing child, from the woman's physical ability to breastfeed and deeply intuitive skills for understanding the whimpering of the newborn, to the man's more objective protector and provider functions. All of these are necessary for the nurturing of the human infant, who takes so many years to develop from gestation to maturity.

6.9. Male sexuality

(See also 2.5, 2.5.3; Examples 2i, George and Gillian; 2l, Larry (and Louise); 4b, Catherine and Claude.)

Puberty is a long-drawn-out experience for the male, with full maturity sometimes taking 10–15 years. During puberty the male develops the ability to produce sperm, to penetrate and to impregnate a female and hence to father children.

A key anxiety for a man of almost any age, which a woman never faces, is the ability to gain and maintain an erection sufficient to penetrate and have 'good enough' sexual intercourse. The young man embarking upon his first sexual intercourse is likely to experience loss of control of his ejaculation. As he becomes more confident or has more experience he can develop greater control. Within a competitive or unsupportive relationship, anxiety may overwhelm him, making it difficult to maintain an erection. In such situations premature ejaculation may occur and become problematic. Social, cultural and religious pressures will affect many of the sexual responses of both the female and male.

Rachel Swift (1993) is concerned about female/male equality.

> A lot of different factors combine to give women a bad start in sexual equality. First the ease with which men can have an orgasm means that many women feel themselves less sexually capable, and therefore something of a sexual underling by comparison. It is for the woman that the man waits: it is for the woman that he extends his foreplay, etc. He doesn't need these things for himself. Because women are sexually more sophisticated they take longer to warm up and they require more skilled lovemaking than men.

Whether a woman is sexually more sophisticated than a man is difficult to demonstrate. However, the rate at which a man or a woman reaches orgasm (and ejaculation for the man) varies. In general, men are aroused and reach orgasm and ejaculation quickly, a characteristic that may slow with age and experience.

Some men are slow to become sexually aroused and may have difficulty with either orgasm or ejaculation. Bancroft (1990) suggests that about 5 per cent of men who present at sexual and relationship clinics have such problems, whilst 13 per cent present with premature ejaculation, and about 50 per cent with erectile difficulties, such as inability to get or maintain an erection or retarded ejaculation; all focus on the penis and its functioning (Bancroft, 1990). With homosexual relationships, though penetration may not be part of the relationship, an erect penis is often felt to be essential.

For heterosexual couples, a disparity can occur between the wishes of the woman and the man regarding penetrative sex. Stated simply, 'Men want sex, and women want relationships' (Mansfield and Collard, 1988; Moir and Jessel, 1991).

> One pattern which we often observe is where the woman is constantly seeking an empathic relationship while the man is nonplussed by this. The man for his

> part seems to need the woman to 'be there' but does not seem to be seeking a close empathic relationship. He may want an active sexual life but seems easily overwhelmed by the woman's wish for more love and understanding. (Crowe and Ridley, 1990)

Gebhard (1978), in a study of 1,607 men and 1,445 women, ranked the various types of marital and sexual problems experienced and found that disagreements over coital frequency were at the top of the list. Twenty per cent of the men and 6 per cent of the older women wanted more frequent intercourse.

The focus, by the male, on an erect penis and penetrative sex may result from the continual production of sperm and consequent need to release the sperm.

A complex situation may arise for the couple when the woman is pregnant. From a physical and biological perspective the woman's womb is occupied with a foetus and therefore she may have little need for penetrative sex. Her partner's body continues its cycle of production of semen and for him, one can hypothesise, there is an ongoing need to penetrate and ejaculate. Because she is pregnant, rather than have a sexual relationship, she may expect her partner to protect her (see 5.2; and 6.3.4, 6.3.4.1) but his need to penetrate and ejaculate may take over at this time and he may either pressurise her for sexual intercourse or seek an affair (see Examples 2h, Janice and Roy; 3c, Douglas and Diane).

An affair at this time can cause much distress since the man may not necessarily feel he has committed an offence, whereas the woman is likely to feel that she has been betrayed (Wellings et al., 1994).

This is a contradictory aspect of the male as he often shows affection and deep feeling for his partner through sexual intercourse. If the woman has grown accustomed to the fact that he shows affection through sexuality, it seems hypocritical when he insists that a brief sexual affair 'means nothing'. Both responses may be honest, if contradictory, evidence that the woman is not alone in being illogical on occasion (see Example 2a, Alan and Amy; 2d, Tim and Tina; 3c, Douglas and Diane).

The developing male's experience of sexual abuse as a child or young man is likely to affect his self-confidence, his understanding of his own sexual needs and his ability to give and receive sexual pleasure. For some men, whose personal journey towards adult sexuality has been uncertain and insecure, promiscuity or prostitution may be the safest outlet for their sexual needs. In such fleeting relationships there is no risk of intimacy.

Once puberty has been reached, a biological reality is that the male can impregnate a female in seconds. He does not necessarily have to penetrate her vaginally for pregnancy to occur. Neither partner needs to have known the other nor to care about each other. Many babies are conceived as a result of one-night stands or rape (Brownmiller, 1991). Sexual abuse of minors, incest and rape, which are predominantly perpetrated by men, may result from the conflicting and ambivalent nature of male sexuality and from their own early experiences of abuse or violence (see 6.8.2).

Although the woman resists and does not want intercourse, her body may have to accept the male sperm and become pregnant against her will. The male may never know whether the female he raped or with whom he had a one-night stand became pregnant. A fundamental difference emerges between the female and male. Once pregnant, she may carry the consequences for the rest of her life while for him there may be no consequences. There is little evidence that the male has much interest in knowing whether the result of rape, or forced intercourse, was indeed to father a child. He does not often have 'post-traumatic stress' following rape or abortion of his child.

For the woman, even if she chooses an abortion, distressing reminders such as vivid dreams may occur. If she is unable to become pregnant later in life she may regret bitterly having once aborted that child.

Sociobiologists (Dawkins, 1976; Johnson, 1994) think that random mating by the male ensures the perpetuation of his genes. Regardless of what hypothesis can explain the behaviour, men can and do father children about whom they have no knowledge or little personal curiosity, often causing distress to the female and hostility against the male. Many other men conceive within a warm, supportive and permanent relationship with both partners experiencing intense pleasure during intercourse.

When assessing the influence of any gender differences on experiences of sexuality, the quality of the relationship must be taken into account. For some couples the search to understand the other's sexual rhythms and responses is a constant source of mystery and discovery, keeping each partner alert to the other's needs; for others frustration and disappointment occur. Sexual closeness, built upon knowledge of gender differences, can be a resource, helping couples survive crises which threaten relationships where gender differences are ignored (see Examples 2a, Alan and Amy; 2d, Tim and Tina; 2h, Janice and Roy; 4b, Catherine and Claude; 4c, Frank and Fiona).

6.10. Male aggression

(See 2.7.3; 4.5; 4.6; Examples 4d, Robert and Rita; 4e, Eustace and Elly.) Male aggression may derive from a need for outlets for a spurt of vigour and energy in adolescence.

> The largest and most consistent psychological sex difference is in aggression. (Pool, 1994)

Whereas Bancroft (1990) and Pool (1994) express certainty that the male is the aggressive gender, O'Leary et al. (1989), using self-report measures of physical aggression in a longitudinal study of marriage in the United States, found that at pre-marriage, at 18 months of marriage and at 30 months:

> women and men did not report significantly different rates of aggression. The modal forms of physical aggression for both women and men were pushing, shoving, and slapping.

The men's movement also questions the assumption that men are more aggressive than women.

In general, the male is stronger and potentially able to inflict damage upon a woman, whereas the opposite may be less possible.

> There is general agreement that the physical damage inflicted by men is greater than that inflicted by women. (O'Leary et al., 1989; see also Berk et al., 1983; Straus et al., 1980.)

6.10.1. What is meant by male aggression?

Is the male potentially a more aggressive creature than the female, and what is meant by aggression? Pool's definition revolves around issues of dominance, stimulus seeking and risk taking. Using self-report questionnaires, he concludes:

> Females get higher scores on tests of nurturance, emotional responsiveness ('notice if someone else is upset') and harm avoidance. Males on the other hand, rate higher on aggression, dominance, stimulus seeking and risk taking. People high in the last two categories tend to enjoy things like parachuting, hang gliding and bungee jumping. (Pool, 1994)

Bancroft (1990) does not attempt to clarify his statement that the:

> only convincing difference which could contribute to sex role differentiation rather than be a result of it is greater male aggression.

An intense dialogue continues regarding the nature and purpose of aggression, well summarised by Parens (1980), who writes of the 2-and-a-half year old boy and girl:

> One aspect of aggressiveness encountered at this time, deriving from a differentiation in the aggressive drive, is what we identify as 'phallic aggressiveness'. We found much evidence of phallic aggressiveness in our boys but not in our girls. In general the little boy's behaviour had a quality of ramminess, at times including gorilla-like posturings as well as the chasing of a little girl with a hard object. By contrast, Mary, for example, who when she crawled had looked like a football tackle, at this developmental period began to look much lighter, much more feminine in appearance and movement. Because we did not find a dominance of phallic aggression in the girls, we postulate here a gender-related distinction between boys and girls. Indeed we found striking differences between girlish and boyish behaviour that preclude application of the term phallic phase to the girls. Their awed, adoring affects and actions at the

> sight of a baby were particularly impressive. This attitude dominated psychic activity in most of our girls for months and in some for years. Boys showed none of this near ecstasy at the sight of a baby. Similarly the boys' rammy, large muscle, heavy locomotor activities were not shared by the girls. In consequence, instead of the phrase phallic phase we substituted the term first genital phase for both boys and girls to emphasise the gender uniqueness of their psychosexual development during the third year of life.

Parens develops the theory that aggression is an aspect of the human animal that is available for self-development and mastery. Having described the 'gender uniqueness' of 'phallic aggression' in the boy's development, disappointingly he does not take this discussion further.

Shaffer et al. (1980) define aggression as:

> an action which it is intended should inflict harm on another ... a high degree of affective arousal is present in much though not all aggressive behaviour.

According to Shaffer et al. (1980) there are female/male differences in aggressive behaviours.

> Sex differences are apparent in aggressive behaviours at the toddler stage of development and are maintained through childhood and adolescence across cultures.

Omark et al. (1973) looked at playground behaviours in the USA, Switzerland and Ethiopia, and noted similar male predominance of hitting and shoving behaviour in all three countries. Whiting and Edwards (1973) were able to replicate these findings in India, Kenya, Okinawa, USA, the Philippines and Mexico.

Maccoby and Jacklin (1975) identified a greater aggressiveness in males, including physical violence, rough and tumble play, and response to aggression by another. Their conclusions are summarised under four headings.

1. Men are generally more aggressive than women in virtually all human societies.
2. Males are more aggressive than females early in life, i.e. during early childhood and the preschool years. 'A time when there is no evidence that differential socialization pressures have been brought to bear by adults to shape aggression differentially in the two sexes.'
3. Greater aggressiveness in males relative to females is found not only in humans but also in primates.
4. Aggression is related to sex hormones and can be influenced by administration of these substances.

Others challenge these conclusions, finding a smaller difference between women and men (Eagly and Steffen, 1986), and suggest that sex differences in aggression diminish with age (Hyde, 1984).

6.10.2. Sexual coercion

Sexual coercion is overwhelmingly committed by men. Data from the National Crime Survey, USA, indicate that less than 1 per cent of offenders are women. According to this survey about 7.3 per cent of the victims of rape are male.

Petrak (1996) uses US studies to show that about one in four women may experience rape or attempted rape at some time in their lives (Russell and Finkelhor, 1984). A survey of outpatients attending a genito-urinary medical clinic in central London also indicated that one in four women and one in ten men report a history of sexual assault at some time in their lives (Petrak, 1996). A survey of 2,000 women in London found that 17 per cent reported completed rape (60 per cent were marital rape) and a further 20 per cent had been victims of attempted rape (Petrak, 1996).

Brownmiller's exhaustive study of rape is a powerful reminder of this aspect of maleness. She writes:

> Man's structural capacity to rape and women's corresponding vulnerability are as basic to the physiology of both our sexes as the primal act of sex itself ... We cannot work around the fact that in terms of human anatomy the possibility of forcible intercourse incontrovertibly exists. This single factor may have been sufficient to have caused the creation of male ideology of rape. When men discovered that they could rape, they proceeded to do it. Later, much later, under certain circumstances they even came to consider rape a crime. (Brownmiller, 1991)

Rape often goes unreported.

> In the United States a mere one in five rapes is reported. (Brownmiller, 1991)

As the reporting of rape is increasingly encouraged and rape crisis centres help to inform the public, so more is learned about the incidence of male rape against females, and male/male rape may be more prevalent than previously acknowledged.

Both women and men are perpetrators of sexual abuse. Although available statistics have focused upon male abuse of the female (Jehu, 1989), there is evidence that male children are abused by men. Lewis (1985), based on samples from the United States, suggested that 16 per cent of men were abused as children; and in Canada a survey revealed that 12 per cent of boys had had an unwanted touching of the 'sex part' of their bodies, and 10 per cent had experienced an attempted or actual sexual assault (National Population Survey Office, 1984). More than 80 per cent of the male victims were aged under 18 years when the abuse occurred. A survey of Britain (Baker and Duncan, 1985) reported 8 per cent to have been sexually abused before the age of 16 years. The data from both the United States (Finkelhor and Russell, 1984) and Canada strongly indicate that sexual offenders against boys are overwhelmingly male.

According to a summary by Jehu (1989):

> prevalence rates of all forms of sexual abuse in the United States are variously reported as 54% by Russell, 53% by Wyatt and Peters and 27% by Lewis.

In Britain, Baker and Duncan (1985) sampled 1,049 women with a face-to-face interview. They were asked if they had ever been sexually abused using the following definition:

> A child (anyone under 16 years) is sexually abused when another person, who is sexually mature, involves the child in any activity which the other person expects to lead to their sexual arousal. This might involve intercourse, touching, exposure of the genital organs, showing pornographic material or talking about sexual things in an erotic way. (Baker and Duncan, 1985)

Of those interviewed, 12 per cent reported sexual abuse had occurred, and 12 per cent refused to answer the question. Where sexual abuse occurred, this involved physical contact in 40 per cent of the cases, and it was intrafamilial in 14 per cent of the cases.

> Overwhelmingly the offenders are male (n = 103, 94%). This is consistent with many other studies (Finkelhor and Russell, 1984; Russell and Finkelhor, 1984) and raises important question about why this gender gap occurs. (Jehu, 1989).

Nicholson (1984) writes of female/male differences:

> The greater overall strength of the adult male can also be traced back to puberty because the more pronounced muscular development of the adolescent boy stems from structural biochemical changes in his muscle cells which once again may stem from the action of the male sex hormone ... By the time they (men) are adults, men have bigger muscles (the muscles of the average adult male are about 15% longer and up to 30–40% thicker than the female's), and some scientists believe that men's muscles are also chemically different from women.

6.10.3. Outlets for male aggression

It would be foolish to assume that the male's physical powerfulness accounts entirely for male aggressiveness. The Western urban way of life provides few creative outlets for male aggression. Warfare, terrorism, rape and crimes of violence against the person are ways in which the male uses his aggressive skills. Warfare is an environment which both sanctions and requires men to use and fine-tune their aggressive abilities. The twentieth century has seen much use of male aggression which entails a preparedness for men to face death for a principle or cause.

Gilligan considers that 'the formal logic of fairness that informs the justice approach of men' informs the way men make moral choices and enables them to fight and, if necessary, sacrifice themselves for others. Women also participate in wars but men carry aggressive roles (Faulks, 1997).

Women have played a passive role, continuing daily routines or supplying food, clothing and the weapons of war to sons, brothers, fathers and partners at war. Gilligan's (1982) vision of maturity thoughtfully combines the ethics of justice (male) with the ethics of care (female) and sees the resolution of these core issues as part of the maturational process of the male and female. They may also explain the reliance of women upon men for protection.

Men are given contradictory messages; on the one hand, to fight and where necessary kill for one's country is seen as heroic, and rape is part of the 'spoils of war' (Brownmiller, 1991). On the other hand, men are being asked to become gentler and more empathic sexual partners and emotionally responsive and nurturing fathers. Within the context of a peaceful society, male aggressiveness is not given adequate acceptable outlets, nor are men helped to understand or contain their aggressive abilities.

6.11. The impact of ageing upon the male

(See 4.3; 4.3.3; Examples 2i, George and Gillian; 3i, Harry and Helen.) The ageing process can be a bewildering critical period for both women and men. Physically both women and men tend to slow down but as knowledge is gained about nutrition, exercise and good health, both genders are living longer and staying active.

Unless illness affects the man's physical abilities, accompanying the general slowing down of physical responses is a slowing down of sexual abilities. While men continue to be fertile into their old age, sexual desire and sexual responsiveness may diminish (Martin, 1981; Hegeler and Mortensen, 1978; Brecher, 1984). Martin (1981) showed that the extent of the decline is a function of the level of sexual activity during early adult life. Those with the highest level of sexual activity when younger showed proportionately the least decline, so that the differences between the high and low activity groups became much more marked in later years.

Martin (1981) found that the least active group in their earlier years were the most likely to have erectile difficulties in later life. He also found that 21 per cent of the sexually least active in their earlier life had ongoing difficulties with premature ejaculation.

> In older men, erections not only take longer to develop, but may require more direct tactile stimulation. The period during which an erection can be sustained gets shorter and may only be a few minutes in those aged over 70. (Bancroft, 1990)

In Brecher's (1984) sample of 2,402 older men, 65 per cent reported that their refractory period was longer (i.e. the ability to get a subsequent erection); 50 per cent took longer to get an erection; 44 per cent said their erection was less rigid when fully erect; and 32 per cent were more likely to lose their erection during sexual activity.

Where a man's self-esteem is focused upon his sexual prowess the adjustments to the ageing process may be difficult. Many men are turning to physical medicine as an aid to extending their sexual abilities instead of allowing themselves to enjoy their older years with less emphasis upon an erect penis and penetrative sex (see Example 4c, Frank and Fiona).

Women are forced to acknowledge the ageing process through the experience of the menopause but there is no similar clear sign to men, making it easier for a man to pretend to himself that he is not ageing. At some point each individual must come to terms with their finiteness. This is one area which both women and men must face.

The same issues confront both sexes: satisfaction or disappointment with personal, family or professional achievements; adjustment to the physical and mental changes which can accompany grand old age; coping with loss of family and friends and, where couples stay together throughout their lives, the inevitable consequence that one partner will die before the other. For less traditional couples the death or illness of past partners or lovers will affect each individual. Gender differences may be less acute in old age and both genders must face up to their achievements, losses and eventual death.

6.12. Discussion of female and male vulnerability

(See 3.2.1, 3.3.1. 3.3.2)

Chapter 6 has focused upon critical periods within the development of the female and male when the individual experiences physical changes that have an impact upon their sense of self and their self-confidence. In this regard a woman's vulnerability revolves around the acceptance of her physical self and its potential. She must learn to adjust to the demands and rhythms of the menstrual cycle, pregnancy, childbirth, breastfeeding, sexuality, the menopause and her own ageing. These often place conflicting and competing demands upon her body and her emotions, which may be at odds with her personal, academic or professional abilities. During these periods of conflicting demands she is often vulnerable.

Her ability to respond to the changing demands of her body may explain why women find it easier than men to relate to, talk about and to understand their own and other's feelings. Many opportunities arise during her life cycle to gain experience and insight into powerful swings of emotion and feelings. Women often worry that their physical and biological make-up puts them at an emotional disadvantage in a male-dominated world of work where little value is placed upon the understanding or expression of vulnerable feelings. This situation may change over time.

A woman is also vulnerable within a physical sexual relationship. Unless her feelings are attended to and she is treated with gentleness, unless her sexual arousal pattern is respected and her need for touch and tenderness understood, her enjoyment of penetrative sex can be affected. Sexual abuse, rape and aggression also affect her sense of self and her pleasure in being female.

It may be appropriate to accept Gilligan's (1982) perspective that women's attributes are not 'vulnerabilities' but strengths. She believes that a discrepancy in both research and thinking about adulthood has disadvantaged women. Researchers such as Broverman et al. (1972) have assumed that the qualities necessary for adulthood are all associated with masculinity. These attributes include autonomous thinking, clear decision-making and responsible action. This has encouraged an attitude that considers women to be deviant or deficient if they do not easily show these attributes. But female attributes which have been seen in the past as weakness in a woman's judgement, and indeed in her adulthood, are as valid as male attributes, though different.

Women should be prepared to accept these differences as strengths. Women's ability to take into consideration complex interactions and be concerned about who gets hurt, women's caring skills or women's intuitive skills should not be discounted, but claimed as strengths in their own right and not judged by male standards. This fundamental point, if recognised, would change many of the ways in which women and men are valued (see 2.2.1).

Men have been seen as the powerful and dominant gender. Politically, socially and economically men have been in control, even though significant numbers of women are reaching positions of authority (Perlberg and Miller, 1990; Evans, 1993; Smart, 1992). As the male world of work becomes less secure it is evident that men have also relied upon a stable work environment for a sense of personal worth (see 2.4.1.1).

Men's vulnerability revolves around the stability of their sexual orientation and their sexual prowess, which is linked to an ability to find a satisfactory relationship within which to have a sexual relationship. Men also find the world of emotions and aggression complicated and may find it easier to express anger or aggression than other emotions. Aggression, its containment or expression may be the arena within which male vulnerability is at its height. The man may be vulnerable during his partner's pregnancy and her preoccupation with child/ren as well as during his own ageing process, retirement or redundancy when his sense of self-worth may be undermined.

The concept of the 'vulnerability' of the man with regard to his sexual orientation is complicated by data which suggest that, within a relationship, a significant difference exists between women and men in their approach to sexuality. Several authors suggest that 'men want sex, and women want relationships' (Mansfield and Collard, 1988; Crowe and Ridley, 1990; Mansfield et al., 1992). Symonds (1979) is dismissive of 'pair bonding' and monogamy and thinks that whilst women may seek intimacy what men seek is the sexual orgasm.

Foucault (1985) sees this dilemma as a moral issue for men.

> The ethical question that was raised was not: which desire? which acts? which pleasures? but rather: with what force is one transported by the pleasures and desires?

These contradictory aspects of maleness, the vulnerability of the sexual orientation coupled with a potential lack of confidence in his masculinity, and the intensity of desire for sexual activity are paradoxical but central to an understanding of maleness. If one adds a tendency to resort to violence when faced with frustration one begins to build a picture of the fragility of the male.

The vulnerability of the male regarding his sexuality and its expression are essential ingredients in his search for intimacy. Unless he can find a safe and trusting relationship where he is not threatened sexually, his self-confidence in his own sexuality and his ability to get and maintain an erection may be affected. He may resort to withdrawal, or a difficulty in expressing his needs, or in some cases to violence. He may occasionally seek solace with prostitutes or one-night stands, or withdraw into work or all-male activities or solitude.

Although it is not possible to verify Money's hypothesis concerning the biological roots of the 'vulnerability' of male sexuality, it is a useful concept in exploring the female/male search for 'intimacy'. It may be relevant to the male's concentration upon erectile difficulties and could partly explain the intensity of performance anxiety for some men. The impact of sexual abuse, rape and violence form pieces in the complex puzzle of female and male vulnerability.

At the same time the man's ability to problem-solve, to be less emotional, to use his greater physical strength to be innovative, to build, protect and provide are essential to the perpetuation of the species.

6.13. Summary

This book is not concerned with social and political areas, but with the private area of interpersonal relationships and the impact of gender upon the intimacy needs of women and men.

In the search for intimacy, both women and men are vulnerable. These vulnerabilities occur at different times and in different ways throughout the life cycle of the individual or couple.

It is argued that:

> Male vulnerability and female vulnerability is inadequately understood by the opposite gender (see 2.2.1).

Chapter 6 has suggested that there are times on the life cycle when each gender is more vulnerable.

The concept of an invisible intimacy screen is used to demonstrate how each gender may seek different elements of intimacy. Gender differences, unless recognised, may exacerbate couple relationships within situations which are emotionally arousing, where there are social pressures, within a physical sexual relationship, where there are different communication styles and ways of expressing aggression.

Even though each tries to support and care for the other, each may feel isolated, misunderstood and lonely within the relationship. Therapists, counsellors and professionals are encouraged to draw upon Chapter 6 together with Part I, where cases are described and alternative interventions offered, for work with couples whose intimacy is in crisis.

References

Absoe D and Thin RN (1996) Prostatic disease, its treatment and sexual functioning. Sexual and Marital Therapy, 11(3): 215–226.

Ainsworth MDS (1991) Attachments and other affectional bonds across the life cycle. In: C Murray Parkes, J Stevenson-Hinde and P Marris (eds) Attachment Across the Life Cycle. London: Routledge.

Aldous J (1996) Family Careers, Rethinking the Developmental Model. London: Sage.

Anderson DY (1996) Gender, Identity and Self Esteem: a new look at. New York: Springer.

Anderson LR and Blanchard PN (1982) Sex differences in task and social-emotional behaviour. Basic and Applied Social Psychology, 3: 109–139.

Anderson S (1994) And the Two Became One. So Easton, MA: Bridges of Hope.

Ardener S(1987) A note on gender iconography: the vagina. In: P Caplan (ed.) The Cultural Construction of Sexuality. London: Routledge.

Austin CR, Edwards RG and Mittwch U (1981) Mechanisms of Sex Differentiation in Animals and Man. London: Academic Press.

Baker AW and Duncan SP (1985) Child sexual abuse: A study of prevalence in Great Britain. Child Abuse and Neglect, 9: 457.

Bales RF (1950) Interaction Process Analysis. Cambridge, MA: Addison Wesley.

Bancroft J (1990) Human Sexuality and its Problems. Edinburgh: Churchill Livingstone.

Bar-Tal D and Frieze IH (1977) Achievement motivation for males and females as determinant of attributions for success and failure. Sex Roles, 3: 301–314.

Bate B (1988) Communication and the Sexes. New York: Harper Row.

Beach SRH, Jouriles EN and O'Leary KD (1985) Extra-marital sex: impact on depression and commitment in couples seeking marital therapy. Journal of Sex and Marital Therapy, 11: 99–108.

Beach SRH, Sandeen EE and O'Leary KD (1990) Depression in Marriage. New York: Guilford Press.

Beach SRH, Whisman MA and O'Leary KD (1994) Marital therapy for depression: Theoretical foundation, current status and future direction. Behaviour Therapy, 25: 345–371.

Beavers WR (1985) Successful Marriage, A Family Systems Approach to Couple Therapy. New York: WW Norton.

Bem SL and Bem DJ (1976) Training the woman to know her place: The power of the nonconscious ideology. In: S Cox (ed.) Female psychology: The Emerging Self, pp 180–190. Chicago: Science Research Associates.

Benjamin J (1988) The Bonds of Love, Psychoanalysis, Feminism and Domination. New York: Pantheon Books.

Berenbaum SA and Hines M (1992) Early androgens are related to childhood sex-typed toy preferences. Psychological Science, 3(3): 203–206.

Bergman MS (1987) The Anatomy of Loving. New York: Columbia University Press.

Berk RS, Berk SF, Loseke DR and Rauma K(1983) Mutual combat and other family violence myths. In: D Finkelhor, RL Gelles, GT Hotaling and MA Straus (eds) The Dark Side of Families: Current Family Violence Research, pp 197–212. Berkeley Hills, CA: Sage.

Bernstein AE and Warner GM (1984) Women Treating Women. New York: International Universities Press.

Bernstein D (1979) Female identity synthesis. In: A Roland and B Harris (eds) Career and Motherhood, pp 104–123. New York: Human Sciences Press.

Bernstein D (1989) The female oedipus complex. In: I Graham (ed.) Personal Myth and Theoretical Streaming. International University Press.

Bernstein D (1990) Female genital anxieties, conflicts and typical mastery modes. International Journal of Psychoanalysis, 71(1): 151–167.

Birtchnell J (1990) Interpersonal theory: criticism, modification and elaboration. Human Relations, 43(12): 1183–1201.

Birtchnell J (1993) How Humans Relate. A New Interpersonal Theory. Westport, CT: Praeger.

Bowlby J (1969) Attachment and Loss. London: Hogarth Press.

Bowlby J (1991) Postcript. In: C Murray Parkes, J Stevenson-Hinde and P Marris (eds) Attachment Across the Life Cycle. London: Routledge.

Bradbury TN and Fincham FD (1988) Individual difference variables in close relationships: A contextual model of marriage as an integrative framework. Journal of Personality and Social Psychology, 54: 713–721.

Bradbury TN and Fincham FD (1989) Behaviour and satisfaction in marriage: Prospective mediating processes. Review of Personality and Social Psychology, 10: 119–143.

Bradbury TN and Fincham FD (1990) Preventing marital dysfunction: review and analysis. In: FD Fincham and TN Bradbury (eds) The Psychology of Marriage: Basic Issues and Applications. New York: Guilford Press.

Bradbury TN and Fincham FD (1993) Assessing dysfunctional cognition in marriage: a reconsideration of the relationship belief inventory. Psychological Assessment, 5(1): 1–10.

Bradbury TN, Beach SRH, Fincham FD and Nelson GM (1996) Attributions and behavior in functional and dysfunctional marriages. Journal of Consulting and Clinical Psychology, 64(3): 1–8.

Brecher EM (1984) Love Sex and Aging, A Consumer Union Report. Boston: Little, Brown.

Breen D (ed.) (1990) The Gender Conundrum. The New Library of Psychoanalysis, 18.

London: Routledge. (Published in association with the Institute of Psychoanalysis, London.)

Briscoe ME (1982) Sex differences in psychological wellbeing. Psychological Medicine, Monograph, Suppl 1.

Briscoe ME (1986) Identification of emotional problems in post-partum women by health visitors. British Medical Journal, 292: 1245–1247.

Briscoe ME (1987) Why do people go to their doctor? Sex differences in the correlates of GP consultation. Social Science and Medicine, 25: 507–513.

Brody LR and Hall JA (1993) Gender and emotions. In: M Lewis and JM Havilland (eds) Handbook of Emotions, pp 447–460. New York: Guilford Press.

Brothers BJ (1991) Intimacy and Autonomy: Connecting. In: BJ Brothers (ed.) Intimate Autonomy–Autonomous Intimacy. New York: Haworth Press.

Broverman I, Vogel S, Broverman D, Clarkson F and Rosenkrantz P (1972) Sex role stereotypes: a current appraisal. Journal of Social Issues, 28: 59–78.

Brown GW and Harris T (1978) The Social Origins of Depression. London: Tavistock.

Brown GW and Harris T (1986) Establishing causal links: The Bedford College studies of depression. In: H Katschnig (ed.) Life Events and Psychiatric Disorders: Controversial Issues. Cambridge University Press.

Brown GW and Harris T (eds) (1989) Life Events and Illness. New York: Guilford Press.

Browne A (1987) When Battered Women Kill. New York: Free Press.

Brownmiller S (1991) Against Our Will. London: Penguin Books.

Burgess AW, Hazelwood RR, Rokous FE, Hartman R and Burgess AG (1988) Serial rapists and their victims: reenactment and repetition. Annals of the New York Academy of Sciences, 528: 277–295.

Buss DM (1994) The Evolution of Desire: Strategies of Human Mating. New York: Basic Books.

Byng-Hall J (1982) Family legends: their significance for the therapist. In A Bentovim, GG Barnes and A Cooklin (eds) Family Therapy. London: Academic Press.

Cahn DD (1992) Conflict in Intimate Relationships. New York: Guilford Press.

Cairns RB and Kroll AB (1994) Developmental perspective on gender differences and similarities. In: M Rutter and DF Hay (eds) Development Through Life, a Handbook for Clinicians, Chapter 15. Oxford: Blackwell Scientific Publications.

Cairns RB, Elder Jr GH, Costello EJ and McGuire A (1995) Developmental Science. New York: Cambridge University Press.

Caplan P (ed.) (1987) The Cultural Construction of Sexuality. London: Routledge.

Carter B and McGoldrick M (1990) The Changing Family Life Cycle. New York: Guilford Press.

Caspi A and Bem DJ (1990) Personality and continuity and change across the life cycle. In: L Pervin (ed.) Handbook of Personality, pp 549–575. New York: Guilford Press.

Champion A (1996) Male cancer and sexual function. Sexual and Marital Therapy, 11(3): 227–244.

Charnofsky S (1992) When Women Leave Men. San Rafael, CA: New World Library.

Chiriboga DA, Catron LS and Associates (1991) Divorce. Crisis, Challenge or Relief? New York: New York University Press.

Chodorow N (1978) The Reproduction of Mothering, Psychoanalysis and the Sociology of Gender. Berkeley,CA: University of California Press.

Christensen A and Heavy CL (1990) Gender and social structure in the demand withdrawal pattern of marital conflict. Journal of Personality and Social Psychology, 59: 73–81.

Coates S. and Wolfe S.(1995) Gender identity disorder in boys: The interface of constitution and early experience. in Psychoanalytic Inquiry, 15(1), pp 6–38. New Jersey: The Analytic Press.

Cohn L (1991) Sex differences in the course of personality development: A meta-analysis. Psychological Bulletin, 109: 252–266.

Colby A and Damon W (1987) Listening to a different voice, a review of Gilligan's In a different voice. In: MR Walsh (ed.) The Psychology of Women, Ongoing Debates. New Haven: CT. Yale University Press.

Conn JH and Kanner L (1974) Children's awareness of sex differences. American Journal of Orthopsychiatry, 10: 747–754.

Crisp AH (1990) Aneroxia Nervosa. Let Me Be. London: Academic Press.

Crooks RL and Stein J (1988) Psychology, Science, Behaviour and Life. New York: Holt, Rinehart and Winston.

Crowe M (1997) Intimacy in relation to couple therapy. Sexual and Marital Therapy, 12(3): 225–236.

Crowe M and Qureshi MJH (1991) Pharmacologically induced penile erections (PIPE) as maintenance treatment for erectile impotence: a report of 41 cases. Sexual and Marital Therapy, 6(3): 273–285.

Crowe M and Ridley J (1986) The negotiated timetable: a new approach to marital conflicts involving male demands and female reluctance for sex. Sexual and Marital Therapy, 1: 157–173.

Crowe M and Ridley J (1990) Therapy with Couples, a Behavioural/Systems Approach to Marital and Sexual Problems. Oxford: Blackwell Scientific Publications.

Dalton K (1987) What is this PMS? In: Walsh MR (ed.) The Psychology of Women. Ongoing Debates. New Haven, CT: Yale University Press.

Dare C (1997) Chronic eating disorders in therapy: clinical stories using family systems and psychoanalytic approaches. Journal of Family Therapy, 19(3): 319–362.

Dare C, Eisler I, Russell G and Szmuckler G (1990) Family therapy for anorexia: implications from the result of a controlled trial of family and individual therapy. Journal of Marital and Family Therapy, 16: 39–57.

Dawkins R (1976) The Selfish Gene. Oxford: Oxford University Press.

Deutsch H (1946) The Psychology of Women; Psychoanalytic Interpretation: Vol. 1, Girlhood; Vol. 2, Motherhood. London: Research Books.

Diamond M (1965) A critical evaluation of the ontogeny of human sexual behaviour. Quarterly Review of Biology, 40: 147–175.

Dickson A (1989) The Mirror Within. A New Look at Sexuality. London: Quartet Books.

Dobash RE and Dobash RP (1979) Violence Against Wives. A Case Against the Patriarchy. New York: Free Press.

Dormor DJ (1992) The Relationship Revolution. Cohabitation, Marriage and Divorce in Contemporary Europe. London: One Plus One.

Douglas AR, Matson IC and Hunter S (1989) Sex therapy for women incestuously abused as children. Sexual and Marital Therapy, 4: 143–159.

Eagly AH (1987), Sex Differences in Social Behaviour: A Social Role Interpretation. Hillsdale, NJ: Erlbaum.

Eagly AH and Steffen FJ (1986) Gender and aggressive behaviour: A meta-analytic review of the social psychological literature. Psychological Bulletin, 100: 309–330.

Ehrhardt AA and Baker SW (1974) Fetal androgens, human central nervous system differentiation and behaviour sex differences. In: RC Friedman, RM Richart and RL Van De Wiele (eds) Sex Differences in Behaviour. New York: Wiley.

Eichenbaum L and Orbach S (1983) Understanding Women. Harmondsworth: Penguin.

Eichenbaum L and Orbach S (1990) What Do Women Want? Glasgow: Fontana Collins.

Elton A (1982) The birth of a baby and the pre-school years. In: A Bentovim, G Gorrell Barnes and A Cooklin (eds) Family Therapy, Chapter 15. London: Academic Press.

Emery RE (1994) Renegotiating Family Relationships: Divorce, Child Custody and Mediation. New York: Guilford Press.

Evans DT (1993) Sexual Citizenship. London: Routledge.

Faderman L (1981) Surpassing the Love of Men. Romantic Friendship and Love between Women from the Renaissance to the Present. London: Junction Books.

Fagan RW, Barnett OW and Patton JB (1988) Reasons for alcohol use in maritally violent men. American Journal of Drug and Alcohol Abuse, 14(3): 371–392.

Fagot BI and Leinbach MD (1993) Gender role development in young children: From discrimination to labelling. Development Review, 13: 205–224.

Family Policy Studies (1993) Fact Sheet 1. Family Studies Centre, London.

Faulks S (1997) Birdsong. London: Vintage.

Fincham FD (1994) Cognition in marriage: current status and future challenges. Applied and Preventive Psychology, 3: 185–189.

Fincham FD and Bradbury TN (1991) Marital conflict: towards a more complete integration of research and treatment. In: Advances in Family Intervention, Assessment and Theory, vol. 5, pp 1–24. London: Jessica Kingsley.

Finkelhor D and Russell DEH (1984) Women as perpetrators: review of the evidence. In: D. Finkelhor (ed.) Child Sexual Abuse: New Theory and Research, pp 171–185. Free Press: New York.

Firth MT (1997) Partners of female victims of child sexual abuse. Sexual and Marital Therapy, 12(2): 159–172.

Fisek MH and Ofshe R (1970) The process of status evolution, Sociometry, 33: 327–346.

Foucault M. (1985) The History of Human Sexuality. New York: Viking.

Frieze IH, Bar-Tal D and Carroll JS (eds) (1979) New Approaches to Social Problems. San Francisco, CA: Jossey Bass.

Ganong LH and Coleman M (1994) Remarried Family Relationships. London: Sage.

Gaylin M (1992) The Male Ego. New York: Viking.

Gebhard PH (1978) Marital stress. In: L Levi (ed.) Society, Stress and Disease, Vol 3. The Productive and Reproductive Age. Oxford: Oxford University Press.

Gesell A (1940) The First Five Years of Life. London: Methuen.

Gibson CS (1994) Dissolving Wedlock. London: Routledge.

Gillan P (1987) Sex Therapy Manual. Oxford: Blackwell Scientific Publications.

Gilligan C (1982) In a Different Voice. Cambridge, MA: Harvard University Press.

Gilligan C.(1987) In a different voice: Women's conception of self and of morality. In MR Walsh (ed.) The Psychology of Women, Chapter 8, Part III. New Haven, CT: Yale University Press.

Gise LH and Paddison P (1988) The violent patient. Psychiatric Clinics of North America, 11(4): 629–648.

Goldner V (1988) Generation and gender: Normative and covert hierarchies. Family Process, 27: 17–31.

Goldner V (1990) Love and violence. Gender paradoxes in volatile attachments. Family Process, 29: 343–364.

Gottman JM (1976) A Couple's Guide to Communication. Champaign: Illinois Research Press.

Gottman JM (1994) What Predicts Divorce. Hillsdale, NJ: Erlbaum.

Gottman JM (1998) What is dysfunctional when a marriage is failing. Paper presented to One Plus One Conference, London, 27 April 1998.

Gottman JM and Levenson RW (1988) The social psychophysiology of marriage. In PN Oller and MA Fitzpatrick (eds) Perspectives in Marital Interaction, pp 182–200. Clivedon: Multilingual Matters.

Green RG (1998) Human Aggression. Theories, Research and the Implication for Social Policy. London: Academic Press.

Greer G (1991) The Change. Women, Ageing and the Menopause. Harmondsworth: Penguin Books.

Grossmann KE and Grossmann K (1991) Attachment quality as an organiser of emotional and behavioural responses in a longitudinal perspective. In: C Murray Parkes, J Stevenson-Hinde and P Marris (eds) Attachment Across the Life Cycle, Chapter 6, Part 2. London: Routledge.

Halford WK and Markman HJ (1997) Clinical Handbook of Marital and Couple Intervention. Chichester: Wiley.

Halpern DF (1992) Sex Differences in Cognitive Abilities. Hillsdale, NJ: Erlbaum.

Hampson E (1990) Estrogen-related variations in human spatial articulatory-motor skills. Psychoneuroendocrinology, 15(2): 97–111.

Harway M (ed.) (1996) Treating the Changing Family, Handling Normative and Unusual Events. Chichester: Wiley.

Hatfield E (1993) Love, Sex and Intimacy: their Psychology, Biology and History. New York: Harper Collins.

Hatfield E (1996) Love and Sex: Cross Cultural Perspectives. Boston: Allyn and Bacon.

Heavy CL, Layne C and Christensen AC (1993) Gender and conflict structure in marital interaction: a replication and extension. Journal of Consulting and Clinical Psychology, 61: 16–27.

Hegeler S, Mortensen M (1978) Sexuality and aging. British Journal of Sexual Medicine, 5(32): 16–19.

Heider F (1958) The Psychology of Interpersonal Relations. New York: Wiley.

Heiman JR and Lo Piccolo J (1988) Becoming Orgasmic. A Sexual and Personal Growth Program for Women. London: Prentice Hall Press.

Heinz WR (1991) Trends and Dilemmas in Life Course Research. Weinheim: Deutscher Studien Verlag.

Heyn D (1992) The Erotic Silence of the American Wife. New York: Turtle Bay Books.

Hines M (1990) Gonadal hormones and human cognitive development. In: J Balthazart (ed.) Hormones, Brain and Behaviour in Vertebrates, pp 51–63. Basel: Karger.

Hinton J (1967) Dying. Harmondsworth: Penguin.

Hite S (1981) The Hite Report on Male Sexuality. London: Optima.

Hooley JM, Orley J and Teasdale JD (1986) Levels of expressed emotion and relapse in depressed patients. British Journal of Psychiatry, 148: 642–647.

Horney K (1932) Feminine Psychology. London: Routledge and Kegan Paul.

Hudson L and Jacot B (1995) Intimate Relations, the Natural History of Desire. New Haven: Yale University Press.

Hunt PA (1964) Responses to marriage counselling. British Journal of Guidance and Counselling, 12(1): 72–83.

Hyde JS (1984) How large are gender differences in aggression? A developmental meta-analysis. Developmental Psychology, 20: 722–736.

Ingoldsby BB and Smith S (1995) Families in Multi-cultural Perspective. New York: Guilford Press.

Jack DC (1991) Silencing the Self, Women and Depression. Cambridge, MA: Harvard University Press.

Jackson M (1987) Facts of Life, or the Eroticisation of Women's Oppression. In: P Caplan (ed.) The Cultural Construction of Sexuality. London: Routledge.

Jehu D (1989) Beyond Sexual Abuse. Chichester: Wiley.

Jacobson NS (1983) Beyond empiricism: the politics of marital therapy. American Journal of Family Therapy, 11: 211–224.

Johnson PE (1994) Darwin on Trial. Crowborough: Monarch.

Johnson SL and Jacob J (1997) Marital interactions of Depressed men and women. Journal of Consulting and Clinical Psychology, 65(1): 15–23.

Kagan J and Moss HA (1962) Birth to Maturity. New York: Wiley.

Kantor D and Okun BF (eds) (1989) Intimate Environments: Sex, Intimacy and Gender. New York: Guilford Press.

Kaplan HS (1981) The Illustrated Manual of Sex Therapy. London: Granada.

Karney R and Bradbury TN (1995) The longitudinal course of marital quality and stability: a review of theory, method and research. Psychological Bulletin, 1: 3–33.

Keller E (1985) Reflections on Gender and Science. New Haven, CT: Yale University Press.

Kendall-Tackett KA, Meyer-Williams L and Finkelhor D (1993) Impact of sexual abuse of children: a review and synthesis of recent empirical findings. Psychological Bulletin, 113: 164–180.

Kerber J (1996) Women and autonomy. Journal of Human Development, 18: 418–427.

Kersten KK and Himle DP (1991) Marital Intimacy: A model for clinical assessment and intervention. In: BJ Brothers (ed.) Intimate Autonomy–Autonomous Intimacy. New York: Haworth Press.

Kestenberg JS (1956) Regression and reintegration in pregnancy. Journal of the American Psychoanalytic Association, 24(5): 213–251.

Kestenberg JS (1961) Menarche. In: S Lorand and H schneer (eds) Adolescence: Psychoanalytic Approach to Problems and Therapy, pp 19–50. New York: Harper.

Kitzinger S (1985) Woman's Experience of Sex. Harmondsworth: Penguin.

Klein M (1932a) The effects of the early anxiety-situation on the sexual development of the girl. In: M Klein, The Psycho-analysis of Children. London: Hogarth Press.

Klein (1932b) The effects of the early anxiety-situation on the sexual development of the boy. In M Klein, The Psycho-analysis of Children. London: Hogarth Press.

Klein M (1952) Development in Psychoanalysis, ed. J Riviere. London: Hogarth Press.

Knedeck LA (1995) Predicting changes in marital satisfaction form husband's and wife's conflict resolution styles. Journal of Marriage and Family, 57(1): 153–164.

Kübler-Ross E (1970) On Death and Dying. London: Tavistock.

Kuebli J and Fivush R (1992) Gender differences in parent-child conversations about past events. Sex Roles, 27: 683–698.

Kurdeck LA and Fine MA (1991) Cognitive correlates of satisfaction for mothers and step fathers in step father families Journal of Marriage and Family, 53(3): 565–572.

Lamanna MA and Reidman A (1997) Marriages and Families. Belmont, CA: Wadsworth Pub Co.

Lavee Y, McCubbin HI and Olson DH (1987) Family stress and wellbeing. Journal of Marriage and the Family, 49: 857–873.

Leff J and Vaughn C (1985) Expressed Emotions in Families. New York: Guilford Press.

Levenson RW and Gottman JM (1985) Physiological and affective predictors of change in relationship satisfaction. Journal of Personality and Social Psychology, 49: 85–94.

Levinger G (1988) Can we picture love? In: RJ Sternberg and ML Barnes (ed.) The Psychology of Love. New Haven, CT: Yale University Press.

Levy DM (1940) Control-situation studies of children's responses to the difference in genitalia. American Journal of Orthopsychiatry, 10: 755–762.

Lewis IA (1985) Los Angeles Times Poll #98, unpublished raw data.

Lindsey K (1978) When battered women strike back: Murder or self-defence? Viva, pp 58–59, 66–74.

Lips HM (1990) Women, Men and Power. Mountain View, CA: Mayfield Pub.

Lips HM (1997) Sex and Gender. Mountain View, CA: Mayfield Pub.

Maccoby E and Jacklin N (1975), The Psychology of Sex Differences. Stanford, CA: Stanford University Press.

Maguire M (1995) Men, Women, Passion and Power. Gender Issues in Psychotherapy. London: Routledge.

Mahler MS, Pine F and Bergman A (1975) The Psychological Birth of the Human Infant. London: Hutchinson.

Mansfield P (1993) Public perceptions: private experiences. In: C Clulow (ed.) Rethinking Marriage: Public and Private Perceptions. London: Karnac.

Mansfield P and Collard J (1988) The Beginning of the Rest of your Life. London: Macmillan Press.

Mansfield P, McAllister F and Collard J (1992) Equality: implications for sexual intimacy in marriage. Sexual and Marital Therapy, 7: 213–220.

Manstead ASR (1992) Gender differences in emotion. In: A Gale and MW Eysenck (eds) Handbook of Individual Difference. Biological Perspectives, London: Wiley. pp 355–387.

Markman HJ and Kraft SA (1989) Men and women in marriage: dealing with gender differences in marital therapy. Behaviour Therapist, 12: 51–56.

Markman HJ, Stanley S and Blumberg S (1994) Fighting for Your Marriage. San Francisco, CA: Jossey Bass.

Markus H and Oyserman D (1989) Gender and thought. The role of the self concept. In M Crawford and M Hamilton (eds) Gender and Thought, pp 100–127. New York: Springer Verlag.

Martin CE (1981) Factors affecting sexual functioning in 60–79 year old married males. Archives of Sexual Behaviour, 10: 399–420.

Martin D (1976) Battered Wives. San Francisco, CA: Glide.

Masters WH and Johnson VE (1966) Human Sexual Response. Boston: Little, Brown and Co.

Masters WH and Johnson VE (1970) Human Sexual Inadequacy. Boston: Little, Brown and Co.

Mijuskovic B (1991) Intimacy and Loneliness. In: BJ Brothers (ed.) Intimate Autonomy: Autonomous Intimacy. New York: Haworth Press.

Miles R (1992) The Rites of Man. Glasgow: Paladin.

Milligan S and Clare A (1994) Depression and How to Survive It. London: Ebury Press.

Moir A and Jessel D (1991) Brain Sex. London: Mandarin.

Money J (1986) Lovemaps. New York: Prometheus Books.

Money J and Ehrhardt AA (1972) Man and Woman, Boy and Girl. Baltimore: Johns Hopkins University Press.

Moore T (1991) Cry of the Damaged Man. Australia: Pan Macmillan,

Murphy CM and Meyer S (1991) Gender, power and violence in marriage. The Behaviour Therapist, 14: 95–100.

Murray Parkes C. (1987) Bereavement and Loss. Harmondsworth: Penguin.

Mussen P and Bouterline-Young H (1964) Relationships between rate of physical maturing and personality among boys of Italian descent. Vita Humana, 7: 186–200.

National Population Survey Office (1984) Sexual Offences Against Children in Canada. Canada.

Nicholson J (1984) Men and Women. Oxford: Oxford University Press.

Nicholson J and Thompson F (1992) Men on Sex. London: Vermillion.

Nolen-Hoeksema S (1987) Sex differences in unipolar depression: Evidence and theory. Psychological Bulletin, 101: 259–283.

Noller P (1993) Gender and emotional communication in marriage. Journal of Language and Social Psychology, 12: 132–154.

O'Leary KD (1988) Physical aggression between spouses. A social learning perspective. In: VB Van Hasselt, RL Morrison, AS Bellack and M Hersen (eds) Handbook of Family Violence, pp 31–55. New York: Plenum.

O'Leary KD and Beach SRH (1990) Marital therapy: a viable treatment for depression and marital discord. American Journal of Psychiatry, 147(2): 183–186.

O'Leary KD and Cascardi M (1989) Frequency of homicide in intimate relationships: A decade of FBI reporting. Unpublished manuscript, Department of Psychology, University of New York, Stony Brook, USA.

O'Leary KD and Vivian D (1990) Physical aggression in marriage. In: Fincham FD and Bradbury TN (eds) The Psychology of Marriage. New York: Guilford Press.

O'Leary KD, Barling J, Arias I, Rosenbaum A, Malone J and Tyree A (1989) Prevalence and stability of physical aggression between spouses: a longitudinal analysis. Journal of Consulting and Clinical Psychology, 57(2): 263–268.

Omark DR, Omark M and Edelman M (1973) Dominance hierarchies in young children. Papers presented at the International Congress of Anthropological and Ethnological Sciences, Chicago, 1973.

OPCS The Office of Population Censuses and Surveys (1993) Marriage and divorce statistics Series FM2, no 21.

Ory MG, Warner HR (eds) (1990) Gender, Health and Longevity, Multidisciplinary Perspectives. New York: Springer.

Oxnard CE (1987) Fossils teeth and sex. New perspectives in human evolution. Seattle: University of Washington Press.

Pagelow MD (1981) Women Battering: Victims and their Experiences. Beverley Hills, CA: Sage.

Papousek H and Papousek M (1974) Mirror image and self recognition in young human infants: a new method of experimental analysis. Developmental Psychology, 7(2): 149–157.

Parens H (1980) The Development of Aggression in Early Childhood. New York: Jason Aronson.

Pauly IB (1974) Female trans-sexualism. Archives of Sexual Behaviour, 3: 487–526.

Paykel ES, Myers JKD, Dienelt MN et al. (1969) Life events and depression: a controlled study. Archives of General Psychiatry, 21: 753–760.

Perlberg RJ and Miller AC (1990) Gender and Power in Families. London: Routledge.

Petrak J (1996) Psychological assessment and treatment of victims of sexual violence. Sexual and Marital Therapy, 11(1): 36–46.

Piaget J (1955) The Child's Construction of Reality. London: Routledge and Kegan Paul.

Pietropinto A and Simenauer J (1977) Beyond the Male Myth. A Nationwide Survey. New York: Time Books.

Pines M (1989) Mirroring and Child Development. Self and Identity, eds T Hones and K Yardley. London: Routledge.

Pool R (1994) Eve's Rib. New York: Crown Publishers.

Pradhan S, Pittrof R and Johanson R (1995) Safe motherhood – a reality? Sexual and Marital Therapy, 10(2): 121–133.

Prager KJ (1989) Intimacy status and couple communication. Journal of Social and Personal Relationships, 6: 435–449.

Quilliam S and Grove-Stephenson I (1992) Super Virility. London: Anaya Publishers.

Rabbon M (1950) Sex-role identification in young children in two diverse social groups. Genet. Psychol. Mon. 42, 81–158.

Rampage C (1994) Power, gender, and marital intimacy. Journal of Family Therapy 16(1): 125–139.

Rancour-Laferriere D (1992) Signs of the Flesh. Bloomington: Indiana Academic Press.

Read J (1997) Sexual Problems and Fertility. London: BICA.

Reibstein J (1997) Rethinking marital love: defining and strengthening key factors in successful partnerships. Sexual and Marital Therapy, 12(3): 237–247.

Reis HT and Shaver P (1988) Intimacy as an interpersonal process. In SW Duck (ed.) Handbook of Personal Relationships: Theory, Research and Interventions, pp 367–389. New York: Wiley.

Revitch E and Schlesinger LB (1988) Annals of the New York Academy of Sciences, 528: 59–61.

Rice FP (1995) Human development: a life span approach. Prentice Hall.

Ridgeway CL and Diekema D (1992) Are gender differences status differences? In: CL Ridgeway (ed.) Gender, Interaction and Inequality. New York: Springer-Verlag.

Ridley J (1993) Gender and couples: do men and women seek different kinds of intimacy? Sexual and Marital Therapy, 8(3): 243–253.

Ridley J (1994) Chronic sorrow. Counselling News, June, pp 18–19.

Riley AJ (1996) Sexuality and ageing in women. Paper delivered to British Association of Sexual and Marital Therapy, Exeter.

Ritvo S (1976) Adolescence to woman. Journal of the American Psychoanalytic Association, 24: 127–138.

Roberts CJ and Krokoff LJ (1990) A time-series analysis of withdrawal, hostility and displeasure in satisfied and dissatisfied marriages. Journal of Marriage and Family 52: 95–105.

Robinson M (1982) Reconstituted families: some implications for the family therapists. In: A Bentovim, GG Barnes and A Cooklin (eds) Family Therapy. London: Academic Press.

Robinson M (1993) Family Transformation Through Divorce and Remarriage. London: Routledge.

Roiphe H and Galenson E (1981) Infantile Origins of Sexual Identity. New York: International Universities Press.

Ross MW, Walinder J, Lundstrom B and Thuwe I (1981) Cross cultural approaches to transsexualism: a comparison between Sweden and Australia. Acta Psychiatrica Scandinavica, 63: 75–82.

Rounsaville BJ, Weissman MM, Prusoff BA et al. (1979) Marital disputes and treatment outcome in depressed women. Comprehensive Psychiatry, 20: 483–490.

Rowbotham S (1983) Dreams and Dilemmas. London: Virago.

Rubin C (1996) Equal Partners. London: Routledge.

Ruble DN and Frieze I (1978) Biosocial aspects of reproduction. In: IH Frieze, JE Parsons, PB Johnson, DN Ruble and GL Zellman (eds) Women and Sex Roles: A Social Psychological Perspective, pp 191–209. New York: Norton.

Ruble DN, Fleming AS, Hackel LS and Stangor C (1988) Changes in the marital relationship during the transition to first time motherhood: effects of violated expectations concerning division of household labor. Journal of Personal and Social Psychology, 55(1): 78–87.

Russell DEH and Finkelhor D (1984) The gender gap amongst the perpetrators of child sexual abuse. In DEH Russell, Sexual Exploitation: Rape, Child Abuse, and Workplace Harassment. Beverley Hills, CA: Sage.

Rutter M (1980) Developmental Psychiatry, Scientific Foundations. London: Heinemann Medical Books.

Rutter M (1981) Maternal Deprivation Reassessed. Harmondsworth: Penguin Modern Psychology.

Rutter M and Hay DF (eds) (1994) Development Through Life, A Handbook for Clinicians. Oxford: Blackwell Scientific Publications.

Samuels A (1985) The Father: Contemporary Jungian Perspectives. London: Free Press Association Books.

Samuels A (1989) The Plural Psyche. London: Routledge.

Satir V (1964) Conjoint Family Therapy. Palo Alto, CA: Science and Behaviour Books.

Saunders DG (1988) Wife abuse, husband abuse, or mutual combat. A feminist perspective on the empirical findings. In: K Yllo and M Bograd (eds) Feminist Perspectives on Wife Abuse, pp 90–113. Beverley Hills, CA: Sage.

Schaap C and Jansan-Nawas C (1987) Marital interaction, affect and conflict resolution. Sexual and Marital Therapy, 2: 35–51.

Scharff DE (1982) The Sexual Relationship. Boston: Routledge and Kegan Paul.

Schover LR (1991) The impact of breast cancer on sexuality, body image and intimate relations. CA – A Journal for Physicians, 41: 112–120.

Schover LR, Evans RB and von Eschenbach, AC (1987) Sexual and marital relationship after radiotherapy for seminoma. Urology, 27: 117–123.

Shaffer D, Heino FL, Meyer-Bahlberg C and Stokman CLJ (1980) The development of aggression. In: Developmental Psychiatry. London: William Heinemann Medical Books.

Sheinberg M and Penn P (1991) Gender dilemmas, gender questions, and the gender mantra. Journal of Marital and Family Therapy, 17(1): 33–44.

Shupe A, Stacey WA and Hazelwood LR (1987) Violent Men, Violent Couples. Lexington USA: Heath.

Slevin ML, Terry Y, Hallett N, Jeffries S, Launder S, Plant R, Wax H and McElwain T (1988) BACUP the first two years: evaluation of a national cancer information service. British Medical Journal, 297: 669–672.

Sluzki CE (1978) Marital therapy from a systems perspective. In: TJ Paolins and BS McCrady (eds) Marriage and Marital Therapy. New York: Brunner/Mazel.

Smart C (ed.) (1992) Regulating Womanhood. Historical Essays on Marriage, Motherhood and Sexuality. London: Routledge.

Smock T (1993) The economic costs of marital disruption for young women over the past two decades. Demography, 30(3): 353–371.

Sommer BY (1983) How does menstruation affect cognitive competence and psychophysiological response? Women and Health, 8 (2/3): 53–90.

Stanko ES (1985) Intimate Intrusions, Women's Experience of Male Violence. London: Routledge and Kegan Paul.

Stanley E (1981) Sex problems in practice, dealing with fear of failure. British Medical Journal, 282: 1–7.

Stanway S (1993) The Loving Touch. London: Little, Brown and Co.

Stern D (1983) Self, other and 'self and other'. Reflections on Self Psychology, eds JD Lichtenberg and S Kaplan. Hillsdale, NJ: Analytic Press.

Stern D (1985) The Interpersonal World of the Infant. New York: Basic Books.

Sternberg RJ (1988) The Psychology of Love. New Haven, CT: Yale University Press.

Stoller RJ (1968) Sex and Gender. New York: International Universities Press.

Stoller RJ (1974) Sex and Gender. New York: Jason Aronson.

Storaasli RD and Markman HJ (1990) Relationship problems in early marriage. Journal of Family Psychology, 4(1): 80–98.

Stout KD and Brown P (1995) Legal and social differences between men and women who kill intimate partners. Affilia, 10(2): 194–205.

Straus MA (1979) Measuring intrafamily conflict and violence: The Conflict Tactics Scales. Journal of Marriage and the Family, 41: 75–86.

Straus MA, Gelles RJ and Steinmetz AK (1980) Behind Closed Doors: Violence in the American Family. New York: Anchor Books.

Swift R (1993) Women's Pleasure or How to Have an Orgasm as Often as You Want. London: Pan Books.

Symonds D (1979) The Evolution of Human Sexuality. Oxford: Oxford University Press.

Tannen D (1990) You Just Don't Understand. New York: William Morrow.

Thomas J (1988) Victims of sexual aggression, introduction. Annals of the New York Academy of Sciences, 528: 274–276.

Tiger L and Fox R (1989) The Imperial Animal, An Owl Book. New York: Henry Holt and Co.

Tyson P (1989) Infantile sexuality, gender identity, and obstacles to oedipal progression. Journal of the American Psychoanalytic Association, 37: 1051–1069.

Tyson P and Tyson R (1990) Psychoanalytic Theories of Development, an Integration. New Haven, CT: Yale University Press.

United Nations Development Project (1994) Gender and Society Working Paper 3. Women's Studies, Birzeit University.

Van Arsdall N (1996) Coming Full Circle, Honouring the Rhythms of Life. Chicago: Third Side Press.

Van de Weil HBM, Weijmar Schultz WCM, Wouda JG and Bouma J (1990) Sexual functioning of partner of gynaecological oncology patients: a pilot study on involvement, support, sexuality and relationship. Sexual and Marital Therapy, 5: 123–129.

Vivian D, Malone J and O'Leary KD (1989) Wife abuse: Impact of severity of abuse on relationship variables. Unpublished manuscript, State University New York, Stony Brook.

Walker L (1984) The Battered Woman Syndrome. New York: Springer.

Wallace C (1991) New patterns of gender identity in youth, or old ones reconstructed. In: WR. Heinz (ed.) The Life Course and Social Change: Comparative Perspectives, pp 43–70. Weinheim: Deutscher Studien Verlag.

Walsh MR (1987) The Psychology of Women. Ongoing debates. New Haven, CT: Yale University Press.

Ward IL (1992) Sexual Behaviour, The product of perinatal hormonal and prepubertal social factors. In: AA Gerall, H Moltz and IL Ward, Handbook of Neurobiology, Vol 11, Sexual Differentiation. New York: Plenum Press.

Watson C (1995) Editorial. Sexual and Marital Therapy, 10(2): 117–119.

Weeks J (1987) Questions of identity. In: P Caplan (ed.) The Cultural Construction of Sexuality. London: Routledge.

Weijmar Schultz WCM, Wiel van de HBM, Hahn DEE and Wouda J (1995) Sexual adjustment of women after gynaecological and breast cancer. Sexual and Marital Therapy, 10(3): 293–306.

Weiss R (1969) The fund of sociability. Transactions, 7: 36–43.

Weiss R (1980) Strategic behavioural marital therapy: Towards a new model for assessment and intervention. In: Advances in Family Intervention, Assessment and Theory, pp 229-271. Greenwich, CJ: JAI Press.

Welldon EV (1992) Mother. Madonna, Whore. The idealisation and denigration of motherhood. London: Tavistock Press.

Wellings K, Field J, Johnson AM and Wadsworth J (1994) Sexual Behaviour in Britain. The National Survey of Sexual Attitudes and Lifestyles. London: Penguin Books.

Whiting B and Edwards CP (1973) A cross cultural analysis of sex differences in the behaviour of children aged three through eleven. Journal of Social Psychology, 91: 171–188.

Whyte MK (1990) Dating, Mating and Marriage. Hawthorne, New York: Aldine.

Wilson N (1993) Gendered interaction in criminal homicide. In: A. Wilson (ed.) Homicide: The Victim-Offender Connection, pp 46–52. Cincinnati, OH: Anderson.

Winnicott DW (1965) The Maternal Process and the Facilitating Environment. London: Hogarth Press.

Winnicott DW (1971) Playing and Reality. London: Penguin Books.

Wolfenden Report (1957) Home Office Report.

Xiaohe X and Whyte MK (1990) Love matches and arranged marriages: A Chinese replication. Journal of Marriage and the Family, 52: 709–722.

Zilbergeld B (1980) Men and Sex. London: Fontana.

Index

EXAMPLES